THE MUSICAL BASIS OF VERSE

THE MUSICAL BASIS OF VERSE

A SCIENTIFIC STUDY OF THE
PRINCIPLES OF POETIC COMPOSITION

By J. P. DABNEY

AMS PRESS
NEW YORK

Reprinted from the edition of 1901, New York
First AMS EDITION published 1970
Manufactured in the United States of America

International Standard Book Number: 0-404-01916-1

Library of Congress Card Catalog Number: 79-119650

AMS PRESS, INC.
NEW YORK, N.Y. 10003

" See deep enough and you see musically."

CARLYLE.

PREFACE

I was led to the inception of this work by my recognition of the need—a need felt grievously in my own studies, but even more in the attempt to direct those of others—of a working hypothesis of the Science of Verse which should be at once rational, coherent, and simple—such a working hypothesis as every music student has at his right hand.

The study of all the *a priori* text-books—founded as they are upon a complicated system which will not fit our modern verse—proved a weariness and vexation to the spirit; for, from Puttenham ("Arte of English Poesie," 1589) to our own day, although there is much delightful reading upon the *essence* of verse, there is little light upon the paths of metre, but endless *ignes fatui*. To follow the various disquisitions of the various metrists is like wandering through a vast Dædalian labyrinth, wherein, if at any time some true clew seems to offer itself, it will be presently snipped away and another diametrical one substituted; and, in the end, all lead no-whither. This, because in every case the supposed true way has been an artificial and arbitrary one, not the natural one founded upon primary law; the primary laws of verse, like those of music, being laid upon the bed-rock of acoustics.

The first clear note of truth we hear struck is from Coleridge, when, in his preface to "Christabel" (1816), he announced that he had discovered a "new principle of versification; to wit, that of accents." This declaration raised a storm of abusive criticism from the "Edinburgh Review," and from other quarters, and there the matter would seem to have ended ; but he had, however elementarily, made as great a discovery as Sir Isaac Newton, when, from a falling apple, he deduced the law of gravitation.

In 1881 Sidney Lanier published his brilliant " Science of English Verse," this being the first deliberate attempt to analyse verse upon its true lines; viz., by musical notation. Lanier's book did not have the revolutionising effect which the promulgation of so great and radical a principle should have had ; partly, perhaps, because the book is somewhat abstruse for the general reader, but also partly, it seems to me, because it is not always wholly logical with itself. Many of the verse-notations, using as they do the foot-divisions and not the true bar-divisions measured from accent to accent, would seem to be an attempt to reconcile quantity with accent; whereas, belonging as they do to different periods, with their differing metrical standards, they have no correlation. Also, I do not comprehend the classing together of such diverse verse as " Hamlet's Soliloquy," Poe's " Raven," and Tennyson's " Charge of the Light Brigade " as *all* in 3-beat measure; because, as I have pointed out (page 49), the 3-beat rhythm cannot exist without such a pre-dominance of three notes (syllables) to a bar as shall give the whole verse its organic stamp.

Lanier's supreme glory is that he was a pioneer. Like Columbus, he plunged boldly into the unknown and dis-covered a new world; and the world is ours, to possess as we will.

In the present work, besides the exposition of primary verse-rhythm, as illustrated by the bar-measurements of music, I have endeavoured to elucidate a quality of verse which I have never seen noticed in any work on metre;

viz., *motion*, and the dynamic relation of verse-motion to its theme.

The purpose of this book being analytic, and not synthetic; dealing with the mechanism of verse rather than with its meaning—though the two are not wholly separable—I must be exonerated from any intention of trenching upon the realm of literary criticism, except as incidental to the exposition and development of the logical lines of my subject.

In all arts there is the art of the art and the science of the art. The former concerns itself chiefly with the subjective genius of the artist; the latter, with his concrete expression, or method; method being another name for universal law, and so reducible to an exact science.

Truth, wherever we find it, is superlatively simple. Through whatever channel we follow the developments of human thought, we shall find it to be a denuding process, a removing of the dead husks which ignorance or superstition or convention have folded about the precious kernel. All true art is at bottom unified and concrete; so also the best exposition, or science, of art will be unified and concrete.

In this treatise upon the " Musical Basis of Verse " I have endeavoured to state, rationally, coherently, and simply, what seem to me to be the principles of verse-technique, these principles being, finally, purely a matter of *vibration*.

I have to acknowledge the courtesy of the various copyright owners who have allowed me to use poems and extracts in illustration of my text: Mrs. Fields; Mrs. Lanier; Mr. John Lane (Mr. William Watson's " Hymn to the Sea " and " England, My Mother," and Mr. Watts Dunton's " The Sonnet's Voice "); Messrs.

Macmillan & Co. (Tennyson, Arnold, and Kingsley);
Messrs. A. & C. Black and The Macmillan Co. (Mr.
Symonds's " Greek Poets "); Messrs. Small, Maynard
& Co., and Messrs. Charles Scribner's Sons. Permission
has also been obtained from Messrs. Ellis & Elvey
to quote D. G. Rossetti's " The Portrait " and " The
Wine of Circe," and from Messrs. Smith, Elder & Co.,
to use extracts from copyright poems by Robert
Browning.

CONTENTS

The Musical Basis of Verse

CHAPTER I

THE INHERENT RELATION BETWEEN MUSIC AND VERSE, HISTORICALLY CONSIDERED

IN the beginning, out of the mists of Time, hand in hand, came those twin sisters of Art, Music and Verse. Man, in the exuberant infancy of the race, instinctively danced, and as he danced he sang. The rhythm of his lips gave the rhythm to his foot, and the rhythm of his foot gave the rhythm to his lips; the two interchangeably linked. Thus was the birth of literature in music.

When we study the history of primitive peoples, we find that their first instinctive expression—before their
Expression of primitive peoples close union with, and sense of, the mystery of nature has been dulled by developing civilisation—is poetic. Imagination dominates in all nascent societies, and the first concrete expression of imagination is song, or more correctly, chanting. It is either connected with religious rites or the rehearsal of the deeds of local heroes. Not infrequently this is accompanied by dance. The ghost-dances, snake-dances, and others, of our Indian tribes, are instances in point in our own day.

The older races connected the origin of music with religion. Emil Nauman, in his "History of Music," says:

" In the 'Rigveda,' one of the four primordial books of the Brahmins, written in Sanscrit and known under the Oldest Hindu name of the ' Vedas,' there are hymns intended songs for music. The existence of these books is supposed to date from the year 1500 B.C. . . . Their (the Hindus') oldest songs are to be found in the ' Vedas.' The sacred songs contained in these holy books were saved from destruction by being written in verse, committed to memory and chanted—a custom common to the civilised peoples of antiquity. . . . We also meet in India with musical dramas, the invention of which is attributed to the demi-god Bharata. Gitagowinda, an idyllic musical drama of very ancient origin, which tells of Krishna's quarrels with the beautiful Radha, consists of the songs of the two lovers, alternating with the chorus of the friends of Radha." (Book I., chap. i.)

Of the Phrygians, Lydians, and Phœnicians, Nauman further says: " Amongst all these people we find sculptured reliefs and mural paintings of women and maidens performing on different instruments, singers beating time with their hands, and dancing youths and maidens playing the tambourine." (Book I., chap. ii.)

Carsten Niebuhr notices " the custom resorted to by Egyptian men and women—so often represented on the oldest Egyptian monuments—of marking the rhythmical measures of their song by clapping hands in the absence of drums to serve this purpose." (Nauman, Book I., chap. ii.)

But it is when we approach the high civilisation of the Greeks that we find the finest efflorescence of the unified arts. I cannot do better here than to insert some passages from John Addington Symonds' " Greek Poets":

" Casting a glance backward into the remote shadows

of antiquity, we find that lyrical poetry, like all art in Greece, took its origin in connection with primitive Na-

Musical rituals of the Greeks ture-worship. The song of Linus, referred to by Homer in his description of the shield of Achilles, was a lament sung by reapers for the beautiful dead youth who symbolised the decay of summer's prime. In the funeral chant for Adonis, women bewailed the fleeting splendour of the spring; and Hyacinthus, loved and slain by Phœbus, whom the Laconian youths and maidens honoured, was again a type of vernal loveliness deflowered. The Bacchic songs of alternating mirth and sadness which gave birth, through the dithyramb, to tragedy, and through the Comus-hymn to comedy, marked the waxing and waning of successive years, the pulses of the heart of Nature, to which men listened as the months passed over them. In their dim beginnings these elements of Greek poetry are hardly to be distinguished from the dirges and the raptures of Asiatic ceremonial, in which the dance and chant and song were mingled in a vague monotony—generation after generation expressing the same emotions according to traditions handed down from their forefathers. But the Greek genius was endowed with the faculty of distinguishing, differentiating, vitalising, what the Oriental nations left hazy and confused and inert. Therefore, with the very earliest stirrings of conscious art in Greece we remark a powerful specialising tendency. Articulation succeeds to mere interjectional utterance. Separate forms of music and of metre are devoted, with the unerring instinct of a truly æsthetic race, to the expression of the several moods and passions of the soul. An unconscious psychology leads by intuitive analysis to the creation of distinct branches of composition, each accurately adapted to its special purpose. . . . (Chap. x.)

" Lyrical poetry in Greece was not produced, like poetry in modern times, for the student, by men who find they have a taste for versifying. It was intimately intertwined with actual life, and was so indispensable that every town had its professional poets and choruses, just as every church in Europe now has its organist of greater or less pretension. . . . From Olympus down to the workshop or the sheepfold, from Jove and Apollo to the wandering mendicant, every rank and degree of the Greek community, divine or human, had its own proper allotment of poetical celebration. The gods had their hymns, nomes, pæans, dithyrambs; great men had their encomia and epinikia; the votaries of pleasure their erotica and symposiaca; the mourner his threnodia and elegies; the vine-dresser had his epilenia; the herdsmen their bucolica; even the beggar his eiresione and chelidonisma. . . . (Chap. x.)

Lyrical poetry an organic growth

" Processional hymns, or prosodia, were strictly lyrical. They were sung at solemn festivals by troops of men and maidens walking, crowned with olive, myrtle, bay, or oleander, to the shrines. Their style varied with the occasion and the character of the deity to whom they were addressed. When Hecuba led her maidens in dire necessity to the shrine of Pallas, the prosodion was solemn and earnest. When Sophocles, with lyre in hand, headed the chorus round the trophy of Salamis, it was victorious and martial. If we wish to present to our mind a picture of these processional ceremonies, we may study the frieze of the Parthenon preserved among the Elgin marbles. Those long lines of maidens and young men, with baskets in their hands, with flowers and palm branches, with censers and sacred emblems, are marching to the sound of flutes and lyres, and to the stately rhythms of antiphonal chanting. When

Processional hymns

they reach the altar of the god, a halt is made; the libations are poured; and now the music changes to a solemn and spondaic measure[1]— for the term spondaic seems to be derived from the fact that the libation hymn was composed in a grave and heavy metre of full feet. . . . (Chap. x.)

" A special kind of prosodia were the Parthenia, or processional hymns of maidens; such, for example, as the Athenian girls sang to Pallas while they climbed the staircase of the Parthenon. . . . A fragment (Bergk, p. 842) only remains to show what they were like.

" ' No more, ye honey-voiced, sweet-singing maidens, can my limbs support me: oh, oh, that I were a cerylus, who skims the flower of the sea with halcyons, of a dauntless heart, the sea-blue bird of spring! ' " (Chap. x.)

Other lyrical forms greatened into the sublime art of tragedy.

" It is certain that tragedy arose from the choruses which danced and sang in honor of Dionysos. These **Origin of** dithyrambs, as they are called, were the last **tragedy** form of lyric poetry to assume a literary shape. . . . This respectable and literary form of dithyramb was early transplanted to Athens, where, under the hands of Lasos, it assumed so elaborate a mimetic character by means of the higher development of music and dancing that (like our ballet) it became almost a drama. . . .

" There was also a rustic and jovial dithyramb common among the lower classes in the same districts, where the choruses imitated the sports and manners of Satyrs in attendance on the god." [2]

I have dwelt thus long upon the poetic rituals of the

---

[1] Observe the interchange of poetic with musical terms. Music, except it were one with verse, could not be called *spondaic.*

[2] MAHAFFY : " Hist. of Classical Greek Literature," vol. i., chap. xiv.

ancients—especially upon those of the Hellenes—to illustrate that, at that period, not only were music and verse regarded as one, but that in this indissoluble union they formed an integral part of the very existence of men. And while it is true that even among the Greeks music was still in swaddling clothes, so to speak, being indeed but the handmaid of poetry, yet the literature to which it was allied stands as the foundation structure for all subsequent culture.   One civilisation moves upon another.   We are the heritors of the ages.   The Greeks bestowed upon us in their literature tragic masterpieces which have never been surpassed; while their singleness of ideal in art and their purity and elevation of style serve as standards for all time.

The revival of learning in the fourteenth and fifteenth centuries—a revival principally stimulated by the inven-
The revival of learning in Europe tion of printing—flung open to the crass European civilisations a treasure of classic lore which, in both Latin and Gothic minds, was to be transmuted " into something new and strange "—into new living literatures for the embodiment of new racial feeling.

There is no nobler vehicle for the expression of poetic thought than is furnished by the English language.   If it
The English language as a verse medium has not that extreme liquidity peculiar to the Italian and Spanish, whose golden syllables seem to melt one over another like ripples upon summer seas, yet it has a splendid, virile melody all its own.   It is strong, incisive, dynamic, while its opulent vocabulary places in the hands of the artist an instrument of many strings, to manipulate at his will.   The preponderance of Anglo-Saxon monosyllables—which may be used either upon accented or non-accented beats at the option of the writer—lends it a peculiar elasticity,

at the same time permitting great possibilities in the matter of terse, concentrated utterance.

Both the simplification and amplification of the language we owe to the Norman.

At the beginning of the eleventh century, with William the Conqueror, came in a new era. He brought to England not only material conquest, but those subtler masteries of the ideal, to which, superimposed upon the sturdy stock of rougher orders, we give the name of civilisation.

Norman invasion

He brought in his train the flower of Norman knighthood, which, imbued as it was with the chivalry, the magnificence, the refinement, and the growing culture of the Continent, speedily made itself felt as a new power throughout the land. In the noble examples of architecture, which even to-day endure, the Normans left a lasting monument to the zeal and taste of that vital period.

But even more revolutionising was their influence upon manners, social customs, literature, and speech.

The revolution extended to the vernacular. The conquerors failed to impose their own language upon the conquered, but they so modified the parent stock which they received, and so infused it with words of Latin origin, that they made of it a new language; made, in fact, out of Anglo-Saxon, *English*. The Norman palate revolted at the Teutonic guttural, and, although we still retain traces of its spelling in such words as *rough, plough, cough*, the Teutonic guttural was discarded. The freer Norman brain also refused to burden itself with a cumbersome system of inflection; and the inflection vanished from the forming speech. But the crowning lingual achievement of the Normans was the substitution in verse of true

Norman influence on literature

rhyme for the Anglo-Saxon alliteration; that is, of end-rhyme for head-rhyme.[1] This, and the enriching of the language with many resonant, polysyllabic words of Latin and Greek origin, which make a splendid foil for the treasury of inflection-freed monosyllables, rendered the fruition of a new literature possible.

English literature may be said to begin with Geoffrey Chaucer. Language, in the infancy of nations, is always more or less fluid, until a master-hand arises to crystallise it into literature, and so bring it from the realm of the primitive to that of the civilised. Such a master was Chaucer. He was

Geoffrey
Chaucer the
father of
English
literature

courtier, traveller, scholar, artist. In his diplomatic journeys to Italy (1372, '74, and '78) he came directly under the inspiration of the great Italian literatures. Dante, Petrarch, Boccaccio, became his teachers. From one he doubtless learned the value of exquisite workmanship; from another how to tell a story in perfect form. Chaucer was preëminently a great artist; one whose mind is an alembic in which all things are, by the magic of genius, dissolved, to be precipitated into divine, new creations. He imbibed the spirit of the Italian revival, but did not become a servile imitator of it. He did not give us sonnet cycles, but instead, " The Canterbury Tales,"—in which " the tale and the verse go together like voice and music,"—" The Legende of Good Women," and " The Compleynte of Venus."

The ten-syllabled couplet, which he seems to have been the first to use, set the model of form which epic

---

[1] Earlier sporadic instances of end-rhyme existed, inspired doubtless by monkish influence; Latin verse having at a very early period attained to great perfection in rhyme. Lanier mentions ("Science of English Verse") an Anglo-Saxon poem with rudimentary end-line rhymes. Also a rhymed poem in Latin by an Anglo-Saxon poet.

or narrative verse was to wear for many generations; and
which, shorn of its rhyme, it wears as blank verse to-day.

> "Thou wert acquainted with Chaucer! Pardie,
>   God save his soul,
>   The first finder of our faire language,"

rhapsodises Occleve.

The times which follow Chaucer are not prolific of
great names until we approach that truly Periclean age
of art, the reign of Elizabeth. But the forces were, nevertheless, gathering. Along the way we find as guide-
lights Occleve, Mallory, Caxton, Shelton, Wyatt, Surrey;
and, shining with an ever-increasing refulgence, Sackville,
Lely, Sidney, Spenser, Bacon, Marlowe; until, from the
summit, flames forth the deathless beacon reared by
Shakespeare.

In spite of the dictum of a prominent English writer
upon music (H. R. Haweis) that the English are not a
musical people, they have from time imme-
morial been ardent lovers of song; and " the
songs of a nation," says Lowell, " are like wild
flowers pressed between the blood-stained pages of history. The Infinite sends its messages to us by untutored
spirits, and the lips of little children, and the unboastful
beauty of simple nature."

The English lovers of song

Byrd, in his " Preface to Psalms, Sonnets, and Songs,"
quaintly says:

" There is not any musike of instruments whatever
comparable to that which is made by the voyces of men;
where the voyces are good, and the same well-sorted and
ordered."

Among the Anglo-Saxons, as well as among the Celtic
and other northern races of Europe, the harp seems to
have been the instrument mostly in use, of course as

accompaniment to the chant, recitation, or song. " The minstrels," says Percy, " were the successors of the ancient bards, who, under different names, were admired and revered from the earliest ages among the people of Gaul, Britain, Ireland, and the North; and indeed by almost all the first inhabitants of Europe, whether of Celtic or Gothic race; but by none more than by our own Teutonic ancestors, particularly by all the Danish tribes. Among these they were distinguished by the name Scalds, a word which denotes ' smoothers and polishers of language.' "

We are told that to possess a harp was the first requirement of a Norman gentleman, and to be able to perform upon it indispensable to his pretensions to gentility. Chaucer mentions in his poems a great number of musical instruments, evidence that the development of music kept pace with that of literature.

When we reach the days of the Tudors we find music in a very advanced stage. Erasmus says of the people of England: " They challenge the prerogative of having the most handsome women, of keeping the best table, and of being the most accomplished in the skill of music of any people." [1] We read of " madrigals, ballets (ballads), and canzonets."

" The ballad and dance-tune," says Ritter, " complemented each other from the very start (of English civilisation) and have remained inseparable companions."

In Elizabeth's time we find the names of such composers as Tye, Marbeck, Tallis, Byrd, Morley, etc.; but,

Music in the time of Elizabeth

before the days of Elizabeth, contrapuntal composition was well advanced. The favourite madrigal—" the light-footed English madrigal," Ritter calls it—seems to have been quite an elabo-

[1] RITTER : " Music in England," chap. ii.

rate affair in several parts. The well-known and quaintly charming " Sumer is icumen in," a canon or " rota " as it is called, was written as early as 1223.

But what concerns us more than any contrapuntal developments is the fact that society in the English Periclean age was simply saturated with musical feeling—that musical feeling which comes of freedom, gayety, and living close to nature. The people of that day were not the sombre, soul-burdened people of post-Revolution times, but a careless, light-hearted race, true children of the Renaissance. There existed a veritable *joie de vivre*, and the universal joyousness rippled, like the joyousness of birds, spontaneously into song.

" In the time of Elizabeth, not only was music a qualification for ladies and gentlemen, but even the city of London advertised the musical abilities of boys educated in Bridewell and Christ's Hospital, as a mode of recommending them as servants, apprentices, and husbandmen. Tinkers sung catches; milkmaids sung ballads; carters whistled; each trade, and even beggars, had their special songs. The bass viol hung in the drawing-room for the amusement of waiting visitors; and the lute, cithern, and virginals, for the amusement of waiting customers, were the necessary furniture of the barber shop. They had music at dinner, music at supper, music at weddings, music at funerals, music at night, music at dawn, music at work, music at play. He who felt not in some degree its soothing influence was viewed as a morose, unmusical being whose converse ought to be shunned and regarded with suspicion and distrust." [1]

[1] CHAPPELL : " Popular Music of the Olden Times," vol. i., chap. iii.
The reader will trace in the foregoing an analogy between these times of rich mental harvest and the lyric days of Greece.

> " If music be the food of love, play on ;
> Give me excess of it, that, surfeiting,
> The appetite may sicken and so die.
> That strain again ; it had a dying fall :
> O, it came o'er my ear like the sweet south,
> That breathes upon a bank of violets,
> Stealing and giving odour ! "

Shakespeare makes the duke sigh in " Twelfth Night."

In Shakespeare the sense of union between music and verse reaches its finest flower.   He was its arch-priest.

Shakespeare's sense of music   His heart beat to the universal rhythms. This is evidenced by his spontaneity and daring in the management of blank verse, which in his hands attained a freedom of movement not reached by any other writer.   It is evidenced by his mastery of all the melodic and metrical resources of his medium ; for he was supreme in every metric device by which verse may be varied and enriched, and he employed methods which in less consummate hands might easily be productive of a chaos of mere chopped prose, but which, in the hands of the master, become a complex and wonderful instrument whence issue immortal strains of power and beauty.

His perfect musical ear is even more demonstrated in the little lyric flights scattered throughout the dramas. We have no songs more spontaneous, or instinct with music, than " Hark, hark, the lark," " Who is Silvia?" " O come unto these yellow sands," " Come away, come away, Death," and a host of others.   They seem literally to sing themselves.   In some indeed the joyous lilt loses itself, for very wanton gladness, in a mere inarticulate ripple.   As

> " It was a lover and his lass,
> With a hey, and a ho, and a hey nonino,

That through the green cornfields did pass
In the spring-time, the only pretty ring-time,
When birds do sing, hey ding a ding ding;
Sweet lovers love the spring."

The high-water mark of the verse of this epoch is also the high-water mark of music.

From Shakespeare on we have to note a steady decadence. It is true that we catch Shakespearean echoes **Decadence** in the verse of Jonson, Beaumont and Fletcher, **after** Campion, Wither, Carew, Herrick, Suckling, **Shakespeare** Lovelace, Waller, and others; but these dwindle with the perspective until, by the time of the Restoration, the English Muse was virtually moribund. It is a far cry from

" Queen and huntress, chaste and fair,"

to the formal rhymed couplet of Dryden's day, " when men wrote in measured thuds, by rule."

" How was it," asks a writer,[1] " that a people could *lose its ear* during a century and a half, as if a violinist should suddenly prefer a tom-tom to his violin?"

The causes of this prolonged decadence are two-fold. In the inevitable barren periods which always follow epochs of great productivity—the fallow seasons of nature —the light of inspiration faded, and a cold formalism fell upon art. Men reverted to a meaningless classicism, and enveloped verse in conventional fetters as inexorable as the tentacles of an octopus. But it is even more due to the great parliamentary and religious struggles which began with the Stuarts. The domination of the Commonwealth sealed the fate both of music and poetry. The Puritans, confounding music with popery, looked

---

[1] WILLIAM R. THAYER : " Review of Reviews," October, 1894.

upon it as the work of the demon, an art of Antichrist, a sacrilege not to be tolerated. Nothing was heard in the land but the droning of psalm-tunes. Artistic inspiration perished beneath the heats of a fanaticism which could not tolerate beauty as " its own excuse for being."

Surely never before were the Muses subjected to such a fury of iconoclastic scourging! Small wonder that they should clasp hands and retire from a people who knew no longer how to appreciate them; and perhaps not less that, when wooed back by passion-laden souls into the splendid Renaissance with which our own century opened, there should no longer be found between them that full and spontaneous union which had before existed.

If we glance down the vistas of history and examine the evidences, we shall perceive one fact, that the two arts of music and poetry have always waxed and waned together. A period of great activity and exceptional merit in the one has been coördinate with a similar manifestation in the other. This is not due to accident. Both impulses spring from the same inspirational fountain. They are different interpretations of

The arts of music and poetry wax and wane together

> " those mighty tones and cries
> That from the giant soul of earth arise,"

which Jubal, far away in the dawn of the world, heard; so

> " That love, hope, rage, and all experience,
>   Were fused in vaster being, fetching thence
>   Concords and discords, cadences and cries,
>   That seemed from some world-shrouded soul to rise,
>   Some rapture more intense, some mightier rage,
>   Some living sea that burst the bounds of man's brief age ! " [1]

[1] GEORGE ELIOT : " The Legend of Jubal."

In those epochs of virtual renascence which civilisation from time to time experiences—high-tides of the soul, Emerson calls them—the minds of men become electrically and rhythmically charged, the outcome being the music of language—poetry—or the more developed emotional expression of pure music, according to the dictates of the creative inspiration of the individual. The great diapason is always the same; but its vibrations differently impress, and are differently interpreted by, differentiating genius.

Thus, of two great artists of our own century whose souls were steeped in poetry—Wagner and Hawthorne—one wrote, not poems (for the opera libretti are subsidiary to the music and would not stand alone as literature), but music-dramas; and the other has given us, again not poems, but the most ideal fiction in the language.

What inspires this differentiation in the expression of the ideal we cannot know. We can only be glad that it is so, and that so great a variety of medium in which to try its wings is furnished to the human soul.

CHAPTER II

THE ARTS OF SOUND

" MAN did not make the laws of music, he only found them out," says Charles Kingsley.

" For poetry was all written before time was, and whenever we are so finely organised that we can penetrate into that region where the air is music, we hear those primal warblings," declares Emerson.

And a little reflection makes us realise that they were saying the same thing; that both men, as all truly poetic souls must be, were conscious of those elemental rhythms—potentially identical—which are developed through the minds of men into harmonious expressions of form and sound.

Music and poetry, arts of sound   Music and poetry—poetry being indeed the music of words—are rhythmic utterances of a cognate order. In other words, *music and poetry are arts of sound*.[1]

---

[1] " Sound is a vibration. Sound, as directly known to us by the sense of hearing, is an impression of a peculiar character, very broadly distinguished from the impressions received through the rest of our senses, and admitting of great variety in its modifications."—J. D. EVERETT : " Natural Philosophy " (" Acoustics ").

" Hauptmann, in ' Harmony and Metre,' says : ' Where sound is to be produced, there is required an elastic, stretched, uniform material, and a trembling or vibrating movement thereof. The parts of the body moved are then alternated in and out of their state of uniform cohesion. The instant of transition into this state of equality or inner unity is that which by our sense of hearing is perceived as sound. Sound is only an element of transition, from arising to passing away of the state of unity. Quickly suc-

Music—the most abstract of the arts, and considered by many to be the highest medium of emotional expression we have—is purely dependent, for the effect upon the mind, upon *vibration*.

Poetry, on the other hand, is only partially dependent upon vibration.

The musician will run his eye over a written score, and there are instantly realised to his mental ear the melodies and harmonies there technically inscribed; but this is because he has already heard similar melodies and chords. To a man born deaf, and who is without any conception of sound, the same page would be but a procession of meaningless lines and dots. Let the deaf man, however, read a verse of poetry, and its intellectual side would immediately be clear to him. He would comprehend the meaning of the words; but the acoustic side, the dynamic force of the rhythm, the melodic effects of rhyme, and all those exquisite *nuances* of colour, which make of a verse of poetry a great art, and which are such a delight to the trained poetic ear, would be lost upon him.

Poetry is of itself a species of music. The merit of true poetry lies largely in its suggestiveness, a suggestiveness only to be fully brought home by oral interpretation.

Poetry should be read aloud

Poetry to be fully interpreted and understood should be read aloud.

There are in our language quantities of lyrics which one

ceeding repetitions of this element make the sound appear continuous.' The swing of molecules affords a vent for the music within the vibrating substance. Two hundred and sixty-four swings per second permit the music hidden in a piano-string to escape in two hundred and sixty-four fragments, which when pieced into a whole produce the tone C. As with the steel wire, so with the vocal cords."—HENRY W. STRATTON: " The Metaphysics of Music " (" Mind," 1899).

2

cannot read, or hear read, without their instantly trans-
lating themselves to music, and, so to speak, singing
themselves. Who has not had, at some time, the experience of hearing, spiritedly rendered, some poem with
which he had before been superficially familiar, and has
experienced thereupon a thrill of revelation, as if a flash-
light had suddenly swept his mental horizon ? It was
my own good fortune to receive my first introduction to
Browning's poems through the medium of a vivid spirit
who not only possessed a deep appreciation of, and insight
into, them, but had the rarer faculty of so interpreting
them as to render them equally luminous to others. The
consequence is, not only that Browning has always meant
another thing to me than if I had come to the study
of him callow and alone, but that to this day I can hear
in the poems then read by this gifted teacher the ringing
tones by which they were brought home to me; and so
the *music* of them lives undying in my thought.

It is difficult to understand why this oral interpretation of poetry is not more studied and taught. To hear
noble poetry adequately rendered is as elevating as to
listen to great music, the modulations of the voice infinitely revealing the subtler significance of the words, as
well as bringing out the full melodic effects of the verse.
But alas! even among the well-educated, good readers
are lamentably few; for, although we consider it a *sine
qua non* that our children should be instructed in music,
not one is really taught to read aloud. We should consider it dry work if our acquaintance with music were
limited to reading the scores to ourselves; yet this is the
silent part we accord to verse.

" People do not understand the music of words,"
said Tennyson. " Sound plays so great a part in the
meaning of all language." He told Miss L—— " to

listen to the sound of the sea " in the line from " Enoch
Arden ":

"The league-long roller thundering on the reef."

Of Tennyson's own reading of poetry Miss Emily
Ritchie writes:

**Tennyson's
reading of
poetry**
"Amongst the experiences of intercourse
with him, nothing was more memorable than
to hear him read his poetry. The roll of his great voice
acted sometimes almost like an incantation, so that when
it was a new poem he was reading, the power of realis-
ing its actual nature was subordinated to the wonder at
the sound of the tones. Sometimes, as in ' The Passing
of Arthur,' it was a long chant, in which the expression
lay chiefly in the value given to each syllable, sometimes
a swell of sound like an organ's; often came tones of infinite pathos, delicate and tender, then others of mighty
volume and passionate strength." [1]

When thus interpreted, we easily perceive that each
syllable of verse is really a separate note of music;
not the dry symbol of an arbitrary system of measurement.

The analogy between music and poetry has always been
more or less consciously recognised. Not only

**The analogy
between
music and
poetry part-
ly recog-
nised**
are musical terms and tropes so constantly used
by the poets that they may be considered an
integral part of verse, but the critics themselves
are continually driven to have recourse to them
to elucidate their own meaning.

Dryden says of Chaucer's verse that " there is the
rude sweetness of a Scotch tune in it."

" Years," says Symonds, writing of Shelley, " filled
with music that will sound as long as English lasts."

[1] HALLAM, LORD TENNYSON : "Life of Tennyson," vol. ii., chap. iii.

" This was a vocal year," comments Gosse in his
" Life of Gray."

Saintsbury, in an analysis of Dryden's " Ode to Anne
Killigrew," remarks, " As a piece of concerted music in
verse it [the first stanza] has not a superior."

Instances might be indefinitely multiplied, but these
suffice to evidence the real thought-current—a current
so strong, so instinctive, so really incontrovertible, that
the only marvel is that scholars have not long since
abandoned themselves to it, instead of endeavouring
to punt up-stream in the cumbersome bateaux of a past
civilisation.

The Gothic genius derived its primary inspiration from
classic culture, but in no sense formulated itself techni-
The Gothic cally upon the classics. The modern poet—
genius and under this term we may include everything post-mediæval—incontinently discarded quantity,
and, with an instinct truer and stronger than tradition
or theory, trusted himself boldly to his ear. For, in the
end, the ear is sole arbiter. Even among those languages developed directly from the Latin we do not find
any imitation. The " Divina Commedia" of Dante and
the " Sonnets " of Petrarch are not derived from classic
prototypes, but are individual evolutions, while nothing
could be freer than the early Spanish dramatists.

The sense of quantity was lost or discarded very early
in the Christian era. " We are told by Christ (' Metrik
Early der Griechen und Römer ') that Ritschl consid-
discarding ered the mill-song of the Lesbian women to be
of quantity an early example of accentual metre in Greek.
. . . In Latin the ' Instructiones ' of the barbarous
Commodianus (about the middle of the third century) is
usually named as the first specimen of accentual verse.
. . . Whatever may be the date of the earliest exist-

ing specimen, there can be no doubt that the feeling for quantity had long before died out among all but the learned few." [1]

We may account for this substitution of accentual for quantitative standards partly by the decline of learning; **Music devel-** but it seems to me even better accounted for **oped with** by the fact that, at the same time that the art **poetry in** **mediæval** of poetry was emerging once more from me- **Europe** diæval night, music was also undergoing a transformation of its own, and emerging, through the Gregorian chant and the early monastic composers, into an independent art. In the cloister were being laid the scientific corner stones,[2] while, outside, the *minnesänger*, the *trouvères*, and the troubadours were pouring into the ears of the people their wild and passionate lays. Imbued with this new and vital sense of rhythm, the poets unconsciously transferred the same to their verse. It was this which imparted to the movement of the Renaissance **English** its splendour. It was not any reproduction of **verse ac-** the old, but literally a new birth. **knowledged** **not to be** Considering the fact that English verse is **quantita-** acknowledgedly *not* quantitative, the efforts **tive** of scholars of all time to prove it so appear, to say the least, herculean. Each man has a system of scansion of his own, opposed to every other man's; each

---

[1] JOSEPH B. MAYOR : "English Metre " (Preface, p. 8).

[2] " Guido of Arezzo (1020) and Franco of Cologne (about 1200—some writers place him much earlier) are the only names worth mentioning at this period. The labours of the first culminated in the rise of descant, *i.e.*, the combination of sounds of unequal length ; or music in which two or more sounds succeed each other while one equal to them in length was sustained. The labours of Franco may be connected with a better system of musical notation, the introduction of sharps and flats, and the *cantus mensurabilis*, or *division of music into bars*." —HAWEIS : " Music and Morals " (book ii., sec. i.).

demolishing the authority before him, to have his own in turn overthrown.   It reminds one of nothing so much as the contests of chivalry, when no errant knight might meet another without putting lance in rest to try which was the better man.

One English metrist, Dr. Guest, holds such stringent ideals of metrical perfection—all based upon quantity— **English** that he would seem to condemn as illegitimate **metrists** a great part of English verse.   Another, Dr. Abbott, would get over the "difficulty of extra sylla-bles" by "effects of slurring."   Mayor disposes sum-marily of a number of his fellow metrists, but has only a fresh pabulum of routine scansion to offer.   Some of the scholars have misgivings; but the fetters of tra-dition are hard to break.   Mr. A. J. Ellis asserts that "the whole subject of English metres requires investi-gation on the basis of accent."   Yet he appears still to scan his verse, and superimposes upon this a system of metrical analysis upon "force, length, pitch, weight, silence," subdivided into forty-five different expression-marks for each syllable to be considered!   This system, he tells us, he has not yet attempted to work out! Professor Sylvester goes so far as to recommend the use of "musical nomenclature in verse," but at the same time does not use it, and offers us a Dædalian maze of lockjaw terminology which is anything but musical. John Addington Symonds tells us that "scansion by time takes the place of scansion by metrical feet; the bars of the musical composer, where different values from the breve to the semi-quaver find their place, sug-gest a truer measure than the longs and shorts of classic feet."

When we turn to American teachers we find them much more radical; yet, though they discard the old,

they have not found their way to the new, and seem to
wander, as it were, in fog-lands and without solid ground
American   under their feet—or at least they place none
metrists   under those of the student.   Professor Gummere has no better way to measure verse than by " a succession of stresses." Professor Hiram Corson also discards
classic traditions and uses for analysis of verse the symbols
XA, AX, XXA, AXX, XAX, etc., a colourless method
which conveys no rhythmic impression to the mind.

It seems admitted by all authorities that English verse
is *accentual and not quantitative;* by the most advanced,
that English verse will not scan; furthermore that we
moderns have lost the feeling for quantity.   Whether
we have lost anything which was worth the keeping I
leave others to decide;[1] but if we *have* lost it, " a God's
name," as Spenser says, let us let it go.   Let us not try
to mete the culture of one age by the measuring-tape of
another.   Let us not put new wine into old bottles.

Yet, if we discard the old, what shall be substituted ?
For there must indubitably *be* a science, a constructive
principle, of verse.   The laws exist whether we recognise
them or not.   The earth revolved around the sun before
Galileo's momentous discovery.   The law of gravitation
flung apples to the ground before Newton arose to give
that law a name.   So, through the centuries, the poets

---

[1] " The distinctive feature of these poets (Melic poets : a term given to
the lyric poets of Greece) was the necessary combination of music, and very
frequently of rhythmical movement or *orchestic* with their text.   When this
dancing came into use, as in the choral poetry of the early Dorian bards,
and of the Attic dramatists, the metre of the words became so complex and
divided into subordinated rhythmical periods, that Cicero tells us such poems
appeared to him like prose, since the necessary music and figured dancing
were indispensable to explain the metrical plan of the poet.   I have no doubt
many modern readers of Pindar will recognise the pertinence of this remark."—MAHAFFY : " History of Greek Literature," vol. i., chap. x.

have been instinctively singing in obedience to the law of musical rhythms, although the fact has not yet received more than a partial recognition.

If we adopt for verse the system of *musical notation,* we cut the Gordian knot of scansion fairly in two. We **Adopt for verse a system of musical notation** should not be forced to the expedient of dividing monosyllables in the middle in order to square a verse of poetry with a particular theory, as one writer has done; nor need we tease our brains over *choriambic, proceleusmatic, dactyl-anapæst, dactyl-iamb, antibacchius, cretic and amphibrach; slurred iambs, metrical metamorphoses, initial truncations,* etc.; nor any of the complicated machineries for smoothing away the so-called difficulties of English verse.

The fact is that, looked at " deep enough " and " seen musically," verse construction becomes a wonderfully simple matter.

As a vehicle of emotional and intellectual expression, music may be said to begin where language ends. We **Verse construction a simple matter** might say that music is thought expressed in the abstraction of sound (vibration), without the interposition of articulate speech. Poetry is thought expressed in articulate speech without any special range in sound. Music is purely abstract, while poetry, in substance, may be either abstract or concrete. Poetry is capable of placing a definite image before the mind, which music, spite of the pretensions of programme music, cannot do.[1]

[1] " Although music is distinctly not a definite means of qualitative emotional expression, it is an exceedingly potent vehicle for such expression. Its quantitative dynamic power is undisputed ; and the qualitative element, which it lacks, is supplied by the performer. Especially is this true of vocal music, in which the quality of emotion is distinctly indicated by the text—from which latter the singer takes his cue."—W. F. APTHORP : " Expression in Music " (" Symphony Notes," 1900).

In such lines as these:

> " How pleasant, as the yellowing sun declines,
> And with long rays and shades the landscape shines,
> To mark the birches' stems all golden light,
> That lit the dark slant woods with silvery white;
> The willow's weeping trees, that twinkling hoar,
> Glanced oft upturn'd along the breezy shore,
> Low bending o'er the colour'd water, fold
> Their moveless boughs and leaves like threads of gold;"

—WORDSWORTH : " An Evening Walk."

we have as distinct a mental picture of that which the words describe as if it were painted before us upon a **Objective verse** canvas. On the other hand, when we read such lines as the following, we realise that we have entered the realm of the abstract, the realm in which music lives and moves and has its being.

> " The gleam,
> The light that never was on sea or land,
> The consecration and the poet's dream;"

Subjective verse

—WORDSWORTH : " Elegiac Stanzas."

> " Sound needed none,
> Nor any voice of joy; his spirit drank
> The spectacle; sensation, soul, and form
> All melted into him; they swallow'd up
> His animal being; in them did he live,
> And by them did he live; they were his life.
> In such access of mind, in such high hour
> Of visitation from the living God,
> Thought was not; in enjoyment it expired."

—WORDSWORTH : " The Excursion."

" The awful shadow of some unseen Power
    Floats though unseen among us ; visiting
    This various world with as inconstant wing
    As summer winds—"
            —SHELLEY : " Hymn to Intellectual Beauty."

        " Believe thou, O my soul,
    Life is a vision shadowy of truth ;
    And vice and anguish and the wormy grave
    Shapes of a dream."
            —COLERIDGE : " Religious Musings."

Technically music and verse overlap but a little way;
therefore, in adopting the symbols of musical notation
for the measurement of verse, we use as models
only the forms of primary music—such simple
rhythmic effects as are found, for example, in
Folk-music, the world over. With the complicated *science* of music, verse has nothing to do. We
speak, by that license which permits the borrowing of a
term from one art to use connotatively in another, of
the *harmonies* in verse; but, technically speaking, harmony is the science of many voices together; and verse
is but a single voice, a solo instrument, a *melody* pure and
simple. Therefore, although in fundamental rhythms
music and verse are identical, the analogy cannot be
pushed beyond the very rudiments of musical form.

Music and poetry are both the result of the discovery
by man that the higher vibrations, either of sound alone,
or of sound with words, when measured off into regular
periods of time, were pleasant to the ear. In substance
this was an instinct. All nature is more or less recog-
nisably rhythmic, and it has been more than once suggested that the length of a breath furnished the primitive

Marginal note: Technically music and verse over-lap only a little way

quotient for verse. This is very likely true of the metrical outlines—early poetry being a species of recitative—and the finer elements of primary rhythm were only gradually evolved.

The basic principle of music is *time;* measurements of time; uniform measurements of time; which measurements are represented by *notes.*

The basic principle of music and of verse The basic principle of verse is *time;* measurements of time; uniform measurements of time; which measurements are represented by *words.*

Now the quality which measures off sound vibrations into regular periods of time is *accent.* In a group of musical beats the mind instinctively emphasises special ones and leaves others unemphasised, thus engendering accent.

Accent the factor of measurement In some cases a natural pause, or silent beat, takes the place of the uttered note; and it is this regular succession of accented beats with unaccented beats, or of accented beats with pauses, which constitutes *primary rhythm.*

"Metre[1] (primary rhythm) in music, is the grouping of two, three, or more tones, as time-units into a whole, or time-integer, called measure, the first part of which (the *thesis*)[2] has an accent, the second part (the *arsis*) either no accent or a weak one.

Definition of primary rhythm

[1] The word *metre*, as applied to verse, refers specifically to the measurement of the line, i.e., to the number of measures (bars or feet), therefore I prefer here to substitute the term *primary rhythm* for what Mr. Cornell designates as *metre*, because it more exactly expresses that basic movement within the bar, repeated from bar to bar, common to both music and verse, and upon which music and verse are both constructed.

In music the word *rhythm* is used to designate somewhat larger and more complex groupings of notes than are contained within the compass of one bar, a conjunction not recognisable in verse.

[2] "The thesis signifies properly the *putting down* of the foot in beating time, in the march or dance ('downward beat'), and the arsis, the *raising* of the foot ('upward beat'). By the Latin grammarians these terms were

Thus the grouping, e.g., of four quarter-notes into a measure, gives the metre whose signature is 4/4, the principal accent being on the first quarter-note, the weak on the third: thus 𝄴 ♩ ♩ ♩ ♩ .   In a piece of music embracing a series of measures, the *rule* is that all measures have (1) the *same number* of time-units of equal length; and (2) a uniform alternation of accent and non-accent; *i.e.*, the accent falls on the same metrical part in one measure as in another.   The regularly recurring accent enables the *ear* to separate the measures one from another; for the *eye* they are separated by means of the vertical line called the *bar*. . . .   To render the metre of a musical thought intelligible to the ear, it is requisite that this thought *exceed the limit of one measure.*   For it is only by the recurrence of the same elements (the same metrical parts) in the second measure that the metre can be recognised by the hearing.'' [1]

I have quoted verbatim these elementary definitions of Professor Cornell, because they apply, in every particular, to verse.   Although verse is not represented by musical notes, nor divided off metrically by bars, it will be convenient in analysing it so to measure it; and I have, therefore, inserted a series of examples farther on.

The same in verse

Sometimes the melody may begin directly upon the

made to mean, respectively, the ending and beginning of a measure.   By a misunderstanding which has prevailed till recently, since the time of Bentley, their true signification has been reversed.   The error mentioned arose from applying to trochaic and dactylic verse a definition which was true only of iambic or anapæstic."—ALLEN and GREENOUGH'S Latin Grammar : " Prosody," chap. ii.

[1] J. H. CORNELL : "Theory and Practice of Musical Form," chaps. i. and ii.

accent of the measure; at others it is led into by one or more unaccented notes called the anacrusis.[1]

The anacrusis is essentially the beginning on a *non-accent*. It neither adds to, nor takes away from, the time-value of the measures, *which are measured from accent to accent*. This is very important to remember in the application of these principles to verse, because a very common form of verse is that beginning upon a non-accented syllable.

Musical no-tation Music is written by a number of signs called notes, regularly graded as to their relative time-valuation.

Thus we have the whole note—*o*—, furnishing the standard of time-value to all.

We have the half-note —*♩*—, two of which are required to furnish the time-value of the whole note.

We have the quarter-note —*♩*—, two of which are required to furnish the time-value of a half-note, and four of which are required to furnish the time-value of a whole note.

We have the eighth-note —*♪*—, two of which are required to furnish the time-value of a quarter-note, and eight of which are required to furnish the time-value of a whole note.

And we have the sixteenth-note —*♪*—, two of which are required to furnish the time-value of the eighth-note, and sixteen of which are required to furnish the time-value of a whole note.

Music-notation runs into much higher denominations,

---

[1] *Anacrusis* is a Greek word, and was borrowed by music from poetry. In verse, the *anacrusis* has also been called a hypermetrical syllable.

but they are omitted here because none smaller than those given could ever be required in verse-notation.

A dot placed after any note means that it is to be held half as long again as its original time-value. Thus we may write a 3-beat measure either | 𝅘𝅥 𝅘𝅥 𝅘𝅥 | or | 𝅘𝅥 𝅘𝅥 | or | 𝅘𝅥· |.

There are also signs for rests, or silences, corresponding in time-values with each note. Thus:

$$o\ —\ ;\ \rho\ —\ ;\ \int \sim\ ;\ \mathcal{D}\ \gamma\ ;\ \mathcal{D}\ \gamma.$$

The rest may take a dot after it in the same way as the note.

As we do not, in verse-notation, have to consider tonality, or pitch, we do not require either the staff or its signatures, but may write our syllabled notes in a single line.

There are only two forms of *primary rhythm;* viz., that based upon *two beats to the measure ;* and that based upon **Two forms of primary rhythm** *three beats to the measure.*   This is rhythm reduced to its units.

Thus:—2-beat rhythm :—

$$\overset{1}{}\ \overset{2}{}\ \overset{1}{}\ \overset{2}{}\ \overset{1}{}\ \overset{2}{}\ \overset{1}{}\ \overset{2}{}\ \overset{1}{}$$
" How sweet the moonlight sleeps upon this bank."

" *How* " being the *anacrusis* is outside of the metric scheme, and we do not begin to measure the metre until we reach the *first accent.*

3-beat rhythm :—

$$\overset{1}{}\ \overset{2}{}\ \overset{3}{}\ \overset{1}{}\ \overset{2}{}\ \overset{3}{}\ \overset{1}{}\ \overset{2}{}\ \overset{3}{}\ \overset{1}{}$$
"There's a bower of roses by Bendemeer's stream."

The same is applicable here; " *There's a* " being the non-accented *anacrusis.*

Now, if we substitute notes for numbers, we shall have the following:

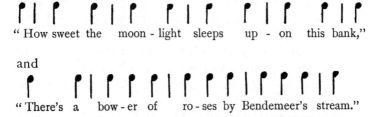

" How sweet the moon - light sleeps up - on this bank,"

and

" There's a bow - er of ro - ses by Bendemeer's stream."

Every syllable represents a note.   The dot may pro-
long it sometimes, and occasionally the rest may represent it; but, as a rule, the measure must be
Every syl- full, or a sufficient number of measures in the
lable repre- verse or line must be full, so as to produce
sents a note
upon the ear the orderly sequence of that rhythm in
which the poem is written.[1]

Roughly speaking, the verse or line may be said to
correspond to the musical phrase; the whole stanza to
the finished melody.

The accent upon dissyllables and polysyllables is always
fixed; that is, it is always upon the same syllable of a
word, in whatever position that word may be
Accents placed, and we cannot alter it.[2]   On the other

---

[1] In music, syncopation—the throwing out of a note, or notes, from the
natural accent—is of course common ; but in these instances other voices,
as those of instrumental accompaniment, or, in the case of folk-dancing, a
stamp of the foot, a snap of the fingers, or a clash of castanets, supply the
missing stroke to the ear.   For the ear *must* keep this sense of accent.
Syncopation in verse is not conceivable.

[2] A study of the literature of the past shows us that formerly it was cus-
tomary often to write with a *wrenched accent ;* that is, throwing the accent
arbitrarily upon a syllable where it does not belong.   Thus :

" That through the green *cornfíelds* did pass."—SHAKESPEARE.

This will pass muster musically because *cornfields* is a compound word, and

hand, monosyllables may be used much as we please, and we may cast them in the verse or line either as accented or unaccented, to suit our own purposes. The same word may, in one and the same sentence, be found first upon the accented beat, and later upon the unaccented beat. But it is bad writing to put upon the accented beat of the measure any weak monosyllable, such as the articles *a* and *the*, the preposition *of*, the conjunction *and*, etc., etc.

In a word of three syllables, if it is cast in 2-beat rhythm, there will fall an accent upon the third syllable as well as upon the first, as this third syllable becomes naturally the *thesis* of the next measure.   Thus:

"How pi - ti - ful the cry of those be-reaved."

On the other hand, if the word *pitiful* be cast in 3-beat rhythm, it will have but *one* accent, upon the *first* syllable. Thus:

"Oh it was   pitiful, near a whole city full."

both syllables are generically *heavy*, so it does not hurt the ear to throw the accent out.   But the following wrenched accent from Swinburne is inadmissible:

" For the stars and the winds are unto her
As raiment, as songs of the harp-playér."

The use of wrenched accent is now rightly condemned ; and the reason is not far to seek.   Although we may vary our metrical schemes to suit, and may take great liberties with colour and melodic effects, we must not disturb the *accent*, because it is the *mensural factor*, the cornerstone upon which rests the whole fabric of primary rhythm.

Inserted below are sixteen examples of notated verse;
twelve from modern poets, and four from Shakespeare.

NO. I.

EXAMPLE OF 2-BEAT RHYTHM.[1]

Calm   soul   of   all   things !   make   it   mine

To   feel,   a - mid   the   ci - ty's   jar,

That   there   a - bides   a   peace   of   thine,

Man   did   not   make   and   can - not   mar.

—MATTHEW ARNOLD : " Lines written in Kensington Gardens."

NO. II.

EXAMPLE OF 2-BEAT RHYTHM.

Love   that   hath   us   in   the   net,

Can   he   pass   and   we   for - get ?

---

[1] In writing these notations, I have followed the usages of musicians.
The student will readily see that the bar counts metrically whether it is
filled out by a rest or not, because the principle of measurement is from
accent to accent.

3

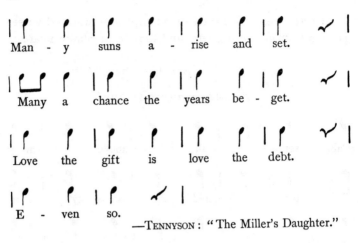

Man - y   suns   a - rise   and   set.

Many   a   chance   the   years   be - get.

Love   the   gift   is   love   the   debt.

E - ven   so.

—TENNYSON : "The Miller's Daughter."

NO. III.

EXAMPLE OF 2-BEAT RHYTHM.

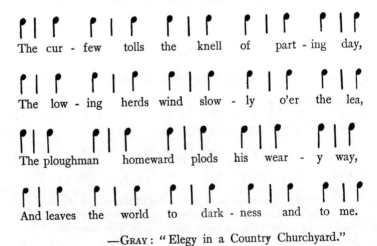

The cur - few   tolls   the   knell   of   part - ing   day,

The low - ing   herds   wind   slow - ly   o'er   the   lea,

The ploughman   homeward   plods   his   wear - y   way,

And leaves   the   world   to   dark - ness   and   to   me.

—GRAY : "Elegy in a Country Churchyard."

NO. IV.

EXAMPLE OF 2-BEAT RHYTHM.

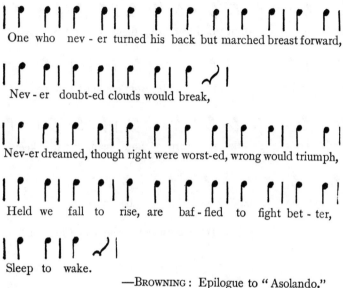

One who nev - er turned his back but marched breast forward,

Nev - er doubt-ed clouds would break,

Nev-er dreamed, though right were worst-ed, wrong would triumph,

Held we fall to rise, are baf - fled to fight bet - ter,

Sleep to wake.

—BROWNING: Epilogue to "Asolando."

NO. V.

EXAMPLE OF 3-BEAT RHYTHM.

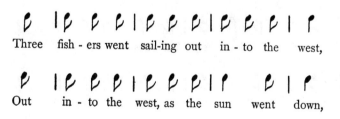

Three fish - ers went sail-ing out in - to the west,

Out in - to the west, as the sun went down,

Each thought of the wom-an who loved him best,

And the chil-dren stood watch-ing them out of the town;

For men must work and wom-en must weep,

And there's lit - tle to earn and man - y to keep,

Though the har - bour bar be moan-ing.

—CHARLES KINGSLEY : " The Three Fishers."

NO. VI.

EXAMPLE OF 3-BEAT RHYTHM.

Where I find her not, beau-ties van - ish;

Whith-er I fol - low her, beau-ties flee ;

Is there no meth - od to tell her in Span-ish

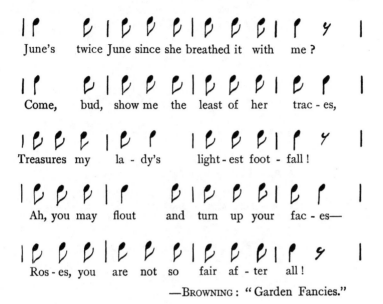

June's   twice June since she breathed it with   me ?

Come,   bud, show me   the   least of   her   trac - es,

Treasures my   la - dy's   light - est foot - fall !

Ah, you may   flout   and turn up your   fac - es—

Ros - es, you   are   not   so   fair af - ter   all !

—BROWNING : " Garden Fancies."

NO. VII.

EXAMPLE OF 3-BEAT RHYTHM.

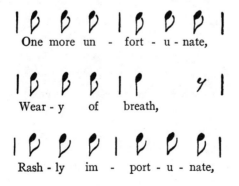

One more un - fort - u - nate,

Wear - y   of   breath,

Rash - ly   im - port - u - nate,

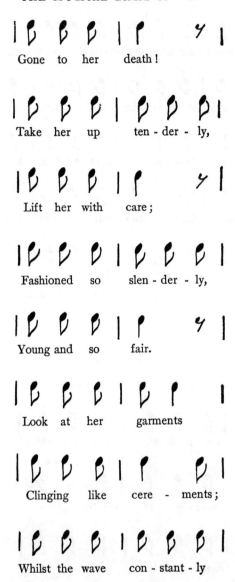

Gone to her death !

Take her up ten - der - ly,

Lift her with care ;

Fashioned so slen - der - ly,

Young and so fair.

Look at her garments

Clinging like cere - ments ;

Whilst the wave con - stant - ly

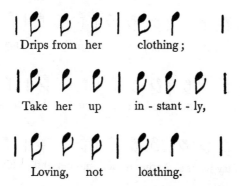

Drips from her   clothing;

Take her up   in - stant - ly,

Loving,   not   loathing.

—THOMAS HOOD: "The Bridge of Sighs."

NO. VIII.

EXAMPLE OF 3-BEAT RHYTHM.

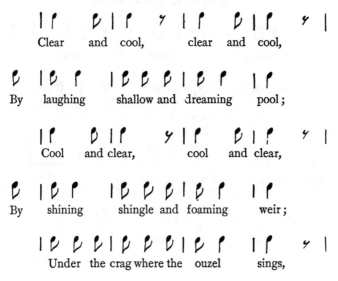

Clear   and cool,   clear   and   cool,

By   laughing   shallow and dreaming   pool;

Cool   and clear,   cool   and clear,

By   shining   shingle and foaming   weir;

Under   the crag where the   ouzel   sings,

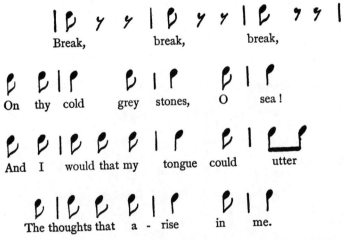

And the   ivied   wall where the church bell rings,

Un - de - filed for the   un - de - filed ;

Play by me, bathe in me, mother and   child.

—Charles Kingsley : "The Song of the River."

NO. IX.

EXAMPLE OF 3-BEAT RHYTHM.

Break,   break,   break,

On   thy cold   grey stones,   O   sea !

And   I   would that my   tongue could   utter

The thoughts that   a - rise   in   me.

—Tennyson : "Break, Break, Break."

NO. X.

EXAMPLE OF 3-BEAT RHYTHM.

Sweet and low,   Sweet and low,

Wind of the western   sea;

Low,   low,   breathe and blow,

Wind of the western   sea!

O - ver the rolling   wa - ters   go,

Come from the dying   moon   and blow,

Blow him a - gain   to   me;

While   my   little   one, while   my   pretty   one   sleeps.

—TENNYSON : "The Princess."

NO. XI.

EXAMPLE OF 2-BEAT RHYTHM.

It's we   two, it's we   two, it's we   two for aye,

All the world and we   two, and heaven be our stay.

Like a laverock in the lift,   sing, O   bonny bride!

All   the world was Adam once with Eve   by his side.

—Jean Ingelow: "Like a Laverock in the Lift."

NO. XII.

EXAMPLE OF 2-BEAT RHYTHM.

'Tis the   middle   of   night by the cas - tle clock,

And the owls   have a-wak-ened the   crow - ing   cock;

Tu - whit!   Tu - whoo!

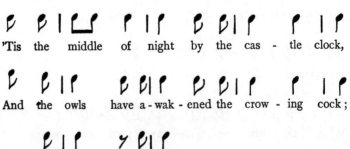

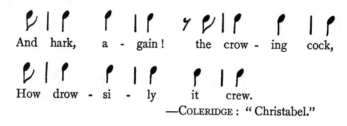

And hark,   a - gain!   the crow - ing   cock,

How drow - si - ly   it   crew.

—Coleridge : " Christabel."

NO. XIII

Song from Shakespeare

2-BEAT RHYTHM

When   dai - sies   pied   and   vio - lets   blue,

And   la - dy - smocks   all   sil - ver   white,

And   cuck - oo - buds   of   yel - low   hue,

Do   paint   the   mead - ows   with   de - light,

The   cuck - oo   then,   on   eve - ry   tree,

Mocks   mar - ried   men;   for   thus   sings   he,

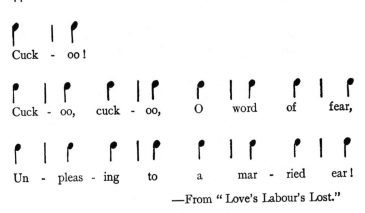

Cuck - oo!

Cuck - oo,   cuck - oo,   O   word   of   fear,

Un - pleas - ing   to   a   mar - ried   ear!

—From " Love's Labour's Lost."

NO. XIV

Song from Shakespeare

2-BEAT RHYTHM

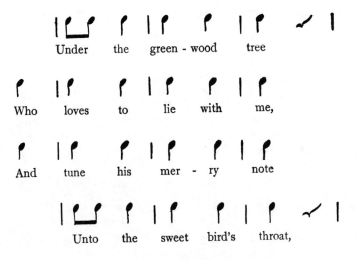

Under   the   green - wood   tree

Who   loves   to   lie   with   me,

And   tune   his   mer - ry   note

Unto   the   sweet   bird's   throat,

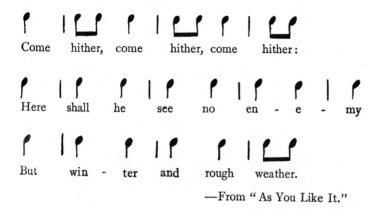

Come hither, come hither, come hither:

Here shall he see no en - e - my

But win - ter and rough weather.

—From " As You Like It."

NO. XV

Song from Shakespeare

2-BEAT RHYTHM

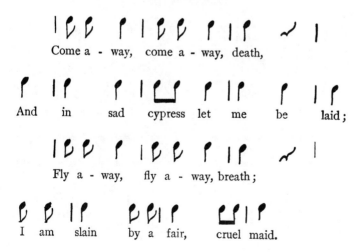

Come a - way, come a - way, death,

And in sad cypress let me be laid;

Fly a - way, fly a - way, breath;

I am slain by a fair, cruel maid.

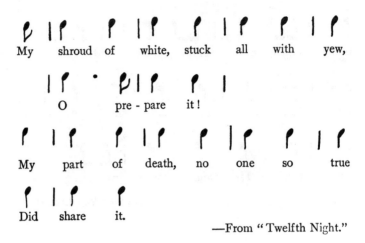

My shroud of white, stuck all with yew,

O pre - pare it!

My part of death, no one so true

Did share it.

—From "Twelfth Night."

NO. XVI

SONG FROM SHAKESPEARE

3-BEAT RHYTHM

When daff - o - dils be - gin to peer,—

With hey! the dox - y o - ver the dale,—

Why, then comes in the sweet o' the year;

For the red blood reigns in the win - ter's pale.

—From "The Winter's Tale."

All verse may be analysed upon this basis. If we
should wish, in analysing a verse of poetry, to use a sig-
All verse nature of time-value, we may write it thus:
analysed
upon this 2/4, which signifies four measures of 2-beat
basis rhythm; or 2/5, which signifies five measures
of 2-beat rhythm; or 3/4, which signifies four measures
of 3-beat rhythm; and so on.

Different There are three different manners of writing
manners verse; viz.: (1) *Strict*, (2) *With direct attack*,
of verse (3) *Free*.

I have given the name *Strict* to that style of verse in
which all the lines begin uniformly with the anacrusis;
as in Numbers I, III, V, XIII, XVI. The use of the
anacrusis imparts a certain elegance and suavity—as it
were, a legato movement—to the verse. Strict verse is
usually employed in the expression of stately and dignified ideas.

Direct attack is, on the other hand, verse written uniformly throughout the poem without the anacrusis; that
is, beginning directly upon the accent of the measure; as
in Numbers II, IV, VI, VII, X. Direct attack is, of
course, also a strict style of another sort. The direct
attack gives a splendid momentum to the rhythmic movement, much like the first launching spring of a swimmer.
Browning, more than any other modern poet, makes
frequent and masterly use of the direct attack. Fine
instances of it are also to be found in Tennyson's
" Charge of the Light Brigade," Campbell's " Battle of
the Baltic," Scott's " Twist ye, Twine ye," and many
others.

Verse is *free* when the lines of a poem may begin either
with or without the anacrusis, according to the rhythmic
feeling of the poet and the effect to be produced; as in
Numbers VIII, IX, XII, XIV, XV. Free verse is very

much less used—because more difficult to handle with the proper rhythmic equilibrium—in 2-beat rhythm than in 3-beat rhythm. In 2-beat verse, unless handled with the finest instinct—an instinct which none but the masters of verse possess—the irregularity is apt to appeal to the ear as superfluous syllables, and to make the rhythm halt upon its feet. Shakespeare was a past-master of these effects, and had so fine an ear that he played upon this not very elastic measure as if it had been an instrument of many strings. In our century, Coleridge has been conspicuous for the same rare faculty.

In 3-beat rhythm, free verse is a very common and most useful medium; and, although in unskilled hands it shows some tendency to slovenliness, it is wonderfully elastic, permitting great freedom of diction and great variety of verse-cadence.

Styles should not be mixed any more than rhythms. If we adopt *strict verse* for our thematic movement—to borrow a term from music—we must preserve this style throughout the poem. If we adopt *direct attack*, direct attack must be uniformly preserved. It is only in the looser, bohemian *free* verse that they may commingle; but even here they need a fine ear for nice contrast in order to produce poetry and not doggerel.

We may now proceed to an analytical examination of the notated poems.

A comparison of Numbers I and II shows that the two poems are rhythmically and metrically identical—that is, Detailed they are both cast in 2/4; but the *direct attack* analyses of of the second example gives a distinctly differ- notated poems ent cadence. It is less formal, and has more motion. Exactly the same, also, as the foregoing poems —the same rhythmically and metrically, but varying in its final cadence—is Longfellow's " Psalm of Life."

" Tell me not, in mournful numbers,
' Life is but an empty dream ! '
For the soul is dead that slumbers,
And things are not what they seem.''

Another variety of cadence is given here by the use,
in the first and third lines, of the *double*,[1] or *feminine*
Feminine rhyme; e.g., *numbers, slumbers.* But the *rhythm*
ending has not been altered thereby; the last measure
is filled out, that is all, instead of ending, as in the first
two examples, upon the first accented word. The *feminine ending* gives an added vibration.

Example Number III varies from Number I only in
having one more measure to the verse or line. It is 2/5.
This is one of the purest examples we have of the *heroic
verse*, so common in English verse, and its greatest
glory. Whether employed in stanzas, rhymed couplets,
or blank verse, it is the most dignified and elevated poetic
medium we have.

Number IV is also in 2-beat rhythm, but it is metrically irregular, the lines being (within the stanza) of different lengths. The poem is not, however, an *irregular
poem*, because the stanzas are alike.

Number V is our first example of triple, or 3-beat,
rhythm. This poem is also *strict*, having the anacrusis
regularly throughout.

As we shall see, by an examination of this and the following poems in triple measure, the full three notes, or
Triple syllables, are not required to appear in *every*
rhythm *bar*, nor indeed in absolutely *every line ;* but
it must be clearly indicated *at the outset*, so that the ear
takes the impression of this rhythm, and it must appear

[1] The *feminine ending* will be found treated with more expansion in
chap. iii.

4

in certainly *every other line*, so that this impression shall be continued and not become weakened or lost. In some extant poems one has to read several lines in order to discover whether the generic rhythm be 3-beat or 2-beat; as in this song from Browning's " Pippa Passes."

> " Overhead the treetops meet,
>   Flowers and grass spring 'neath one's feet;
>   There was naught above me, naught below
>   My childhood had not learned to know :
>   For what are the voices of birds
>   —Ay and of beasts—but words, our words,
>   Only so much more sweet? "

This poem is really in 3-beat rhythm, but there is nothing in the first two lines to indicate this; they are plain 2-beat. The true rhythm is first indicated—none too clearly—in the anacrusis of the third line, and does not distinctly take possession of the ear until the fifth line. This has always seemed to me an artistic defect. The rhythmic key-note should be clearly struck at the beginning, so that the ear become imbued with it; and, if irregularities are to occur, they should come later.

Numbers V and VI are rhythmically and metrically identical—both being 3/4; but, as we saw in a previous instance, the *direct attack* of " The Flower's Name " gives it more vibration; the presence of the feminine ending in the first and third lines of every quatrain varying the cadence still further.

We have in the " Bridge of Sighs "—Number VII— a very melodious poem, although, less well handled, so short a line might easily have a choppy, grotesque effect; —*vide* some of the " Bab Ballads." It has one slight defect to my ear; and this is that, the *direct attack* having been basically adopted, the irregularity of an anacrusis

has been allowed to creep into several of the later stanzas,
thus preventing entire artistic perfection.

Very similar in movement is James Hogg's " Skylark."

> "｛ Bird of the wilderness,
>   Blythesome and cumberless,
> Sweet be thy matin o'er moorland and lea !
>   Emblem of happiness,
>   Blest is thy dwelling-place—
> O to abide in the desert with thee ! "

Here the increased length of the third and sixth lines
gives a good balance to the shorter ones.

In Number VIII we have our first example of *free verse*.
There is nothing in the English language more melodious
Free or more rhythmically suggestive than this little
verse lyric. Observe the perfect manner in which
the lines with *direct attack* are contrasted with the *strict*
lines, making beautiful verse. Also the prolonged syllables of the first and third lines seem to give a liquid
suggestion, as of gliding waters. The equilibrium between the full and non-full bars is very nice; and the
full beats of the last line seem to impart to it an accelerated motion, as if the gliding changed to rushing.

Of Number IX I might almost repeat my remarks as
to the suggestive effects of the rhythmic management,
except that in " Break, Break, Break " the impression intended is of breaking, not gliding, waters. This is admirably done by the staccato syllables followed by rests.
We seem to get the very impact of the surf. The key to
the rhythm is distinctly struck in the anacrusis of the
second line, and it sweeps in fully in the third. There
is never the slightest doubt.

Number X is also an excellent example of the equilibrium of measures with the *direct attack* preserved uni-

formly throughout. Observe the lulling sound of the long, full-barred line at the end. These *nuances* are due, not to accident, but are the subtle touches of great masters of verse.

In Number XI we have a lyric famous for its spirited cadences; but few persons analyse closely enough to detect that there is in it quite a Shakespearean freedom in the handling of the 2-beat rhythm. The prolonged syllables *we* and *Eve* give a fine swing, increased by the use of the *direct attack*, while the solitary opening anacrusis appeals to the ear, as in some of Shakespeare's songs, as quite legitimate, if sporadic.

" Christabel "—Number XII—is rhythmically, perhaps, the most remarkable of modern poems, inasmuch as Coleridge, more than any other modern poet, seems **Doubled notes** to have quite caught that Elizabethan faculty of doubling syllables without giving the slightest sense of superfluous syllables. The rhythmic balance here is quite as perfect as in Shakespeare's lyrics.

It may be asked why are not these lines, where the doubled notes, or syllables, occur, in regular triple rhythm ? They are not in triple rhythm because the extra syllables are *sporadic*, not *organic;* that is, the whole poem scheme is in 2-beat rhythm, and the sense of the two beats remains undisturbed to the ear by these extra syllables, which naturally settle themselves into the doubled notes indicated in the notations. This power of writing doubled notes is, however, a ticklish business and requires the feeling of a master. It may be studied in its very perfection in the two songs from Shakespeare given in Numbers XIV and XV. If the doubled notes are compared with the pure 3-beat movement of Number XVI, the radical difference will be easily apparent.

The 2-beat rhythm and the 3-beat rhythm are as an-
tipodal and as distinct from each other as oil and water,
Rhythms and quite as impossible to mix as those incon-
cannot be
inter- gruous elements. They are not interchange-
changed able, and one may never be substituted for the
other. To introduce measures of one into a poem cast
in the other is to commit a fault against artistic purity,
and is productive, not of poetry, but of doggerel. No
musical composer would think of writing a piece of music
with one or two bars in 3/8 time, the next in 4/4 time,
another in 12/8, and so on, because this would result in
musical chaos. But the movement which he selects is
adhered to uniformly throughout the piece.[1] Thus is the
composition homogeneous. The same is true of verse.

Of course no poet who is at the same time an artist
ever does confuse them; but there are some who, for the
elevation of their thought and their eloquence of diction,
take high rank, yet whose ears are too defective for true
rhythmic perfection. There is scarcely a poem of Emerson's where this artistic solecism is not committed, the
confusions of rhythm giving to much of his verse that
halting quality, often so painful to the ears of even his
best lovers. Wordsworth too, though in a very much less
degree, was defective of ear. Witness his " Ode to a
Skylark," which opens with a panting triple beat:

" Up with me, up with me into the clouds ! "

but before the end of the first stanza it flats out into a
somewhat broken 2-beat measure, and never regains the
first rhythmic fervour.

This is not to say that music or verse may not be legi-

[1] It must always be borne in mind that, in these comparisons, I am re-
ferring only to the simplest forms of musical composition.

timately *switched off* upon another track, if desired. When, in music, it is desired to change the rhythm, **The barring** there is a double bar drawn across the staff, **off of verse** and a new signature—the signature of the new measure—is written in. So, with a distinct demarkation —a mental *barring off*, as it were—we may introduce songs into longer compositions, or we may divide a long poem into distinct parts. In Swinburne's "Atalanta in Caledon," after the chief huntsman's invocation to Artemis, which is in blank verse (2/5), there comes that brilliant bit of verbal melody, the hunting chorus, in ringing 3-beat rhythm.

> " When the hounds of spring are on winter's traces,
>   The mother of months in meadow or plain
> Fills the shadows and windy places
>   With lisp of leaves and ripple of rain ;
> And the brown bright nightingale amourous
>   Is half assuaged for Itylus,
> For the Thracian ships and the foreign faces,
>   The tongueless vigil, and all the pain.''

Another example is in Browning's "Paracelsus," where, from the meditative speech in blank verse, ending:

> " This is my record ; and my voice the wind's,''

Paracelsus breaks into a song with bounding triple movement very suggestive of the swell of the seas of which it sings.

> " Over the sea our galleys went,
>   With cleaving prows in order brave,
> To a speeding wind and a bounding wave,
>   A gallant armament : ''

Still another example is found in the exquisite little lyrics scattered, like dainty *intermezzi*, through the

pages of Tennyson's " Princess.'' But perhaps the most
notable instance of verse *barring off* is to be found in
" Maud,'' where the story is told, not in dramatic form,
nor even in that of the romantic narrative—as in Browning's " Ivan Ivanovitch,'' " Donald,'' and others—but in
a succession of fervid lyrics, each cast in a separate metrical mould.

We have seen how we may vary the cadence of our
rhythms by writing the verse in different styles, and by
Lines of
different
lengths
within the
stanza the use of the feminine ending. We can give
further metrical variety by employing, and con-
trasting with each other, lines of different
lengths within the stanza. This varies the
phrase effects and prevents monotony. The adjustment
of lines of different lengths contrasted in a stanza is not
an arbitrary thing, a question merely of caprice, but is
determined by a natural pause, or breathing-place, in the
rhetoric or in the rhythm alone. When these pauses
occur at the end of a line it is called *end-stopped*. Similar
pauses occurring in the middle of the verse are known as
cæsuras or *cæsural pauses*.[1] Exactly in the same way in
music is a melody divided naturally into its component
phrases.

It will be found on comparison that, as a rule, very
long lines do not balance well set against very short ones;
also, that lines of an uneven number of measures balance
each other better than alternations of even and uneven.
Thus a line of five measures naturally calls for an alternating line of three measures rather than one of four,
etc. But for effects of this sort rules cannot be laid

---

[1] Cæsura (from *cædo*, to cut) means a cutting. This term, as well as
anacrusis, is extensively used in music, the interchangeability of nomenclatures in this and other terms demonstrating anew the close structural relation between the two arts.

down. They are a matter of a trained ear, which the student must develop for himself.

We also find that the ear will not carry as a unit a very long line; but that lines of more than five measures are **Cæsural** apt mentally to divide themselves into two **division** periods, because of the very strong cæsura always found in the middle. The poet may at his option write these long phrases either in one period or two periods.

Thus " Locksley Hall " is written:

" Love took up the harp of Life, and smote on all the chords with
        might ;
Smote the chord of Self, that, trembling, passed in music out
        of sight.''

But they more naturally fall into two rhythmic periods, thus:

        " Love took up the harp of Life,
            And smote on all the chords with might ;
        Smote the chord of Self, that, trembling,
            Passed in music out of sight.''

The same is true of the " May Queen," and some others. The *English Ballad Metre*—the oldest lyric form we have—will be found sometimes written out in long lines with rhymed couplets, as in Chapman's Homer ; sometimes in the shorter quatrains, each alternate line rhymed, as in Macaulay's " Lays of Ancient Rome.''

When we come to irregular poems—poems with lines of irregular lengths, and not divided into uniform stanzas **Equilibrium** —the equilibrium between long and short must **of irregular** be very nicely preserved, or we shall get an **poems.** effect of chopped prose merely, and not a sense of that perfect metrical balance required for a real poem. Not having the equipoise afforded by the formal stanza, we have only the natural pauses to guide us, and these are sometimes so subtle as to require a very fine ear for perfect adjustment. Tennyson has given us many irregular poems, all marvellously balanced. The " Lotos Eaters " is an example. Observe, in the lines quoted below, the longer and longer roll to each succeeding line, like the lazy up-roll of an incoming tide. The effect is most musical.

" Here are cool mosses deep,
And thro' the moss the ivies creep,
And in the stream the long-leaved flowers weep,
And from the craggy ledge the poppy hangs in sleep."

Wordsworth's ode on the " Intimations of Immortality " is a beautifully balanced poem. The cæsural effects fall naturally and with great simplicity, and the melody moves harmoniously throughout. It is a fine touch, at the last, to drop entirely into the always stately heroic verse.

Lowell's " Commemoration Ode," on the contrary, has always impressed me as not well balanced, and very mechanically divided. The ear gets no sense of natural pauses, and the theme moves upon hard, cold numbers.

Sidney Lanier was fond of the irregular form, and has left us some most melodious poems in it; but one of the most perfect specimens of irregular composition which I have ever come across is Mrs. James T. Fields's limpid little " Ode to Spring," which, as it is short, I insert entire:

" I wakened to the singing of a bird;
I heard the bird of spring.
And lo !
At his sweet note

The flowers began to grow,
Grass, leaves, and everything,
As if the green world heard
The trumpet of his tiny throat
From end to end, and winter and despair
Fled at his melody, and passed in air.

" I heard at dawn the music of a voice.
O my belovèd, then I said, the spring
Can visit only once the waiting year ;
The bird can bring
Only the season's song, nor his the choice
To waken smiles or the remembering tear !
But thou dost bring
Springtime to every day, and at thy call
The flowers of life unfold, though leaves of autumn fall.''

There is in verse a secondary accent concerning the
verse, the *accent of emphasis*—called by some prosodists
Secondary   the *rhetorical accent* or the *logical accent*,—
accent   which not only serves to indicate the meaning
of the words, but further brings out the larger metric
swing of the whole line.

Some writers have much discussion about *word accent*
and *verse accent*, and their correlation; but it seems so
obvious a proposition that the accent of emphasis shall
coincide with the rhythmic accent—that is, that it shall
fall upon a strong syllable, already accented,—as scarcely
to need formal statement.

Lanier concerns himself with some hair-splitting dis-
quisition upon further expression marks; but verse reading is a species of *tempo rubato*, dependent for expression
upon the interpretive genius of the reader, and, therefore,
if it were advisable to formulate rules upon these lines—
which it seems to me it is not—they would belong rather

to the province of elocution, and would have no place in a work upon the science of verse.

To sum up the foregoing chapter, we find:

1. That music and verse are both arts of sound, or

Summary of vibration.

foregoing 2. That both music and verse are measured

chapter by a natural accent, recurring at regular intervals, and dividing the notes, or syllables, into successive groups.

3. That these groups are all uniform, each having the same time-value as every other.

4. That the measurement of these groups is always to be made, not necessarily from the opening note, or syllable, but from *accent to accent*.

Or to formulate still more condensedly:

Music and verse are both dependent for existence as such, and distinguished from chaos, upon continual, balanced rhythm.

In concluding this chapter, I should like to urge upon the student of verse the advisability of taking with his

Advisabil- studies in prosody a coördinate elementary

ity of study course in music; if possible, vocal, since the

of music voice—song—is the connecting medium between music and verse. It need not be with any view to becoming a musical performer, but should be rudimentarily constructive as far as the developing the understanding of metre (primary rhythm), simple phrase division, and pure melody. The musically-drilled ear will instinctively construct rhythmic and melodic verse; while any student so deficient in these perceptions as to be unable to grasp the elements of music may be sure that, even by any poetical license, he will never be able to produce anything resembling real poetry.

CHAPTER III

DIFFERENTIATED MOTION

THERE is a vital quality in which verse and music resemble each other and by which they are essentially differentiated from the other arts, and that is *motion*.

Music has much more motion than poetry, and may therefore be considered the freest of all vehicles for emotional expression. The other arts are station-

Fixity of other arts ary. They are intellectual snap-shots; bits of life snatched from time and space and immutably fixed upon the mental plates. They catch for us a single impression; they perpetuate for us a single moment of human experience. In such a picture as Millet's "Angelus"—to use a universally-known example—a brown, nubbly harvest field stretches away indefinitely from us, until it melts into the paling perspective. In the foreground, beside a rude barrow, stand two of the harvesters, a woman and a man. They have heard the echo of the far-away angelus, the bell of evening prayer, and stand with bent heads, devoutly murmuring their orisons. Time passes; but in the picture it does not pass. Still the tenebrous field rolls itself into the gloaming; still, in the foreground, stand the two reverent figures, fixed in their attitudes of devotion.

In sculpture we have exactly the same momentary conditions. All emotional expression is as stationary as the figures upon Keats's "Grecian Urn."

> " Fair youth, beneath the trees, thou canst not leave
> Thy song, nor ever can those trees be bare ;

Bold lover, never, never canst thou kiss,
    Though winning near the goal—"

Laocoön stands before us in his petrified extremity,
forever striving to uncoil those never-uncoiled serpents.
The Discus Player waits with body bent and discus
poised—but never hurled. The Dying Gladiator droops
in mortal agony above his shield—but the final moment
never arrives; he does not die.

But with poetry what a difference! Here we have
motion, progression, vibration; in short, the concrete
Motion manifestation of energy; and energy, the sci-
of poetry entist tells us, "manifests itself as motion, heat,
light, chemical action, sound."

Poetry moves, not only abstractly by the unfoldment
of the thought—pictorial, dramatic, spiritual—moving in
orderly sequence from premise to conclusion; but concretely, by the rhythmic vibration of its numbers. We
have in verse, not a solitary impression, but a succession
of impressions; not a single pictorial moment, but a whole
mental panorama. Moved by the master-hand of the
artist, like men upon a chessboard, there pass before us
marvellous presentments of that strange game called
Life. In company with Roland we turn loathingly from
the "hoary cripple with malicious eyes," and plunge
into the "ignoble country." We follow across the
"sudden little river," where he fears to set his foot
"upon a dead man's cheek," on to the "bit of stubbed
ground once a wood," through the marsh, and over the
country of "blotches rankling, coloured gay and grim,"
until we arrive at the mountains:

    "Those two hills on the right,
Crouched like two bulls locked horn in horn in fight;
While to the left a tall scalped mountain——"

and perceive suddenly, as he did, the " Dark Tower"
itself:

> " The round squat turret, blind as the fool's heart,"

Our own nerves quiver in creepy and sympathetic sus-
pense as Roland, dauntless and provocative, sets the
slug-horn to his lips and blows:

> " Childe Roland to the Dark Tower came ! "

So, too, we live over with Guinevere her passionate and
guilty tragedy, from

> " The golden days
> In which she saw him first, when Launcelot came,
> Reputed the best knight and goodliest man,
> Ambassador, to lead her to his lord
> Arthur, and led her forth, and far ahead
> Of his and her retinue moving, they,
> Rapt in sweet talk or lively, all on love
> And sport and tilts and pleasure (for the time
> Was Maytime, and as yet no sin was dream'd),
> Rode under groves that look'd a paradise
> Of blossom,"

to those last direful days when, flying from the conse-
quences of her sin, she seeks asylum in " the holy house
at Almesbury," and one day hears through the sombre
cloisters the dread, whispered word, " The King!"

> " She sat
> Stiff-stricken, listening; but when armed feet
> Thro' the long gallery from the outer doors
> Rang coming, prone from off her seat she fell,
> And grovell'd with her face against the floor :
> There with her milk-white arms and shadowy hair
> She made her face a darkness from the King :
> And in the darkness heard his armed feet
> Pause by her."

But it is not only thus abstractly, upon the progression of its themes, that poetry moves. It has further a specific, concrete vibration within the measured bar; a vibration which imparts to the ear a greater or less sense of velocity correlative with the rhythm, metre, and manner employed.

Motion of rhythm and metre

In the famous Virgilian line:

" *Quadrupedante putrem sonitu quatit ungula campum* "

we are aware of the galloping of the horse, not so much because the poet informs us that

" He shakes the quivering earth with the four-footed bound of the hoofs,"

as because, in the rapid beat of the dactylic measure— 1, 2, 3; 1, 2, 3; 1, 2, 3; 1, 2, 3; 1, 2, 3; 1, 2—there is the verisimilitude of the clatter of galloping horsehoofs. Furthermore, there is, in the accelerated vibration of the triple beat, a rush, a vigour, a sense of onward movement, very distinct and dynamic.

We perceive this sense of velocity even more clearly in the short, crisp lines of the " Charge of the Light Brigade ":

> " Half a league, half a league,
>   Half a league onward,
>   All in the valley of Death
>   Rode the six hundred.
>   ' Forward, the Light Brigade !
>   Charge for the guns ! ' he said :
>   Into the valley of Death
>   Rode the six hundred.
>   .   -   .   .
> " Cannon to right of them,
>   Cannon to left of them,

Cannon in front of them
Volley'd and thunder'd ;
Storm'd at with shot and shell,
Boldly they rode and well,
Into the jaws of Death,
Into the mouth of Hell
Rode the six hundred.''

Should we feel the breathless impact of this poem if it were cast, for example, in heroic blank verse, or in the 2/4 measure of " The White Doe of Rylstone " ? I think not. For it is in the rhythmic rush, quite as much as in the words, that the impression is conveyed to the imagination. The technical movement of a poem has then not a little to do with the impression which it makes upon us; and this sense of the movement in verse varies with the varying metre and rhythm of the numbers.

Sources of motion The primal source of motion in verse is to be found in *rhythm.*

A second, lesser, source of motion is found in the *direct attack;* which, as has already been pointed out, has a strong propulsive force, and seems, as it were, to launch the verse out into the deeps.

A third, still lesser, source of motion is found in the *feminine ending;* the second, or unaccented syllable, giving a little back swing, like that of a pendulum.

The feminine ending is the ending of a verse of poetry with the *non-accent*, or second beat in the bar; as *pleasure,*

Feminine ending *treasure ; dying, crying; faster, vaster ;* etc. It is so called in contradistinction to the masculine ending, which is upon an accent—either a monosyllable or the accented final syllable of a polysyllable,— the first beat in the bar. Two words may be used instead of a dissyllable, in which case it is called, not the feminine ending, but the double ending. If the endings are rhymed, they are designated as feminine, or double *rhymes;* if unrhymed, merely as *endings*.

The feminine ending is a wonderful factor in relieving metric monotony and producing melodic and motive contrast; but it must be used with discretion, or it is liable to produce, upon the English ear, a cloying effect. In many of Longfellow's poems, Moore's, and Byron's, we may observe instances of its possibilities of effeminacy. It seems used without object, and merely to tickle the ear, becoming an idle melodic tinkle. Professor Corson has pointed out the fact that Byron, whenever he wishes to express the trivial or the grotesque, lapses into it. Thus:

> " Sweet is the vintage when the showering grapes
>   In Bacchanal profusion reel to earth,
> Purple and gushing; sweet are our escapes
>   From civic revelry to rural mirth :
> Sweet to the miser are his glittering heaps,
>   Sweet to the father is his first-born's birth,
> Sweet is revenge—especially to women,
> Pillage to soldiers, prize-money to seamen.

> " Sweet is a legacy, and passing sweet
>   The unexpected death of some old lady
> Or gentleman of seventy years complete,
>   Who've made ' us youth ' wait too—too long already
> For an estate, or cash, or country seat,
>   Still breaking, but with stamina so steady
> That all the Israelites are fit to mob its
> Next owner for their double-damned post-obits."
>   —" Don Juan," canto i., stanzas 124, 125.

There is, however, nothing intrinsically meretricious in the feminine ending; quite the contrary. In the hands

5

of a master, it can be made to give out nothing but strains of pure beauty. Browning, more than any other poet, has exploited the feminine ending, and has handled it with " imperial grace."

The 2-beat rhythm has less internal vibration, therefore less motion, than is to be found in the 3-beat rhythm. Purely ethical poets—poets of a contemplative order, cold and without passional fires—affect it chiefly and make imperfect, if any, use of the more motive 3-beat rhythm. We cannot turn the pages of Wordsworth, Coleridge, Arnold, Emerson, without recognising this to be the chief resource of their muse. It is the full-rounded artists, whose inspiration runs the whole gamut of human experience, who have discovered and utilised the cadence variety possible to the 3-beat rhythm.

Generally speaking, we might, therefore, characterise **Poetry of** the 2-beat rhythm as the medium of the *Poetry* **reflection** *of Reflection;* and the 3-beat rhythm as **and poetry** **of motion** more specifically the medium of the *Poetry* *of Motion.*

The noblest expression of 2-beat rhythm is to be found in strict 2/5 verse, or the line of five bars with two beats to the bar. ·It is always dignified, while shorter metrical divisions may be trivial, and longer are awkward for long-sustained themes. In blank verse—the medium best suited to heroic themes—it reaches its greatest elevation, and also its most elastic presentment; because, blank verse not being, strictly speaking, *song*, but rather a species of recitative, it admits of greater irregularity of notation than is possible within the close stanza.[1]

---

[1] " The Italians called it *stanza*, as if we should say a resting-place."— PUTTENHAM : "Art of English Poesie!"

" So named from the stop or halt at the end of it. Cognate with English *stand*."—SKEATS'S " Etymological Dictionary."

Stateliness of heroic verse The ordinary heroic quatrain is stately, but, long continued, bears a certain stamp of monotony.

" Still doth the soul, from its lone fastness high,
Upon our life a ruling effluence send ;
And when it fails, fight as we will, we die,
And while it lasts, we cannot wholly end."
        —MATTHEW ARNOLD : " Palladium."

This stanza, because of its common selection for elegy, is known in English as the elegiac stanza. It must not be confounded with the classical elegiac verse.

In the Spenserian stanza, with the varied rhyme-melody and the stately rounding of the final Alexandrine, we have a noble verse-form.

The stanza of Shelley's " Ode to the West Wind "— bits of Italian *terza rima*, separated at regular intervals into stanzas by a rhymed couplet—is felicitous and beautiful.

There are plenty of other beautiful variants of 2/5 verse —some with the break of an occasional shorter line, like Keats's " Ode to a Nightingale," Arnold's " Scholar Gypsy," etc., but the reader will easily find them for himself.

Of all the metric forms we have, the strict 2/4 verse **Monotony of common quatrain** (verse of four bars of two beats to the bar) has the least internal music. Its cadences are tame and flat, with an inevitable aroma of monotony.

The feeblest of all vehicles for poetic expression is, perhaps, the quatrain of alternating lines of 2/4 and 2/3.[1]

---

[1] Known in the hymn books as *common metre*.

> " I travell'd among unknown men,
>   In lands beyond the sea ;
>   Nor, England ! did I know till then
>   What love I bore to thee."
> —Wordsworth : " I Travell'd among Unknown Men."

Verse in this form runs great danger of degenerating into the utterly commonplace, and ringing out, not poetry, but the mere sing-song of a nursery jingle. We get more music in Tennyson's " Brook," where the addition of the feminine ending seems to give it a fresh swing, and imparts to it a terminal ripple eminently suggestive.

> " I come from haunts of coot and hern,
>   I make a sudden sally,
>   And sparkle out among the fern,
>   To bicker down a valley."

A shorter line—2/3 or even 2/2—has more movement, owing perhaps to the rapid succession of metric divisions.

> " When spring comes laughing
>   By vale and hill,
>   By wind-flower walking
>   And daffodil,—
>   Sing stars of morning,
>   Sing morning skies,
>   Sing blue of speedwell,
>   And my Love's eyes."
> —Austin Dobson : " A Song of the Four Seasons."

Let us now examine and see how we can, as it were, **How to build** *build up motion* in the 2/4 quatrain. We will **up motion** take a series of progressive examples in verse-motion to show the larger and larger rhythmic swing possible.

" Art thou a statesman, in the van
  Of public business train'd and bred ?
First learn to love one living man !
  Then mayst thou think upon the dead."
        —WORDSWORTH : " A Poet's Epitaph."

" 'Tis sweet to him, who all the week
  Through city crowds must push his way,
To stroll alone through fields and woods,
  And hallow thus the Sabbath day."
        —COLERIDGE : " Homesick."

" Thy summer voice, Musketaquit,
  Repeats the music of the rain ;
But sweeter rivers pulsing flit
  Through thee, as thou through Concord Plain."
        —EMERSON : " Two Rivers."

" Like driftwood spars, which meet and pass
  Upon the boundless ocean-plain,
So on the sea of life, alas !
  Man meets man—meets, and quits again."
        —ARNOLD : " The Terrace at Berne."

This verse certainly moves upon a dead level of utter monotony. But the direct attack will give it fresh impulse.

" I am old, but let me drink ;
  Bring me spices, bring me wine ;
I remember, when I think,
  That my youth was half divine."
        —TENNYSON : " The Vision of Sin."

With both the direct attack and the feminine ending, we get still more motion.

" ' Guidarello Guidarelli ! '
    Rang the cry from street and tower,
    As our Guido rode to battle
    In Ravenna's darkest hour."
—S. Weir Mitchell: " Guidarello Guidarelli."

In the beautiful little spinning song given below, we seem to get the acme of motion possible to 2-beat verse. It is achieved partly by the use of the direct attack and alternate feminine endings, but a great deal by the effect of the long swinging line.   One seems to catch the very whir of the wheel.

" Moon in heaven's garden, among the clouds that wander,
    Crescent moon so young to see, above the April ways,
    Whiten, bloom not yet, not yet, within the twilight yonder;
    All my spinning is not done, for all the loitering days.

" Oh, my heart has two wild wings that ever would be flying !
    Oh, my heart's a meadow lark that ever would be free !
    Well it is that I must spin until the light be dying;
    Well it is the little wheel must turn all day for me ! "
        —Josephine Preston Peabody: " Spinning in April."

Many poets have employed the 2/4 verse in rhymed couplets for long poems, but it seems an inadequate measure for sustained action.   It has not the staying power of the heroic verse, and the limited swing of the shorter line renders the constantly recurring rhyme tiresome and mechanical, like the *clip clip* of a woodman's hatchet chopping a fagot into lengths.   Wordsworth has written " The White Doe of Rylstone " and other poems in it; Byron has used it extensively; and Scott has cast most of his longer poems in it.   He probably used this measure because, like Byron and other young men of that day, he was much under

Use of the short couplet

the ascendency of Wordsworth. Scott's diction is, however, bold and ringing; and the interspersion, at intervals, of the shorter 2/3 line seems to divide the text.
roughly into stanzas, and gives, as it were, a breathing
space. But at best it is a poor vehicle beside 2/5 verse,
and all of these poems would have gained in dignity and
power had they been cast in blank verse, or even in heroic
rhymed couplets.

Scott's instincts were those of the true artist, but his
muse was too facile for a nature not self-exacting, and he
suffered, like Byron, from too universal a popularity and
absence of criticism to achieve the highest artistic results.

Neither Wordsworth, Coleridge, nor Emerson was a
metric artist of a high order. Arnold was artistically
much greater, yet, it seems to me, not really great. His
critical judgment of what art should be certainly exceeds
that of any person, yet in his own work he made use of
a very limited number of forms, and easily lapses into a
monotonous 2/4 measure.

Let us examine now how Tennyson—a past-master of
artistic technique—handled the 2-beat rhythm. Tenny-
Tennyson's son's use of heroic verse is always pure, ele-
use of 2-beat vated, and resonant. He was opulent of re-
rhythm source and sure of touch. His use of forms is
never a lottery as with lesser craftsmen. Whatever
effects of rhythm or melody he employs, it is always with
distinct and unerring purpose. For dignity, melody,
fluidity, *enjambement*,[1] and perfect cæsural balance, his
blank verse is virtually beyond criticism. It will be
treated more at large in a future chapter, and we will
confine ourselves here to an analysis of some of his lyric
forms. He employs 2/4 verse very little in its baldest

---

[1] *Enjambement.* Running of a verse into the next line to complete the
sense.

shape, but, when he does do so, he contrives to endow it with some subtle virtue of melody.   More often we find variants, as in " Mariana."

> " With blackest moss the flower-plots
>   Were thickly crusted, one and all ;
>   The rusted nails fell from the knots
>   That held the pear to the gable-wall.
>   The broken sheds look'd sad and strange :
>   Unlifted was the clinking latch ;
>   Weeded and worn the ancient thatch
>   Upon the lonely moated grange.
>   She only said, ' My life is dreary,
>   He cometh not,' she said ;
>   She said, ' I am aweary, aweary,
>   I would that I were dead ! ' "

Here we have a stanza composed of three quatrains; the first, in ordinary strict 2/4 measure with alternating rhyme; the second, with the first and fourth lines rhymed, the two central ones rhyming together (this variation alone is a refreshment to the ear); and in the third (again an alternating quatrain), the second and fourth lines are shortened a bar, while the first and third carry the fcminine ending.   Yet so homogeneous is the stanza that the ordinary reader would not be aware that the metrical scheme was not uniform throughout.

In this song from " The Miller's Daughter "—not a quatrain, by the way, but a sestet—note the sweet insistence of the rhyme.

> " Love that hath us in the net,
>   Can he pass, and we forget ?
>   Many suns arise and set.
>   Many a chance the years beget.
>   Love the gift is Love the debt.
>   Even so."

Here we have the impulse of the direct attack, and the pretty touch of the little half-phrase, like a sighing echo, at the end.

In " The Lady of Shalott " we have the same melodic idea of repeated rhyme; but the stanza is divided with central and terminal rhymes, the last line being shortened to 2/3, which rounds it well off. This poem is an example of free verse, somewhat rare, and difficult to do well, in 2-beat rhythm.

> " On either side the river lie
> Long fields of barley and of rye,
> That clothe the wold and meet the sky ;
> And thro' the field the road runs by
> To many-tower'd Camelot ;
> And up and down the people go,
> Gazing where the lilies blow
> Round an island there below,
> The island of Shalott."

And in this song from " Maud " what an ecstatic, spring-like lilt we catch in the direct 2/3 verse!

> " Go not, happy day,
> From the shining fields,
> Go not, happy day,
> Till the maiden yields.
> Rosy is the West,
> Rosy is the South,
> Roses are her cheeks,
> And a rose her mouth."

In " The Two Voices " we have three uniform-rhymed lines. This gives " a close emphasised stanza. The poem consists in a great part of a succession of short, epigrammatic arguments, *pro* and *con*, to which the stanza is well adapted." [1]

> " A still small voice spake unto me,
>   ' Thou art so full of misery,
>   Were it not better not to be ? '
>
> " Then to the still small voice I said :
>   ' Let me not cast in endless shade
>   What is so wonderfully made.'
>
> " To which the voice did urge reply:
>   ' To-day I saw the dragon-fly
>   Come from the wells where he did lie.
>
> " ' An inner impulse rent the veil
>   Of his old husk: from head to tail
>   Came out clear plates of sapphire mail.' "

In " The Palace of Art," the stanza is a quatrain of which the first line is 2/5 verse; the second, 2/4 verse; the third, again 2/5 verse; and the fourth drops into the still shorter 2/3 verse.

> " One seem'd all dark and red—a tract of sand,
>   With some one pacing there alone,
>   Who paced for ever in a glimmering land,
>   Lit with a low large moon.
>
> " One show'd an iron coast and angry waves.
>   You seem'd to hear them climb and fall
>   And roar rock-thwarted under bellowing caves,
>   Beneath the windy wall.
>
> " And one, a full-fed river winding slow
>   By herds upon an endless plain,
>   The ragged rims of thunder brooding low,
>   With shadow-streaks of rain."

[1] HIRAM CORSON : " Primer of English Verse," chap. vi., p. 78.

Of this stanza Peter Bayne says, " It is novel, and it is only by degrees that its exquisite adaptation to the style and thought of the poem is perceived. The ear instinctively demands in the second and fourth lines a body of sound not much less than that of the first and third; but in Tennyson's stanza, the fall in the fourth line is complete; the body of sound in the second and fourth lines is not nearly sufficient to balance that in the first and third; the consequence is that the ear dwells on the alternate lines, especially on the fourth, stopping there to listen to the whole verse, to gather up its whole sound and sense. I do not know whether Tennyson ever contemplated scientifically the effect of this. I should think it far more likely, and indicative of far higher genius, that he did not. But no means could be conceived for setting forth to more advantage those separate pictures, ' each a perfect whole,' which constitute so great a portion of the poem." [1]

Most writers agree that, as an adaptation of means to ends, no stanza is more felicitous than that employed in " In Memoriam." A certain elegiac monotony—a minor key of verse—being desired, it is found in the 2/4 quatrain, not in its usual form of alternating rhymes, but with the two central lines rhymed, the first line waiting for its complement until the last.[2]

" By the rhyme-scheme of the quatrain, the terminal rhyme emphasis of the stanza is reduced, the second and third verses being the most clearly braced by the rhyme. The stanza is thus admirably adapted to that sweet con-

[1] See " Primer of English Verse," p. 81.

[2] " This stanza is not original with Tennyson, Ben Jonson having employed it in an elegy in his ' Underwoods ; ' and Dante Gabriel Rossetti, just before ' In Memoriam ' appeared, in ' My Sister's Sleep.' "—HIRAM CORSON : " A Primer of English Verse," p. 70.

tinuity of flow, free from abrupt checks, demanded by
the spiritualised sorrow which it bears along.   Alternate
rhyme would have wrought an entire change in the tone
of the poem.'' [1]

> '' Sweet after showers, ambrosial air,
>   That rollest from the gorgeous gloom
>   Of evening over brake and bloom
> And meadow, slowly breathing bare
>
> '' The round of space, and rapt below
>   Thro' all the dewy-tassell'd wood,
>   And shadowing down the horned flood
> In ripples, fan my brows and blow
>
> '' The fever from my cheek, and sigh
>   The full new life that feeds thy breath
>   Throughout my frame, till Doubt and Death,
> Ill brethren, let the fancy fly
>
> '' From belt to belt of crimson seas
>   On leagues of odour streaming far,
>   To where in yonder orient star
> A hundred spirits whisper ' Peace.' ''

The 3-beat rhythm is instinct with motion.   It has an
inherent bounding swiftness which the 2-beat rhythm

Mobile quality of 3-beat rhythm entirely lacks.   It runs, it leaps, it laughs, it
flies, it gallops; therefore poets have instinct-
ively selected it as the vehicle of their most
fervid thought.   Wherever rapid or passionate action is
to be expressed, it will be found a most effective medium.   '' The good news '' is carried from Ghent to Aix
upon it; Pheidippides runs in it; the Light Brigade
charges to it; the Sea Fairies dance to it; the pace of

---

[1] Hiram Corson : '' A Primer of English Verse,'' chap. vi., p. 70.

Arethusa's melodious flight is tuned to it; and upon its numbers a thousand imperishable love lyrics breathe out their impassioned music.

With the resource of invention, such as we know it to-day, the 3-beat rhythm seems to be a very late development. In the centuries preceding ours it appears conspicuous by its absence. The Elizabethans seem not to have been acquainted with it, or certainly never to have used it consciously; another proof, if any were needed, of how entirely free the technique of the Renaissance literature was from any influence from the classics. They had the models of the classic dactyls and anapæsts, which they might have imitated, and in which some men—more pedants than creators—did write; but it never became germane to the language and left no permanent imprint.

Absence of triple movement in Elizabethan poetry

Says Edmund Gosse, " The dactylic and anapæstic movement was conspicuously unknown to the Elizabethans. I purposely take no note here of the experiments in tumbling, rimeless measure made by certain Elizabethans. These were purely exotic, and, even in the hands of Campion himself, neither natural nor successful." [1]

Sir Philip Sidney, Fulke Greville, Gabriel Harvey, and others—even the most melodious Edmund Spenser—proposed wild schemes for bringing English verse under the restrictions of the classic laws of quantity. Spenser seems, however, to have soon recovered from his " artificial fever," and, in one of his letters to Harvey, he exclaims fervently: " Why, a God's name, may not we, as else the Greeks, have the kingdom of our own language, and *measure our accents by the sound*, reserving quantity to the verse?"

[1] EDMUND GOSSE : " From Shakespeare to Pope," p. 9.

The tide of feeling for true rhythmic values was too strong to be stemmed; and English verse went on its way rejoicing, taking cognisance neither of theory nor theorist, but singing itself out according to its own divine instinct.

Previous to Elizabeth there are a few sporadic traces of 3-beat rhythm; although here, too, was the sugges-

Triple rhythm previous to Elizabeth tion in the Anglo-Saxon verse, which, although not measured by syllables, is divided into certain heavy stresses, resembling an imperfect triple movement.

There is a very old comedy entitled " Gammer Gurton's Needle " (see page 199 of this book) in which is inserted a song—undoubtedly much older than the play —the chorus of which has a distinct triple lilt.

> " Back and side go bare, go bare,
>   Both hand and foot go cold;
> But belly, God send thee good ale enough
>   Whether't be new or old."

Lanier gives a " Song of Ever and Never," belonging to the early part of the sixteenth century; and " The Battle of Agincourt,"[1] also early sixteenth century, both of which are in 3-beat measure, and may be older than the foregoing.

> " Agincourt, Agincourt !
> Know ye not Agincourt ?
> Where English slue and hurt
>   All their French foemen ?
> With our pikes and bills brown,
> How the French were beat downe,
>   Shot by our bowmen."

[1] From appendix to vol. ii., Hale's and Furnivall's " Bishop Percy's Folio Manuscript." There are also in the " Reliques " a number of ballads with triple movement.

There is also a " Battle of Agincourt " by Michael Drayton (1563–1631) which may have been imitated from the preceding.[1]

> " Fair stood the wind for France
> When we our sails advance,
> Nor now to prove our chance
> Longer will tarry ;
> But putting to the main,
> At Kaux, the mouth of Seine,
> With all his martial train,
> Landed King Harry.''

Shakespeare, saturated as he was with music, ripples wonderfully near the triple rhythm, and occasionally breaks, for a few exotic bars, into the true lilt. As:

Shakespeare's use of triple rhythm

> " 'Ban, 'Ban, Ca—Caliban,
> Has a new master—get a new man.''

Yet it is clear it has no part in his intention as a special form; and the only plays in which I find it deliberately used in a song are " The Winter's Tale " and " Othello." Desdemona's song is famous.

> " The poor soul sat sighing by a sycamore tree,
>   Sing all a green willow;
> Her hand on her bosom, her head on her knee,
>   Sing willow, willow, willow :
> The fresh streams ran by her, and murmur'd her moans ;
>   Sing willow, willow, willow :
> Her salt tears fell from her, and soften'd the stones ; "

[1] We notice that Longfellow's famous " Skeleton in Armor " is modelled upon this poem.

The rhythmic balance is here not perfectly true, for the ear loses the movement in the refrain. These lines are from an old ballad called "A Lover's Complaint, being Forsaken of his Love." The entire ballad is given in "Percy's Reliques." There it is the plaint of a man; Shakespeare assigns it to a woman.

The other songs are put into the mouth of that delightful vagabond, Autolycus, and have a rollicking, exuberant lilt.

> " When daffodils begin to peer,—
> With hey ! the doxy over the dale,—
> Why, then comes in the sweet o' the year ;
> For the red blood reigns in the winter's pale."

And later comes the jolly catch:

> " Jog on, jog on, the footpath way,
> And merrily hent the stile-a:
> A merry heart goes all the day,
> Your sad tires in a mile-a." [1]

"The Winter's Tale" was among the last known works to leave the poet's hand. Had he lived to the ripe age of a Wordsworth or a Tennyson, it is very possible that the 3-beat rhythm would not have had to wait for the days of Waller and Cleveland for its exposition. According to Mr. Gosse, Waller seems the first poet to

---

[1] I find a number of instances of single couplets throughout the dramas ; also a portion of a song of Silence's in the second part of "Henry IV," which shows rough triple rhythm. The fool's catch in "Lear," "Have more than thou showest," and several other of his short strains, have the ring of triple time ; while Iago's drinking song (one stanza) in "Othello," "And let me the canakin clink, clink," is quite pure in movement. With the exception of Desdemona's song, this measure seems to be always put into the mouths of rogues or clowns, which would point to its being less a matter of invention than a reversion to the refrains of the people.

make deliberate use of the triple rhythm. " Up to his (Cleveland's) time, and to that of Waller, the triple or **Waller the** anapæstic cadence, which is now so familiar **first to make** to us, and which the facilities of its use have **conscious** **use of triple** even vulgarised, had not been used at all. The **rhythm** great Elizabethan poets had achieved their marvellous effects without its ever occurring to them that they had at their elbow a dancing or lilting cadence which the very ballads of the peasantry might have revealed to them. . . . Shakespeare, of course, in such songs as ' Come away, come away, Death,'[1] glides into the triple cadence; and so, as my friend Coventry Patmore points out, does the early Elizabethan, Phaer, in his version of the ' Æneid.' I have remarked another instance in a ballad of Bishop Corbet's. But these felicities were the result either of accident or, in the case of Shakespeare, for instance, of an art above art. . . . In Waller's 1645 volume of poems there is a copy of verses called ' Chloris and Hilas,' which is written in faltering but unmistakable dactyls. Waller, long afterwards, said that it was composed to imitate the motions of a *Sarabande.* Here are portions of it, those in which the triple cadence is most audible:

> " ' Hilas, O Hilas, why sit we mute
>   Now that each bird saluteth the spring ?
> Wind up the slackenèd strings of thy lute,
>   Never canst thou want matter to sing !
>
> .   .   .   .   .
>
> " ' Sweetest, you know the sweetest of things,
>   Of various flowers the bees do compose,
> Yet no particular taste it brings
>   Of violet, woodbine, pink or rose.' "

[1] I have already shown in chap. ii. that " Come away, come away, Death " is not true triple rhythm.

6

Waller would seem to have hit upon this movement " almost by chance, by his surprising quickness of ear," **Cleveland's use of triple rhythm** and not to have prosecuted the experiment. " Cleveland, on the other hand, deliberately studied, not once, but repeatedly, anapæstic effects of a really very delicate kind. The first edition of Cleveland's poems was published in 1647; but on this we can build no theory of Waller's priority of composition. Born eight years earlier than Cleveland, Waller is likely to have been first in the field. But as Cleveland's lyrical poems are, I believe, practically unknown, even to scholars, and as this point of the introduction of the triple cadence is one of greatest interest, I will quote one or two examples. In a strange, half-mad, indecorous lyric called ' Mark Anthony,' I find these lines:

> " ' When as the nightingale chanted her vespers,
>   And the wild forester crouched on the ground ;
>   Venus invited me in th' evening whispers
>   Unto a fragrant field with roses crowned.'

" This drags a little; but the intention is incontestable. This is better:

> " ' Mystical grammar of amourous glances,
>   Feeling of pulses, the physic of love,
>   Rhetorical courtings and musical dances,
>   Numb'ring of kisses arithmetic prove.'

" Another poem, called ' Square-Cap,' evidently written at Cambridge in the author's undergraduate days, gives us a totally distinct variety of the anapæstic [1] cadence:

[1] Mr. Gosse's use of " anapæst " and " dactyl " is purely conventional, for none of these poems are strictly either.

" ' Come hither Apollo's bouncing girl,
    And in a whole Hippocrene of sherry,
    Let's drink a round till our brains do whirl,
    Tuning our pipes to make ourselves merry ;
    A Cambridge lass, Venus-like, born of the froth
    Of an old half-filled jug of barley-broth,
      She, she is my mistress, her suitors are many,
      But she'll have a square-cap if e'er she have any.'

" There is quite a ring of John Byrom or of Shenstone in these last lines, the precursors of so much that has pleased the ear of the eighteenth and nineteenth centuries." [1]

Towards the end of the eighteenth century we find a formal triple movement coming more and more into **Eighteenth-century triple rhythm** use, and, by the early part of this century, becoming quite general. Scott, Campbell, Moore, Byron, and a host of their contemporaries used it freely, but still in somewhat mechanical numbers. For it is the nice adjustment of prolonged syllables and of pause effects which make the balance of melody in 3-beat verse.

Steady, full bars, unless used, as by Victorian poets, for a distinct impressional purpose, become wearisome to the ear. Here are a few typical strains.

" When forced the fair nymph to forego,
    What anguish I felt at my heart !
    Yet I thought—but it might not be so—
    'Twas with pain that she saw me depart.
    She gazed as I slowly withdrew ;
    My path I could scarcely discern :
    So sweetly she bade me adieu,
    I thought that she bade me return."
              —WILLIAM SHENSTONE : " Absence."

[1] EDMUND GOSSE : " From Shakespeare to Pope :—The Reaction."

  " Would my Delia know if I love, let her take
  My last thought at night and the first when I wake ;
  When my prayers and best wishes preferred for her sake.

 " Let her guess what I muse on, when, rambling alone,
  I stride o'er the stubble each day with my gun,
  Never ready to shoot till the covey is flown.

 " Let her think what odd whimsies I have in my brain,
  When I read one page over and over again,
  And discover at last that I read it in vain."
      —WILLIAM COWPER : " The Symptoms of Love."

 " Come, rest on this bosom, my own stricken deer !
  Tho' the herd have fled from thee, thy home is still here,
  Here still is the smile that no cloud can o'ercast,
  And the heart and the hand, all thine own to the last.

 " Oh ! what was love made for, if 'tis not the same
  Thro' joy and thro' torments, thro' glory and shame ?
  I know not—I ask not—if guilt's in that heart,
  I but know that I love thee, whatever thou art."
      —THOMAS MOORE : " Come Rest on this Bosom."

  These are certainly elementary, and full of what Carlyle calls " a rocking-horse canter." They also strike
Nineteenth- a false note in sentiment, which makes the mat-
century
triple ter worse. The following, though the same
rhythm in metrical method, is more elevated, because
more genuine, and has the touch of the Byronic fire of
diction.

 " The Assyrian came down like the wolf on the fold,
  And his cohorts were gleaming in purple and gold ;
  And the sheen of their spears was like stars on the sea,
  When the blue wave rolls nightly on deep Galilee.

" Like the leaves of the forest when summer is green,
That host with their banners at sunset were seen :
Like the leaves of the forest when autumn hath blown,
That host on the morrow lay wither'd and strown."
                —Byron : " The Destruction of Sennacherib."

And in the following—metrically more compact—we sweep truly melodious chords:

" Since our Country, our God—O my Sire !
Demand that thy daughter expire ;
Since thy triumph was bought by thy vow—
Strike the bosom that's bared for thee now !

" And the voice of my mourning is o'er,
And the mountains behold me no more :
If the hand that I love lay me low,
There cannot be pain in the blow."
                —Byron : " Jephtha's Daughter."

Byron, though he lacked the spiritual ideal necessary to the making of the greatest of poets, was a brilliant artist, a master of technique.

Shelley, who drank infinitely deeper from the fountains of true inspiration than his contemporaries, has given us beautiful music in triple movement, but none more motive and sparkling than his " Arethusa," a direct precursor of some of the perfected motion of our own time.

" Arethusa arose
From her couch of snows
In the Acroceraunian mountains,—
From cloud and from crag,
With many a jag,
Shepherding her bright fountains.

She leapt down the rocks,
With her rainbow locks
Streaming among the streams;
Her steps paved with green
The downward ravine
Which slopes to the western gleams:
And gliding and springing
She went, ever singing
In murmurs as soft as sleep.
The earth seemed to love her,
And Heaven smiled above her,
As she lingered toward the deep.''

—SHELLEY: '' Arethusa.''

But none of the Georgian poets ever wholly fathomed the music of the 3-beat rhythm—such varied cadences as we get in '' Break, Break, Break ''; '' Cool and Clear ''; '' Come into the Garden, Maud '';

The perfect triple movement only came in with Victorian poets

and a host of other lyrics. This crowning achievement remained for the masters of the Victorian era; and such consummate handling of it have they given us, and some—notably Tennyson and Browning—have so played upon this triple rhythm, in such an infinity of metrical combinations, that it would almost seem as if art could go no farther.

In triple rhythm the line of four bars is not open to the same objection as in 2-beat rhythm, and has not that suggestion of thinness and monotony. The fuller bars —for, whether represented by the full complement of notes, or by notes and pauses, the bar *is* fuller—give in effect a body of sound equivalent to a longer line of the other rhythm. In fact a very long line in triple rhythm is not perfectly easy to handle well, and requires the most perfect cæsural balance to present to the ear a sense of harmonious unity.

We find lines of 3/4 and 3/3 the commonest and most
Examples of easily satisfactory presentment of this rhythm.
perfect
triple
I give, from modern verse, a few illustrative
rhythm examples of developed triple rhythm.

> " Strong, free, with a regal ease,
>   Over the scrub and the scrag,
> His nostrils spread to the spicy breeze,
>   Bounds the majestic stag.

> " He tosses his head with the antlers wide
>   Till he sweeps his loin with the horn ;
> Splendid he is in his power and pride,
>   Beautiful in his scorn !

> " What shall tire him, what shall break
>   The furious rush of his power ?
> Lives there a creature can overtake
>   The stag in his sovereign hour?

> " Oh, fierce, fierce is that strenuous heat
>   As it sweeps from holt to hollow ;
> But fleet, fleet are the fateful feet
>   Of the unleashed hounds which follow.

> .　　　.　　　.　　　.　　　.

> " Now, on a bank where the weeds grow rank,
>   He turns as the death-pang grips ;
> The sweat breaks dank from his quivering flank,
>   And the blood-foam froths his lips."
> 　　　—John Bass : " The Hunting of the Stag."

The *free verse* of this poem is admirably adapted to its
rushing spirit, and the strain springs loosely and buoyantly
along. The prolonged syllables are specially effective.
Observe that the words *strong* (first stanza), *fierce* and
fleet (fourth stanza) are held through the bar—three whole
beats. This gives a momentary *reining-in* effect, after
which the full bars seem to bound recklessly forward.

This same elastic measure lends itself wonderfully to the vivid numbers of one of our great love-lyrics, thus expressing the *motion of passion*.   In the first stanza the word *come* is twice held through the bar, giving the same pause-effect as in the preceding example; after which the music sweeps in with rich, balanced cadences.

> " Come into the garden, Maud,
>> For the black bat, night, has flown,
> Come into the garden, Maud,
>> I am here at the gate alone;
> And the woodbine spices are wafted abroad,
>> And the musk of the roses blown.
>
> .   .   .   .   .
>
> " There has fallen a splendid tear
>> From the passion-flower at the gate.
> She is coming, my dove, my dear;
>> She is coming, my life, my fate;
> The red rose cries, ' She is near, she is near;'
>> And the white rose weeps, ' She is late;'
> The larkspur listens, ' I hear, I hear;'
>> And the lily whispers, ' I wait.'
>
> " She is coming, my own, my sweet;
>> Were it ever so airy a tread,
> My heart would hear her and beat,
>> Were it earth in an earthy bed;
> My dust would hear her and beat,
>> Had I lain for a century dead;
> Would start and tremble under her feet,
>> And blossom in purple and red."
>> —Tennyson: " Maud." [1]

---

[1] It is significant that, in this passionate lyric-drama, almost every single section is in triple measure, as though the fires were too hot for anything less vibratory.

The next two quotations are examples of triple rhythm as expressing rapid motion. The impression to be conveyed to the ear is that of speed—superlative speed;—an impression which is, by means of the full, reiterated beats, certainly attained.

" I sprang to the stirrup, and Joris, and he ;
I galloped, Dirck galloped, we galloped all three ;
' Good speed !' cried the watch, as the gate-bolts undrew ;
' Speed !' echoed the wall to us galloping through ;
Behind shut the postern, the lights sank to rest,
And into the midnight we galloped abreast.

" Not a word to each other ; we kept the great pace
Neck by neck, stride by stride, never changing our place ;
I turned in my saddle and made its girths tight,
Then shortened each stirrup, and set the pique right,
Rebuckled the cheek-strap, chained slacker the bit,
Nor galloped less steadily Roland a whit."
—BROWNING : " How They Brought the Good News from Ghent to Aix."

Here again we have the galloping hoof-beats, only even more accentuated by the short line closely bound by the rhymes. This poem is in strict verse—advisedly so. Free verse could not have given the uniform clang of the hoof-beats. The anacrusis is required for the cumulative effect; and so vivid is the verisimilitude that the reader himself becomes the actor, and, as the breathless periods pile up, finds himself rushing, break-neck, through the sleeping towns, to drop—exhausted but triumphant—in the market-place at Aix.

Here is another example of speed.

" Archons of Athens, topped by the tettix, see, I return!
See, 'tis myself here standing alive, no spectre that speaks!

Crowned with the myrtle, did you command me, Athens
and you,
' Run Pheidippides, run and race, reach Sparta for aid !
Persia has come, we are here, where is She ? ' Your command
I obeyed,
Ran and raced : like stubble, some field which a fire runs
through,
Was the space between city and city : two days, two nights did
I burn
Over the hills, under the dales, down pits and up peaks.

" Into their midst I broke : breath served but for ' Persia has
come !
Persia bids Athens proffer slaves'-tribute, water and earth ;
Razed to the ground is Eretria—but Athens, shall Athens
sink,
Drop into dust and die—the flower of Hellas utterly die,
Die, with the wide world spitting at Sparta, the stupid, the
stander-by ?
Answer me quick, what help, what hand do you stretch o'er
destruction's brink ?
How,—when ? No care for my limbs !—there's lightning in
all and some—
Fresh and fit your message to bear, once lips give it birth ! ' ''
—BROWNING : '' Pheidippides.''

In these long lines we have the panting heats of the
foot-racer.   Not the full, uninterrupted beats of the galloping horse, but plenty of prolonged syllables, as a man
might draw his breath irregularly, slackening, as his wind
failed a little, then accelerating once more.

The next two poems are 3-beat rhythm illustrative of
sea-motion.   The first has already been given in another
chapter as an example of verse-notation ; but I repeat it
here because, as an example of *broken* motion, I know of
no other so good.

" Break, break, break,
 On thy cold grey stones, O Sea!
And I would that my tongue could utter
 The thoughts that arise in me.

" O well for the fisherman's boy,
 That he shouts with his sister at play !
O well for the sailor lad,
 That he sings in his boat on the bay !

" And the stately ships go on
 To their haven under the hill ;
But O for the touch of a vanish'd hand,
 And the sound of a voice that is still !

" Break, break, break,
 At the foot of thy crags, O Sea !
But the tender grace of a day that is dead
 Will never come back to me."
   —TENNYSON : " Break, Break, Break."

Almost all verse may be regarded as *legato* in quality; but in the first line of the first and last stanzas of this poem we get a graphic *staccato ;* one syllable (or note) then two rests—short, sharp, incisive—the very impact of breaking surf. With the second stanza comes in the *legato* movement, which reaches its fullest sweep in the last two lines of the third stanza. Then, in a fresh burst of grief, once more the sharp, reiterated *staccato*. These repetitions intensify the accent. Two, would have failed of the effect; four, would have overdone it. Merely as a piece of technique, and quite without regard to its literary value, I know of nothing more organically express- ive than this little surf song, so full of storm and stress, and foiled effort.

In the next poem we get the slow swing of deep-sea
rhythms.

" Come, dear children, let us away ;
  Down and away below !
  Now my brothers call from the bay,
  Now the great winds shoreward blow,
  Now the salt tides seaward flow ;
  Now the wild white horses play,
  Champ and chafe and toss in the spray.
  Children dear, let us away !
  This way, this way !
    .   .   .   .   .

" Children dear, was it yesterday
  (Call yet once) that she went away ?
  Once she sate with you and me,
  On a red gold throne in the heart of the sea,
  And the youngest sat on her knee.
  She comb'd its bright hair, and she tended it well,
  When down swung the sound of a far-off bell.
  She sigh'd, she look'd up through the clear green sea ;
  She said : ' I must go, for my kinsfolk pray
  In the little grey church on the shore to-day.
  'Twill be Easter-time in the world—ah me !
  And I lose my poor soul, Merman ! here with thee.'
  I said : ' Go up, dear heart, through the waves ;
  Say thy prayer, and come back to the kind sea-caves ! '
  She smiled, she went up through the surf in the bay."
        —MATTHEW ARNOLD : " The Forsaken Merman."

In this poem we get a distinct impression of undula-
tion ; not the restless surface agitation of comber and
surge and surf, but a full, fluid movement, suggestive of
great sea deeps, where the long, slow swell laps the
ledges and fringes out the great fronds of algæ.   The

triple rhythm gives, of course, the primary motion; but
the undulatory effect is due to the metric irregularity of
the lines, which, uneven, yet rising and falling with perfect cæsural balance, reproduce marvellously the irregular
regularity of wave-motion,—the sighing, sounding, surging dithyrambs of the sea.

A very short triple rhythm has an exuberant play.

> " Christmas is here :
> Winds whistle shrill,
> Icy and chill,
> Little care we :
> Little we fear
> Weather without,
> Sheltered about
> The Mahogany Tree."
> —THACKERAY : " The Mahogany Tree."

Another well-known poem—one of luminous aspiration
—begins with the same metric scheme, but sweeps into
larger cadences. Observe that the 3/4 lines of the latter
part of the poem simply double the 3/2 lines of the first
half; but this sustained sweep at the end gives a fulness
and dignity which the short, equal metric periods of the
previous poem lack.

> " All that I know
> Of a certain star
> Is, it can throw
> (Like the angled spar)
> Now a dart of red,
> Now a dart of blue ;
> Till my friends have said
> They would fain see, too,
> My star that dartles the red and the blue !

> Then it stops like a bird; like a flower hangs furled:
> They must solace themselves with the Saturn above it.
> What matter to me if their star is a world ?
> Mine has opened its soul to me; therefore I love it."
> —BROWNING : " My Star."

We have already studied, farther back, the intense, rushing movement of the " Charge of the Light Brigade." Probably no poem in the language is imbued with a more concentrated motion than this one. This motion is achieved by the triple rhythm, by the direct attack, by the feminine cadences of the rhyming lines, and, last but not least, by the short line with its incisive cæsural effects. These are all the sources of verse-motion focussed into one movement.

It has been suggested that the " Charge of the Light Brigade " was modelled upon the " Battle of Agincourt ";[1] but that such a master-craftsman as Tennyson should consciously *imitate* anything is not conceivable. The probable fact is that, all forms and all possibilities of forms being latent in his mind, when the theme agitated and heated the imagination, that form instinctively presented itself which should most adequately express speed, impetuous impact, and emotional fire.

It is my belief that, where real inspiration is present, form is virtually self-selective; for there is a deeper **Form virtually self-selective** internal relation between the thought and its material expression than the passing reader detects. By some psychological law, not yet clearly understood, but which we may class as a law of

[1] Those who are interested will find in Sidney Lanier's " Science of English Verse," p. 175, a comparison of five battle songs, from the seventh to the nineteenth centuries, in which is traced cleverly the fit metric analogy.

sympathetic vibration, the super-heated thought[1] correlates to itself words, and syntax (the construction of
sentences), and metric forms, which are best suited to
embody and express its particular spirit.   In other words
it correlates to itself forms of *harmonious motion.*   For
in the heats of creation matter and manner become one.
Only thus may we explain the concrete verisimilitude,
the wonderful organic correspondence, between form and
sense which we find in all the deeply true poems of the
world.   For a grave thought, a solemn *adagio* measure;
for a delicate or rapid conception, an equally delicate or
rapid movement.   Any sacrifice of this inherent fitness
destroys the vividness of the impression.   One could
not, for example, imagine Shelley's "Skylark"[2] cast in
the elephant paces of Whitman; nor Ariel's aëry messages hammered out in the Dryden rhymed-couplet.

I do not mean by this that nothing is retouched in a
poem.   Words may supplement each other; whole lines,
or even whole stanzas, be recast; but the general form
in which the poem, in the heats of creation, took shape,
will remain uninfringed, because it is an integral part
with the birth of the thought.   Be very sure that the
man who has to beat about for his form has within him
no inspirational fire, but only some farthing dip which he
believes to be such.

The improvisational or spontaneous character of all
the best poetry is well known.[3]   We read in Tennyson's

---

[1] The scientific definition of heat is : a manifestation of molecular motion.   The greater the motion, the greater the heat.

[2] "The quick pulses of his panting measure seem to give us the very
beats of those quivering wings," is the vivid comment made by Richard
Hutton upon the rhythmic *animus* of this beautiful poem.

[3] "I appeal to the poets of the present day, whether it is not an error to
assert that the finest passages of poetry are produced by labour and study."
—SHELLEY : "Defence of Poetry."

"Life" how, pacing beneath his trees at Farringford, many of his most beautiful numbers burst like lyric lavas from his brain,—perfect, and wearing the imperishable forms by which we know them to-day. We are told by his son, in the "Life," that "many of his shorter poems were made in a flash."

Browning "wrote most frequently under that lyrical inspiration in which the idea and the form are least separable from each other." "Mrs. Browning told Mr. Prinsep that her husband could never alter the wording of a poem without rewriting it, practically converting it into another."[1]

Shelley, nervous and impatient, and with a poetic faculty simply immense, threw off his verse in its first panting heats and retouched little; being reproached by his contemporaries for this seeming carelessness.

"He composed with all his faculties, mental, emotional, and physical, at the utmost strain, at a white heat of intense fervour, striving to attain one object, the truest and most passionate investiture for the thoughts which had inflamed his ever-quick imagination. . . . He was intolerant of detail, and thus failed to model with the roundness that we find in Goethe's works."[2]

Lowell, we are told, "in a sort of poetic frenzy, that lasted forty-eight hours, almost without food or sleep," composed the "Vision of Sir Launfal."[3]

When Shakespeare wishes to introduce to us the fairy folk of his imagination, he does so in dancing lilts of delicate rhythms and gossamer imagery. Caliban, coarse and earthy, speaks in crude measures which befit his elemental condition.

Form correlated to the informing thought

[1] Mrs. Sutherland Orr: "Life of Browning," chap. xviii.
[2] John Addington Symonds: "Life of Shelley," chap. viii.
[3] William Cranston Lawton: "New England Poets :—Lowell."

Browning sings us a song of a " Toccata of Galuppi's," all through the voluptuous images of which he permits us to catch echoes of this somewhat formal, and now extinct, musical form. In " Abt Vogler," on the other hand, with the swell of the organ in his ears, it gets itself into the poem, which is uttered in verse-equivalent of chords;—long, full, sustained metric periods, and long, full, almost over-weighted stanzas. And what could be more expressive than the " Grammarian's Funeral," with the lengthy, almost dithyrambic line contrasted so abruptly with the short, ecstatic one, suggesting the rough, stiff scramble up the mountain side, interspersed with celebrant song ?

Yet are none of these effects of deliberate intention, else could they not be so happy. But rather are they intuitional, the instinctive action of that vibratory centre upon which in all men thought plays, and which, in the artist, becomes of peculiar sensitiveness.[1]

Professor Masson advances the theory that " at a certain pitch of fervour or feeling, the voice does instinctively lift itself into song. All extreme passion tends to cadence. . . . When the mind of man is either excited to a certain pitch, or engaged in a certain kind of exercise, its trans-actions adjust themselves in a more express manner than usual to *time*, as meted out in beats or intervals. . . . The law, as stated hypothetically, is, that the mind, *either* when excited to a certain pitch, *or* when engaged in a

---

[1] This, of course, does not obviate the intellectual processes by which a poem—especially the larger works of art—is conceived, rounded out, polished, and perfected. Yet I am sure that, even in such stupendous objective art as we have, for instance, in Dante or Milton, those lines and passages which live immortal were less the product of reason than the revelation of the vision.

The conscious working in of such material is what Wordsworth means when he speaks of " emotion recollected in tranquillity."

particular kind of exercise, takes on in its transactions a marked concordance with time as measured by beats."[1]

I should not go so far as to claim that *all* super-heated thought resolves itself rhythmically; because the mind of a mathematician, or of a scientist, or of a capitalist, might be, and often is, "excited to a certain pitch or fervour of feeling," and the voice will certainly *not* "lift itself into song"; but it is quite true that, with the accelerated mental vibration incident to the stress of a great idea or a great passion, thought ceases to be an intellectual process and becomes an emotional, or intuitional one. And the largest vehicles for emotional expression are, either poetry proper, or that more etherealised poetry—music. So that, if a man's habit of thought be already rhythmic, if he be a natural poet or musician, the expression of this emotion will of necessity be rhythmic.

Creation—true creation—is a *raptus,* in which vision is clarified and thought becomes ebullient, a volcano of living possibilities. Within this psychic agitation lie, fluid and intermingled—as in the material molten forces —all elements; words, tropes, images, rhythms, metres, colours, proportions; to issue thence, when the perfect moment arrives, in lyric fusion—white-hot.

[1] DAVID MASSON : "Essays :—Theories of Poetry."

CHAPTER IV

MELODY

SHOULD poetry be rhymed ?

How the poets formulate poetry We may answer this question by another: what, essentially, and as differentiated from prose, constitutes poetry ? Here are a few definitions from the initiate themselves.

" Poetry is a part of learning, in measure of words for the most part restrained, but in all other parts extremely licensed, and doth truly refer to the imagination."—BACON.

"That art,
Which you say adds to nature, is an art
That nature makes."—SHAKESPEARE.

" Poetry is articulate music."—DRYDEN.

" The vision and the faculty divine."—COLERIDGE.

" Poetry is emotion recollected in tranquillity." —WORDSWORTH.

" The best and happiest moments of the best and happiest minds."—SHELLEY.

" Poetry is the utterance of a passion for truth, beauty, and power, embodying and illustrating its conception by imagination and fancy, and modulating its language on the principle of variety in uniformity."—LEIGH HUNT.

" Poetry is thought and art in one."—MATTHEW ARNOLD.

Professor Corson, in his lectures on " The Æsthetics of

Verse," has defined poetry as " definite thought wedded
to music which is indefinite."

According to Emerson, " the Zoroastrian definition of
poetry, mystical, yet exact, is ' Apparent pictures of
unapparent natures.' " Emerson's own definition is,
" Poetry is the perpetual endeavour to express the spirit
of the thing." And again he calls it, " This delirious
music in the brain."

These definitions are, however, vague and altogether
inconclusive. They deal with abstractions and not with
potentialities. They do not define wherein poetry as an
art differentiates from prose as an art; because the elements with which they deal are as much concomitants of
all ideal prose as of poetry. Professor Corson comes
nearest to the truth by claiming for poetry its indissoluble union with music; but he is still generalising, and
evades the final issue. Because, when we examine
closely, we perceive that the radical difference between
prose and poetry is organic,—is not one of *essence* but
purely of *form*.

I should say that the distinctive quality of poetry, and
that which differentiates it from prose, is dependent upon

**Form the
quality which
differentiates
poetry from
prose** three conditions: viz.:

1. *Uniform and interconsistent accent* (engendering primary rhythm).

2. *Balanced pause-effects* (giving metrical
divisions of verse and stanza).

3. *Melody.*

Says Professor Corson: " The fusing or combining principle of a verse is *Melody*. We often meet with verses
which scan, as we say, all right, and yet we feel that
they have no vitality as verses. This may, in most cases,
be attributed to their purely mechanical or cold-blooded
structure. They are not the product of feeling, which

attracts to itself (a great fact) vocal elements, **either**
vowels or consonants, which chime well together and in
accord with the feeling; but they are rather the product
of literary skill. The writer had no song, no music in
his soul." [1]

Of the three conditions of verse enumerated above,
none can be omitted and the resultant composition be
poetry. The first two have already been treated in
chapters ii and iii. In this chapter we will try to elucidate the principles of Melody.

The most palpable and also the largest factor in melody is *rhyme*. While it is possible to attain melody with
Factors of subtler devices, and to dispense with rhyme,
verse- this has seldom been, in English, a successful
melody experiment, and the instances are few in which
unrhymed verse can be truly called poetry. I except
blank verse, which will be treated by itself.

Other sources of melody are: (1) Tone-colour and Phonetic Consonance; (2) Alliteration and Onomatopœia;
(3) Repetitions and Refrains.

If we go once more to the sister art of poetry, music,
we may find a logical acoustic reason for the demand of
the human ear for rhyme.

It is a general canon of composition that a simple melody shall end upon its *tonic*, or key-note.[2]   Otherwise
Principle of there is not produced upon the ear a sensation
the tonic of repose or completion. The reason of this
is that, in the tonic chord, or triad,—that is, the key-note
of a melody, with the super-addition of the third above
it and the fifth above it,—we have the only *perfect*
cadence producible in music. When preceded by the

---

[1] Hiram Corson : "A Primer of English Verse," chap. ii.
[2] It must be borne in mind that in all these technical comparisons of
verse with music, I confine myself to the very simplest melodic forms.

dominant, it is called the *perfect authentic cadence*. This is because there is in other chords a sense of incompleteness,—a quality which requires to go on, to modulate or progress into some further chord. In the tonic chord alone the ear makes no demand for further progression because, for that theme, it is the end—is complete in itself. Thus it is that, through however many modulations the ear may be dragged, (and in much of the music of our own day a tonal labyrinth it is!) we must drop at last upon the tonic for rest. Browning has beautifully symbolised this in "Abt Vogler" where, after restless progressions of vision and image and speculation, the spirit drops back for anchorage to the simple starting-point—the soul-centre—the spiritual key-note.

" Well, it is earth with me ; silence resumes her reign :
    I will be patient and proud, and soberly acquiesce.
  Give me the keys.   I feel for the common chord again,[1]
    Sliding by semitones, till I sink to the minor,—yes,
  And I blunt it into a ninth, and I stand alien ground,
    Surveying awhile the heights I rolled from into the deep ;
  Which, hark, I have dared and done, for my resting-place is
      found,
    The C Major of this life : so, now I will try to sleep."

I have gone at some length into these elements of melodic balance, for it seems to me that in them we detect the logical reason why rhymed verse—some form of rhymed verse—has so far presented, and probably will

---

[1] The common chord is the chord of C Major, thus :

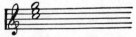

This chord, and the scale it represents, is selected as typical and to furnish the model for other scales, because it is written upon the staff as it stands, without the need of accidentals (sharps or flats).

always continue to present, to the human ear the most satisfying results. I will insert here a little melody of Mozart's—selecting purposely a theme almost universally known—by way of elucidating further this fundamental idea.

Reading the treble staff (where the thematic movement is given) it will be observed that this melody is divided into two phrases, the first—or out-swinging half (A to B)—poising itself as it were in air, (to be technical, upon a note of the dominant chord); the second (B to C), by a return-swing of the mental pendulum, bringing us once more to rest upon the *tonic*, or key-note. It is exactly at this point that the analogy between the verse-scheme and the music-scheme comes in. The chord of the dominant is called the *half-cadence* because it leads directly into the chord of the tonic, or full cadence; therefore at B there is *prepared* a tone which the tonic, at C, is required to *complete*. In exactly the same way, in any rhymed stanza, the first word of the rhyme prepares or introduces a tone which the last rhyme is required to complete. Take for example an ordinary quatrain, which is what this little theme practically represents. Thus:

Analogy between music and verse as to cadence correspondence

> " Once more the gate behind me falls ;
> Once more before my face
> I see the moulder'd Abbey walls,
> That stand within the chace."

[1] First eight bars of Trio of Minuet, from Mozart's Symphony in E♭, Op. 58. (Arr. for pianoforte, four hands.)

Here the word *face* stands for the half-cadence and requires the answering word, *chace*, to make tonal completeness.   Half-way between A and B, in the theme given on page 103, there is a place where the music swings away from cadence: these two points have their correspondence in the stanza in the words *falls* and *walls*, of the first and third lines.   This is a secondary sequence, which, as it is not required for the tonal completeness of the stanza, we may call the *off-rhymes ;* while the rhymes *face* and *chace* of the second and fourth lines, as they *are* required for tonal completeness, we call the *finish-rhymes.*

Stanzas with more complex and irregular rhyme-schemes may be compared with more irregular melodic themes, where, through modulation, the final tonic is delayed ; but of course such comparisons are elementary and cannot be pushed far.

Rhyme we must then regard as the *cadence-correspondence* of verse.   Man, Emerson tells us,

" Through worlds, and races, and terms, and times,
    Saw musical order and pairing rhymes."

The melodic balance of a stanza seems to lie in the last
The melodic line.   If rhyme exist in previous lines and not
balance of a in the last, the ear will not receive an impres-
stanza lies
in last line sion of tonal finish.   Thus if the foregoing
stanza stood as follows :

" Once more the gate behind me falls ;
    Once more before my face
I see the moulder'd Abbey walls,
    That stand within the wood,"

we could not call the stanza a rhymed stanza, because, although the first and third lines rhyme, there is no terminal rhyme, and so to the ear no sense of melodic completeness. Therefore, although we may easily omit *off-rhymes*, we cannot omit *finish-rhymes*, and maintain melodic completeness.

For the same reason it is obvious that, when rhymes are placed irregularly through a stanza, they must not **Rhymes** be too far apart for the ear to correlate them **must not be** and carry them as a tonal unit. " Pheidip-**too far apart** pides " has, I think, somewhat this defect, the rhyme-scheme being needlessly complex. There are eight lines to the stanza, the first four each having a different tonal ending. The last four reverse the scheme, the fifth rhyming with the fourth, the sixth with the third, while the last two are again twisted about, the seventh rhyming with the first, and the eighth with the second. Melodic coherence is thus, in a measure, destroyed—the very long line being a further erasive factor, —and, except in the two central lines, the ear catches no distinct tonal impression.

It is always best to use, among rhymes, a large proportion of monosyllables. The strength of our language lies in its monosyllables. Thus, such rhymed tones as *suddenly, universally*, lack strength, and the lines wherein they occur would gain in virility should one of the rhymes be instead a monosyllable, as *sky*.

In English, in order to have rhyme, it is necessary to have absolute coincidence of the terminal consonant **Rhyme** sounds. We also require coincidence of ter-**involves** **absolute co-** minal vowel sounds; but some stretching of **incidence** these is permissible, while none at all is per-**of terminal** **consonant** missible in the consonant sounds. Thus *art* **sounds but** and *wert* may be considered as rhymes, but **not of** **vowels** *time* and *fine* may not. Words need not be spelled alike—indeed in our unphonetic language we may not compel such a condition,—but they must strike the

same tone; as *hear, sphere; shoe, through; news, confuse.*
Certain words which are spelled differently but pronounced exactly alike, both as to consonant and vowel
sounds,—such as *air, heir; there, their; sent, scent, cent*
—cannot be considered rhymes because they are not contrasted tones, but, both in vowel and consonant sounds,
phonetically identical.

It has become the custom in these latter days—with
that tendency of eras barren in production—to riot in
hyper-criticism, which hyper-criticism rules out as imperfect and untrue all rhymes not absolutely coincident
in vowel cadence.   Such rhymes as the following: *De-
fender, Leander:* (Keats).   *Valley, melancholy:* (Keats).
Near it, spirit, inherit: (Shelley).   *Wert, art:* (Shelley).
Moon, alone: (Tennyson).   *With her, together:* (Tennyson).   *Valleys, lilies:* (Tennyson).   *Chatters, waters:*
(Wordsworth).   *Weary, sanctuary:* (Wordsworth).   *Re-
turning, morning:* (Gray).   *Beech, stretch:* (Gray).

The question arises, why—if these rhymes are inadmissible, because tonally defective—have the greatest
Imperfect   and best artists of verse, of all time, used
cadence   them ?   The fact is that they are *not* tonally
defective.   We have already examined the tonic chord,
or perfect authentic cadence, of music, and see that it
consists of the tonic or key-note, with the addition of its
third and fifth, which complete it tonally.   Now it is
quite as correct for a melody to end upon either the third
or the fifth as upon the tonic, because either of these
notes is a component of the perfect chord, the correlating
ear instinctively supplying the fundamental note.   This
sort of ending is called the *Imperfect Authentic Cadence.*

Now, in verse, when vowel sounds are so closely related as to give practically a coincident vibration, we
may consider them in the light of the musical imperfect

cadence and so admit them to use. Such rhymes as the
list given above belong to the verse imperfect cadence,
and, used with discretion, are just as tonally satisfying
to the ear as the perfect cadence; because, although they
have not the sense of absolute finality of the tonic, or
true rhyme, they produce upon the ear the same tonal
impression. Of course it requires much nicety of ear to
distinguish between tones which are correlated and those
which are not. A conspicuous absence of this discrim-
inative faculty is observable in the odd, flashing, often
wonderfully prismatic, bits of verse—bits, rather than
coherent verses—of the late Emily Dickinson; where are
frequent such startling tonal combinations as *denied,
smiled; book, think; all, soul; own, young;* etc.

No, we cannot rule out the imperfect cadence. In
a language which admits six sounds of A; six sounds of
E; three sounds of I; five sounds of O; and five sounds
of U—not to mention combined vowel sounds,—should
we discard all the beautiful melodic effects possible with
this factor, we should have verse-poverty indeed, instead
of, as we really have, great opulence.

And the fact remains that in the end it is the poets,
and not the critics, who determine what words or rhymes
shall be used, simply by *using them.* They present us
with a coin which passes current by reason of its very
adaptability. They fill our literature with tones attuned
to finer cadences than is ever pedagogically attainable.
" We, the musicians, know," says Abt Vogler.

We have already seen how the feminine ending becomes an added factor in motion. In the same way
Feminine ending a factor of melody feminine rhymes become an added factor in
melody by prolonging the cadence. Double
or feminine rhymes must, of course, always be
used with restraint and a good ear. It is not quite such

good art to set two monosyllables against a dissyllable
as to have both composed of either dissyllables or monosyllables.   Thus *Aurora* and *for her* is not so pure as *for
her* and *bore her*.   Such rhymes as *fabric* and *dab brick*
—used by Browning—are entirely inadmissible, because
over-strained, grotesque, and cacophonous.   Many of
Mrs. Browning's double rhymes are also questionable.
Rhymes should be apposite in sound as well as in sentiment.

Triple rhymes are apt to have a grotesque effect, but
a notable exception is Hood's " Bridge of Sighs," where
Triple   they are so handled as to seem to add a note
rhymes   of pathos to the theme.   Remarkable com-
apt to be
grotesque   binations of them may be found in the " Bab
Ballads "; and in Browning's " Pacchiarotto " and " Flight
of the Duchess " there are some wonderful triple rhymes,
but they impress one almost more as tonal gymnastics
than as legitimate music.   As a rule it is best to avoid
rhymes of more than two syllables, as it adds nothing to
the melody of, and is apt to detract from, the dignity of
a poem.

I have already pointed out that rhymes should not be
too far apart for the ear to coördinate them tonally.
Rhyme   But it is quite as bad to overload rhyme need-
should not be lessly and produce tonal indigestion.   Very
overloaded   wonderful effects are producible by rhyme-
repetitions when they are organic and for a purpose—as
I shall presently show—but they need the finest perception to adjust.   It is invaluable to study and analyse the
rhyme-schemes of the best verse, and to determine for
one's self wherein the melodic secret lies.   In the sonnet
—a metric form so perfect that its use has suffered no
eclipse in five centuries—the intrinsic virtue lies in the
rhymed sequences.   Kindred to it in basic purpose is

the beautiful Spenserian stanza. The rhyme-groupings in Keats's odes are balanced with wonderful delicacy, giving them that melodious flow which makes of the poems perennial music. Verse rhyme-schemes will be treated in detail in the next chapter.

There is a certain coördination of thought by which the concept of one sound seems to draw to it, as the magnet draws the steel, cognate or related sounds, so that all impinge upon the ear as a harmonious whole. This tonal inter-relation or correspondence is only another manifestation of that law of sympathetic vibration previously noted, which, in this conjunction, operates to the fluency of melody within the verse. Thus we see that the poet not so much seeks his effects as they seek him; and, to the trained imagination, tone combinations present themselves naturally, as by right divine.

Within this law of inter-related tones is comprehended Rhyme and its two great coefficients, Tone-colour and **Tone-colour** Alliteration. Refrains would seem to be a **of verse** little further differentiated.

The term *Tone-colour* (the word *colour* being borrowed from a visual art, painting, and *tone* from poetry's sister art, music) means those gradations of melodic light and shade producible to the ear by nice adjustments of vowel consonances and contrasts within the verse and stanza.[1]

[1] "When the voice utters the sound denoted by the English character A, it makes, not a single tone, but a tone composed of a number of other tones. When it utters the sound denoted by the English character O, it again utters a tone which is not single, but composed of a number of other tones ; and the difference between the two sounds, by which the ear distinguishes A from O, is due to the fact that certain of the ingredient sounds are prominent in A, while certain others are prominent in O. As in making the colour purple

Professor Max Müller tells us, in the " Science of Language," concretely just what vowels are. " What we
What   call vowels are neither more nor less than the
vowels are   qualities, or colours, or *timbres* of our voice,
and these are determined by the form of the vibrations,
which form again is determined by the form of the buccal
tubes. . . . Vowels are produced by the form of the
vibrations. They vary like the *timbre* of different instruments, and we in reality change the instruments on which
we speak when we change the buccal tubes in order to
pronounce a, e, i, o, u." (Lecture iii.)

Thus when we speak of Keats as " a great colourist,"
and Wordsworth as *not* " a great colourist," we mean that
the verse of the former is filled with rich and varying
tone-combinations, while in that of the latter this richness and variety are virtually absent.

Coleridge, who at his best had a fine feeling for colour,
used to call the attention of his children to the melody
of such a verse as this, from " Love ":

out of a composition of red and violet, we should have different shades of
purple according as we should make the red or violet more prominent in the
mixture ; so in making up a sound, the buccal cavity manages, by coördina-
tions of muscles which are learned in childhood, to render now one, now
another ingredient-sound more prominent, and thus to bring out different
shades of tone. It is a certain shade of tone which we call A, another
which we call O, another which we call E, another which we call U; and
so on : and the ear discriminates one of these shades of tone from another,
as the eye discriminates one shade of colour from another. It is this analogy
between processes belonging to sound and processes belonging to light which
has originated the very expressive term, ' Tone-colour' in acoustics."—SID-
NEY LANIER : " The Science of English Verse," chap. xi.

" The tongue, the cavity of the fauces, the lips, teeth, and palate, with
its velum pendulum and uvula performing the office of a valve between the
throat and nostrils, as well as the cavity of the nostrils themselves, are all
concerned in modifying the impulse given to the breath as it issues from the
larynx, and in producing the various vowels and consonants."—MAX MÜL-
LER : " Science of Language," Second Series, lecture iii.

' I played a soft and doleful air,
    I sang an old and moving story,
    An old rude song, that suited well
    That ruin, wild and hoary.''

Here O and U are the vowels played upon; but often
the *nuances* will slide through the whole gamut of vowel
Effects of sounds, subtly interweaving them one with
toning another. The ear takes pleasure in having the
tone-impression renewed, recombined, and contrasted,
drinking in as a melodic whole both the variation and the
repetition. Certain tones repeated bear a subtle relation
to the interweaved figures in musical compositions.

To attempt to lay down lines for the melodic effects
achieved through toning would be futile, as these depend
entirely upon the feeling and auditory sensitiveness of
the artist. The most valuable course of training in this
particular is to study the great colourists among the poets,
and so to saturate one's self with the underlying spirit
of verse-tones that, when composing, the right ones will
instinctively present themselves. I give a few illustrative examples of rich vowel effects; but the student will
find plenty upon every page of the great poets.

" At last they heard a horne that shrillèd cleare
    Throughout the wood that ecchoëd againe,
    And made the forrest ring, as it would rive in twaine.''
            —SPENSER : " Faerie Queene,'' ii., 3, 20.

" How sweet the moonlight sleeps upon this bank !
    Here will we sit, and let the sounds of music
    Creep in our ears : soft stillness and the night
    Become the touches of sweet harmony.
    Sit, Jessica. Look, how the floor of heaven
    Is thick inlaid with patines of bright gold :

> There's not the smallest orb which thou behold'st
> But in his motion like an angel sings,
> Still quiring to the young-eyed cherubims:
> Such harmony is in immortal souls;"
> —SHAKESPEARE : " The Merchant of Venice," v. i.

> " She was a gordian shape of dazzling hue,
> Vermilion-spotted, golden, green, and blue ;
> Striped like a zebra, freckled like a pard,
> Eyed like a peacock, and all crimson barr'd ;
> And full of silver moons, that, as she breathed,
> Dissolved, or brighter shone, or interwreathed
> Their lustres with the gloomier tapestries—"
> —KEATS : " Lamia."

> " Then saw they how there hove a dusky barge,
> Dark as a funeral scarf from stem to stern,
> Beneath them ; and descending they were ware
> That all the decks were dense with stately forms
> Black-stoled, black-hooded, like a dream—by these
> Three queens with crowns of gold—and from them rose
> A cry that shivered to the tingling stars,"
> —TENNYSON : " The Passing of Arthur."

> " The lady sprang up suddenly,
> The lovely lady, Christabel !
> It moaned as near, as near can be,
> But what it is she cannot tell.—
> On the other side it seems to be,
> Of the huge, broad-breasted old oak tree."
> —COLERIDGE : " Christabel."

Of this last quotation Professor Corson remarks: " The form of this stanza is quite perfect. Note the suggestiveness of the abrupt vowels in the first verse, the abatement required for the proper elocution in the second verse, the prolongable vowels and sub-vowels of the third, and then the short vowels again in the fourth. Then note how the vowels in the last verse swell responsive to the poet's conception, and how encased they are in a strong framework of consonants."[1]

Verse-toning depends quite as much upon the concordance and melodic adjustment of consonant sounds as upon the skilful variation and adaptation of the vowel sounds.

Turning again to the " Science of Language," we find consonants scientifically defined. " There is no **What consonants are** reason why languages should not have been entirely formed of vowels. There are words consisting of vowels only, such as Latin *eo*, I go; *ea*, she; *eoa*, eastern; the Greek *eioeis* (but for the final *s*); the Hawaiian *hooiaioai*, to testify, (but for its initial breathing). Yet these very words show how unpleasant the effect of such a language would have been. Something else was wanted to supply the *bones of language*, namely, the consonants. Consonants are called in Sanscrit *vyanjana*, which means ' rendering distinct or manifest,' while the vowels are called *svara*, sounds." (Lecture iii.)

In casting a verse of poetry, harsh or barbarous contrasts of consonants, and juxtapositions of those difficult to be pronounced together, must, as a rule, be avoided. We all remember the unpronounceable catches with which, as children, we used to test each other's powers of articulation. For instance:

> " 'Midst thickest mists and stiffest frosts,
> With strongest fists and stoutest boasts,
> He thrusts his fists against the posts,
> And still insists he sees the ghosts."

[1] " Primer of English Verse," chap. ii.

8

This quatrain is not poetry, not so much because of absence of meaning, as because it is, from beginning to
Phonetic end, the most racking cacophony; and cacoph-
consonance ony can never be poetry. We must steer clear of the "consonantal rocks," as some one has felicitously put it. Thus the whole verse becomes tonally organic. Word fits to word with such perfection of rhetorical join-ery that the poem flows with the unified impulse of a running stream. To this consonantal fitness some give the name of *phonetic consonance.* I much prefer it to the jaw-breaking term *phonetic syzygy* [1] employed by Syl-vester, and followed by Lanier and others. It is not necessary to give special examples of phonetic con-sonance, as these form a large part of all toning, con-trasting and separating the vowel *nuances.* Neither this nor alliteration—which is a form of phonetic consonance —are really separable from the general studies in colour, as all are integral parts of one melodic purpose.

Dissonances are also, at times and for special ends, permissible. Shakespeare, where it serves the theme, has many instances of sharp, even harsh, consonantal contrasts. Browning—who may be called the Wagner of verse—abounds with them; and he has so enlarged the scope of verse that he may be pardoned if, like his great contemporary, he sometimes loses the tonal cen-tre of gravity and slips over into pure, unmitigated cacophony. [2]

[1] From the Greek *syzygos :* yoked together.
[2] Browning's roughnesses will be found to be not metric, but always in the diction. Moreover, in a great number of instances—whether with the best artistic taste or not—this is done with intention and a view to produc-ing a special effect. We see this in "Holy Cross Day," which opens with a movement almost grotesque, but flows out, as the theme deepens, into large, forcible, solemn measures. Another example is "The Grammarian's Funeral," which begins with an onomatopœic scramble, but deepens into

In the eyes of many metrists, colour-toning is of more importance even than rhyme, since rhyme furnishes only the terminal tones, whereas tone-colour furnishes the internal music which is inherent in all true poetry whether verse be rhymed or not. In blank verse all the melody lies, of course, in the internal toning.

Next to tone-colour, and rivalling it in the distribution of tone-values, stands alliteration, with its subdivision of onomatopœia. **Alliteration** Alliteration is the repetition of a letter—generally a consonant—at the beginning of, or within, several contiguous words of a verse, or words almost contiguous. Thus:

" With *l*isp of *l*eaves, and *r*ipple of *r*ain."—SWINBURNE.

" St*inging*, *r*inging sp*i*ndri*f*t, nor the *f*ulmar *f* lying *f*ree."
—KIPLING.

" *M*ur*m*u*r*ing fro*m* Gla*r*a*m*a*r*a's in*m*ost caves."—WORDSWORTH.

" An*d d*rowsy tink*l*ings *l*u*ll* the *d*istant fo*ld*s."—GRAY.

" The *l*eague-*l*ong *r*o*ll*er thunde*r*ing on the *r*eef."—TENNYSON.

" The *m*oan of doves i*n* i*m*memoria*l* e*l*ms,
    And *m*ur*m*uring of i*nn*u*m*era*bl*e *b*ees."—TENNYSON.

" The *b*are, *bl*ack c*l*iff c*l*anged round him."—TENNYSON.

These repetitions give a tone-consonance very closely related to rhyme, and bind together special words within the verse exactly in the same manner in which rhyme

splendid meteoric climax. Browning can be melodic enough, too, when he chooses. " The Flower's Name," " Rabbi Ben Ezra," " Over the Sea our Galleys Went," " Heap Cassia Buds," " One Way of Love," " Meeting at Night," " A Toccata of Galuppi's," " Memorabilia," " There's a Woman Like a Dew-drop," " One Word More," and a host of others, are full of a " rich and haunting music " not easily to be matched in English verse.

binds together, and tonally unifies, special verses within the stanza.

Thus, in the first quotation, *l* correlates *lisp* and *leaves*, while *r* correlates *ripple* and *rain*. In the second quotation the alliteration extends to whole groups of letters: *inging, inging, in, i;* and then the *f* in *spindrift* introduces the second alliteration on *f*. In the third, the alliteration is upon *m* and *r*. In the fourth, it plays between the letters *d* and *l;* this and the following ones taking on that more subtle correspondence of initial with internal alliteration. In the fifth, the play is upon *l* and *r*. The sixth is a very subtle web of *m, n,* and *l*. This internal alliteration does not appeal so quickly to the eye as initial alliteration, and many persons would read this passage without in the least detecting the relation of sounds, merely having an æsthetic pleasure in the harmonious flow of the verse. In the seventh, we have again initial alliteration, sharp and resonant, upon *b* and *cl;* the *l* and *ck* in *black* introducing the second alliterative tone.

The key to harmonious alliteration lies, I think, in the etymological grouping of consonants, these being along **The key to** purely phonetic lines. English teachers do **harmonious** not make much of these groupings, and we **alliteration** have to turn to the Greek grammar for suggestions in making a table of them.

Table of Consonant Groups

Liquids :—*l, m, n, r.*   (*l* and *r* are also called *trills.*)
Aspirate :—*h*.
Sibillant :—(or spirant) *s*.

	Smooth.	Middle.	Rough.
Labials :—	*p*.	*b*.	*ph* or *f*.
Palatals :—	*k*.	*g* (hard).	*ch* (guttural).
Linguals :—	*t*.	*d*.	*th*.

Of the consonants not included in the above table, *c* is either *s* or *k*, according as it is hard or soft. *J* and soft *g*, which do not exist phonetically in Greek, Professor Müller classes as *soft aspirates*. *Q* is another sound of *k*. *V* is another sound of *f*. *W* and *y* we consider phonetically vowels.

X and *z* are called by the Greeks *double consonants* because they are compound in sound, *x* being composed of *k* sound and *s* sound; *z* being composed of *d* and soft *s*. But none of the letters indicated in this last paragraph are often used alliteratively.

Now it is evident that, if the alliterative letters come from the same group, the sound of the verse will be peculiarly suave; and, conversely, if they come from contrasted groups, the sound will be more dissonant. Thus, " The league-long roller," etc., has its alliterations from the same consonant group; while " The bare, black cliff," etc., has them from sharply contrasted groups, and thus gives phonetically the desired impression of harshness.

The feeling for alliteration lies deep at the core of English speech. It is our one inheritance from the literature **Deep feeling** of the Anglo-Saxons; and a priceless one it is! **for allit-** It becomes difficult to imagine how harsh Eng-**eration in** **English** lish diction would be, wanting this softening **verse** and binding element. In Anglo-Saxon verse alliteration took the place of rhyme. The introduction in the fourteenth century of French and Italian forms swept aside the clumsier Teutonic methods, and made of the new speech something more melodious and plastic. Chaucer, giving it classic form, caught, and interwove with echoes of the warm southern tones, this fine, native melodic element. Spenser may be said to clasp hands with Chaucer across two centuries—for between them lie no great English poets—and such melodic hints as the older artist left, the younger caught up and developed into a lofty music which has never been surpassed. Subsequent poets owe much of their tonal inspiration to Spenser; but it was particularly in his rescue and elaboration of alliteration—his genius putting upon the coin a stamp which made it current for all time—that he laid a debt upon his countrymen. Here are some examples from the older poets.

> " The heraudes lefte hir priking up and doun ;
> Now ringen trompes loude and clarioun ;
> Ther is namore to seyn but west and est
> In goon the speres ful sadly in arest ;
> In goth the sharpe spore into the syde.
> Ther seen men who can juste and who can ryde ;
> Ther shiveren shaftes upon sheeldes thikke ;
> He feleth thurgh the herte-spoon the prikke.
> Up springen speres twenty foot on highte ;
> Out goon the swerdes as the silver brighte."
> —CHAUCER : " Canterbury Tales," 2601.

> " By this the northerne wagoner had set
>   His sevenfold teme behind the stedfast starre
> That was in ocean waves yet never wet,
>   But firme is fixt, and sendeth light from farre
>   To al that in the wide deepe wandring arre ; "
> SPENSER : " Faerie Queene," ii. 1.

> " Love in a humour play'd the prodigal,
> And bade my senses to a solemn feast ;
> Yet more to grace the company withal,
> Invites my heart to be the chiefest guest :"
> —MICHAEL DRAYTON : Sonnet.

> " Upon her head she wears a crown of stars,
> Through which her orient hair waves to her waist,
> By which believing mortals hold her fast,

And in those golden cords are carried even,
Till with her breath she blows them up to heaven.
She wears a robe enchased with eagles' eyes,
To signify her sight in mysteries:
Upon each shoulder sits a milk-white dove,
And at her feet do witty serpents move.''
    —BEN JONSON: " Truth," from " Hymenæi.''

" Care-charmer Sleepe, Sonne of the sable night,
Brother to death, in silent darkness born,
Relieve my languish and restore the light;
With dark forgetting of my care returne,
And let the day be time enough to mourne
The ship-wracke of my ill-adventured youth:
Let waking eyes suffice to waile their scorn
Without the torment of the night's untruth.''
    —SAMUEL DANIEL: Sonnet.

" Come live with me, and be my love,
And we will all the pleasures prove,
That valleys, groves, or hill, or field,
Or woods and steepy mountains yield;

" Where we will sit upon the rocks,
And see the shepherds feed their flocks,
By shallow rivers, to whose falls
Melodious birds sing madrigals.''
—CHRISTOPHER MARLOWE: " The Passionate Shepherd to his
Love.''

" Lay a garland on my hearse
 Of the dismal yew;
Maidens, willow branches bear,
 Say I died true.

> " My love was false, but I was firm
> From my hour of birth.
> Upon my buried body lie
> Lightly, gentle earth ! "
> —BEAUMONT and FLETCHER : " The Maid's Tragedy."

"Oberon. My gentle Puck, come hither.   Thou rememberest
Since once I sat upon a promontory,
And heard a mermaid on a dolphin's back
Uttering such dulcet and harmonious breath
That the rude sea grew civil at her song
And certain stars shot madly from their spheres,
To hear the sea-maid's music.
"Puck: I remember.
"Oberon. That very time I saw, but thou couldst not,
Flying between the cold moon and the earth,
Cupid all armed : a certain aim he took
At a fair vestal throned by the west,
And loosed his love-shaft smartly from his bow,
As it should pierce a hundred thousand hearts :
But I might see young Cupid's fiery shaft
Quenched in the chaste beams of the watery moon,
And the imperial votaress passed on
In maiden meditation, fancy-free."
—SHAKESPEARE : " Midsummer Night's Dream," ii. 1.

Alliteration makes resounding music, but its abuse is
too easy.   It requires a master-touch and the finest of
self-restraint to use it with that subtlety which
charms, and not wearies the ear.   One must
not " hunte the letter to the death," admon-
ishes George Gascoigne.   A radical defect in much of
Swinburne's verse is that it is bitten by what John Burroughs aptly calls " a leprosy of alliteration."

Alliteration easily abused (margin)

" Onomatopœia [1] is that principle in language by which

[1] From the Greek *Onoma*, name ; and *poieo*, make.

words are formed in imitation of natural sounds," says the Standard Dictionary. Also, "an imitative word."

Onomato- Max Müller tells us that "interjections, though **pœia** they cannot be treated as parts of speech, are nevertheless ingredients of our conversation; so are the clicks of the Bushmen and Hottentots, which have been well described as remnants of animal speech. Again there are in many languages words, if we may call them so, consisting of the mere imitations of the cries of animals or the sounds of nature, and some of them have béen carried along by the stream of language into the current of nouns and verbs," (Lecture vii.).

Such words as *clinch, split, roar, murmur, bubble, whisper, sibillant, thundering*, etc., are onomatopœic.

Onomatopœia is distinctly connotative. An onomatopœic word is a species of trope which, merely by the sound, makes to the mind an image or picture of that which the word rhetorically expresses.

The examples given on page 115 for alliteration are all more or less onomatopœic. In the line " Murmuring from Glaramara," etc., the alliterated letters are *m* and *r*, which, interweaved with tones of the vowel *a*, give a subdued murmurous echo, very suggestive of the soft, reverberant music of hidden waters. In the " league-long roller " the prolonged vowel cadence could mean nothing else but what it does mean, and it is capped by the strong onomatopœic word " thundering." In the two lines beginning "And moan of doves " the web of *m* and *n* and *l* makes a subtle onomatopœic murmurous effect all through the quotation. There is a fine reverberation in such lines as these of Kipling:

> " Jehovah of the Thunders,
> Lord, God of Battles, aid ! "

In the following lines from " Paradise Lost " the sub-
stantives, adjectives, and verbs are distinctly onomatopœic, giving by their very sound the sense of unwieldi-
ness:

> " That sea-beast
> Leviathan, which God of all his works
> Created hugest that swim the ocean stream."

This effect is heightened by the doubled notes in the bar
" hugest that."   And again:

> —" part, huge of bulk,
> Wallowing unwieldy, enormous in their gait,
> Tempest the ocean."

These effects are what Tennyson meant by the term
" the marriage of sense with sound; " and happy is the
poet who possesses that superlative feeling for tone
which instinctively supplies the right word in colour as
well as meaning.

There is a golden thread of onomatopœia running all
through language.   In the imaginative diction of verse
it becomes more apparent, and is especially so in alliterative effects.   That alliteration will be most vivid and
organic which is at the same time the most onomatopœic.

The foregoing elements of verse are indissolubly linked
together; they govern the euphonious distribution of
vowel and consonant tones, and so fuse and combine into
a perfect whole the entire verse, that one may justly
apply to it the beautiful term, " articulate music."

I have elsewhere pointed out the danger of over-harp-
ing upon one rhyme.   When rhyme-repetition is used
arbitrarily, and without purpose, it is likely to become

as deadly to the ear as the grind of a hand-organ. But in a certain class of poems, and when used with **Rhyme-** discrimination, rhyme repetition and phrase-**repetition as** repetition (refrains) may be made to play an **a factor of** important part in the melody of verse. **verse**

melody In the rhyme-groups below, from Tennyson's " Lotos Eaters," the iterated tone produces upon the ear a soothing, lulling impression, which is heightened in the first example by adding a bar to each successive line, so that it gives the effect of the incoming of a lazy tide.

" Here are cool mosses deep,
    And thro' the moss the ivies creep,
    And in the stream the long-leaved flowers weep,
    And from the craggy ledge the poppy hangs in sleep.

      .   .   .   .   .

" How sweet it were, hearing the downward stream,
    With half-shut eyes ever to seem
    Falling asleep in a half-dream !

      .   .   .   .   .

" Music that gentlier on the spirit lies
    Than tired eyelids upon tired eyes ;
    Music that brings sweet sleep down from the blissful skies."

Browning's " A Toccata of Galuppi's " is made into wonderful cadences by binding together each stanza by a single tone.

" O Galuppi, Baldassaro, this is very sad to find !
    I can hardly misconceive you ; it would prove me deaf and blind ;
    But although I take your meaning, 'tis with such a heavy mind !

" Here you come with your old music, and here's all the good
        it brings.
    What, they lived once thus at Venice where the merchants were
        the kings,
    Where St. Mark's is, where the Doges used to wed the sea with
        rings ?

    .   .   .   .   .

" Was a lady such a lady, cheeks so round and lips so red,—
    On her neck the small face buoyant, like a bell-flower on its
        bed,
    O'er the breast's superb abundance where a man might base his
        head ? "

Titania, in " Midsummer Night's Dream " (iii. 1), exhorts the fairies to care for Bottom in a stanza of honeyed
rhyme-repetition.

        " Be kind and courteous to this gentleman;
          Hop in his walks and gambol in his eyes;
          Feed him with apricocks and dew-berries,
          With purple grapes, green figs and mulberries;
          The honey-bags steal from the humble-bees,
          And for night-tapers crop their waxen thighs,
          And light them at the fiery glow-worm's eyes,
          To have my love to bed and to arise;
          And pluck the wings from painted butterflies
          To fan the moonbeams from his sleeping eyes:
          Nod to him, elves, and do him courtesies."

This certainly is " linked sweetness long drawn out."
It would seem as if rhyme could be pushed no farther;
yet it can.   In " Through the Metidja," Browning has
achieved a marvellous desert effect by the use, through
five stanzas—in all, forty lines—of a single tone.   No
picture-drawing in words could convey to the mind

a more poignant impression than does this word-organ-
point of the immeasurable monotony of the great desert.[1]
It is a consummate touch.

> " As I ride, as I ride,
>   With a full heart for my guide,
>   So its tide rocks my side,
>   As I ride, as I ride,
>   That, as I were double-eyed,
>   He in whom our Tribes confide,
>   Is descried, ways untried,
>   As I ride, as I ride.

> " As I ride, as I ride
>   To our Chief and his Allied,
>   Who dares chide my heart's pride
>   As I ride, as I ride ?
>   Or are witnesses denied—
>   Through the desert waste and wide
>   Do I glide unespied
>   As I ride, as I ride ? "

As in the foregoing poem, we often find central rhymes
balancing terminal rhymes and producing, as in internal
Balance of alliteration, much more subtle effects than the
central with obvious terminal consonance. The internal
terminal
cadence music of the following song from Tennyson's
" Princess " is very delicate.

---

[1] Wagner achieves a similar effect in " Rheingold," where the superimposed melodies of the Rhine daughters are rippled over one tremendous
major triad, held from beginning to end. By this cataract of monotonous
tone, he makes the listener *feel* the eternal pulse of the waters. Both these
effects are *emotional* impressions.

" The splendour falls on castle walls
    And snowy summits old in story;
The long light shakes across the lakes,
    And the wild cataract leaps in glory.
Blow, bugle, blow, set the wild echoes flying,
Blow, bugle; answer, echoes, dying, dying, dying.

" O hark, O hear! how thin and clear,
    And thinner, clearer, farther going;
O sweet and far, from cliff and scar,
    The horns of elfland faintly blowing!
Blow, let us hear the purple glens replying:
Blow, bugle; answer, echoes, dying, dying, dying.

" O love, they die in yon rich sky,
    They faint on hill or field or river:
Our echoes roll from soul to soul,
    And grow forever and forever.
Blow, bugle, blow, set the wild echoes flying,
And answer, echoes, answer, dying, dying, dying."

In the following excerpt from a poem entitled
" Grishna," by Sir Edwin Arnold, there is a splendid
sensuous music produced by the central rhyme-repe-
titions, which are everywhere very warm in tone.

" With fierce noons beaming, moons of glory gleaming,
    Full conduits streaming, where fair bathers lie;
With sunsets splendid, when the strong day, ended,
    Melts into peace, like a tired lover's sigh—
                    So cometh summer nigh.

" And nights of ebon blackness, laced with lustres
    From starry clusters; courts of calm retreat,
Where wan rills warble over glistening marble;
    Cold jewels, and the sandal, moist and sweet—
                    These for the time are meet."

But perhaps the crowning example of repeated tones, internal and external—producing, as it were, a succession of tonal waves upon the ear—is to be found in Poe's "Raven."

"Once upon a midnight dreary, while I pondered weak and
      weary,
Over many a quaint and curious volume of forgotten lore—
While I nodded, nearly napping, suddenly there came a tap-
      ping
As of some one gently rapping, rapping at my chamber door.
'Tis some visitor,' I muttered, 'tapping at my chamber door—
      Only this and nothing more.'

"Ah, distinctly I remember it was in the bleak December,
And each separate dying ember wrought its ghost upon the
      floor.
Eagerly I wished the morrow;—vainly I had sought to borrow
From my books surcease of sorrow—sorrow for the lost Lenore—
For the rare and radiant maiden whom the angels name
      Lenore—
      Nameless here forevermore.

"And the silken sad uncertain rustling of each purple curtain
Thrilled me—filled me with fantastic terrors never felt before;
So that now, to still the beating of my heart, I stood repeating
'Tis some visitor entreating entrance at my chamber door—
Some late visitor entreating entrance at my chamber door;
      .This it is and nothing more.'

  .   .   .   .

"And the Raven, never flitting, still is sitting, still is sitting
On the pallid bust of Pallas just above my chamber door;
And his eyes have all the seeming of a demon's that is dreaming,
And the lamplight o'er him streaming throws his shadow on
      the floor;
And my soul from out that shadow that lies floating on the floor,
      Shall be lifted—nevermore."

The rich interweaved tones, the rhyme-correspond-
ences, with feminine cadence, and the repetitions and
refrains make this poem, melodically, one of the most
remarkable in our language. The whole rings with
a weird melody very consonant with the theme. Poe,
more than any other poet, has exploited this peculiar
grace of verse; but in the " Raven " he has touched high-
water mark. Some of his other poems—" Ullalume "
for instance—are of such tenuity that one examines them
more as essays in verse-tones than as meaning poems.

This brings us directly to the cognate division of *Refrains.* A refrain (or burden) is the repetition of a single
Refrains as phrase at the end of each stanza of a poem.
a factor of Occasionally it comes in the middle of the
melody stanza; more seldom, at every two or three
stanzas. Here is a ringing refrain.

> " My heart is wasted with my woe,
>   Oriana.
> There is no rest for me below,
>   Oriana.
> When the long dun wolds are ribb'd with snow,
> And loud the Norland whirlwinds blow,
>   Oriana,
> Alone I wander to and fro,
>   Oriana.
>
>   .   .   .   .   .
> " She stood upon the castle wall,
>   Oriana :
> She watch'd my crest among them all,
>   Oriana :
> She saw me fight, she heard me call,
> When forth there stepp'd a foeman tall,
>   Oriana,
> Atween me and the castle wall,
>   Oriana.

" The bitter arrow went aside,
   Oriana :
The false, false arrow went aside,
   Oriana :
The damned arrow glanced aside,
And pierc'd thy heart, my love, my bride,
   Oriana !
Thy heart, my life, my love, my bride,
   Oriana ! "
      —TENNYSON : " The Ballad of Oriana."

The solemn iteration of this refrain is like the tolling
of a bell, and thrills the nerves in the same way.

Belonging in the same category is the " Sands of Dee."
The constant repetition of fateful, connotative phrases
holds the imagination suspended and intensifies the
tragedy of the situation.

" ' O Mary, go and call the cattle home,
   And call the cattle home,
   And call the cattle home,
   Across the sands o' Dee ; '
The western wind was wild and dank wi' foam,
   And all alone went she.

" The creeping tide came up along the sand,
   And o'er and o'er the sand,
   And round and round the sand,
   As far as eye could see ;
The blinding mist came down and hid the land—
   And never home came she.

" ' O, is it weed, or fish, or floating hair—
   A tress o' golden hair,
   O' drownèd maiden's hair,
   Above the nets at sea ?

9

Was never salmon yet that shone so fair,
　　Among the stokes on Dee.'

" They rowed her in across the rolling foam,
　　The cruel, crawling foam,
　　The cruel, hungry foam,
　To her grave beside the sea ;
But still the boatmen hear her call the cattle home
　Across the sands o' Dee."

　　　　　　—CHARLES KINGSLEY : " The Sands of Dee."

In our next quotation we catch the music of waters.
Compare this echoing, melodious rush with the adjective-
clang of " How the Water Comes Down at Lodore."
Here, as in the " Raven," we find the internal consonances saturating with colour the verse, which is crowned
by the melodious refrain.

" Out of the hills of Habersham,
　Down the valleys of Hall,
I hurry amain to reach the plain,
Run the rapid and leap the fall,
Split at the rock and together again,
Accept my bed, or narrow or wide,
And flee from folly on every side
With a lover's pain to attain the plain
　Far from the hills of Habersham,
　Far from the valleys of Hall.

" All down the hills of Habersham,
　All through the valleys of Hall,
The rushes cried *Abide, abide,*
The wilful waterweed held me thrall,
The laving laurel turned my tide,

The ferns and the fondling grass said *Stay*,
The dewberry dipped for to work delay,
And the little reed sighed *Abide, abide,*
   Here in the hills of Habersham,
   Here in the valleys of Hall."
—SIDNEY LANIER : " Song of the Chattahoochee."[1]

Delicate melodic effects are sometimes obtained by refrain-inversions. Thus in " The Song of the River "
Refrain-inversions (see page 39) we read in the first line " Clear and cool, clear and cool," and the third " Cool and clear, cool and clear," the inversion giving variety to the repetend. A charming effect of refrain-inversion —being indeed the making of it—occurs in the following little lyric.

" There is no spring, though skies be blue and tender,
   And soft the warm breath of a gentler air ;
Though scarves of green veil all the birches slender,
   And blossoms star the open everywhere.
Though beauty breathe in every living thing,
Except thou lovest me—there is no spring.

" There is no winter, though the sky may darken,
   And chilly death hide all the world in snow ;
No sound of spring, though all the soul may hearken,
   No message from the flowers tombed below.
Though desolate the earth, the air, the sea,
There is no winter—if thou lovest me ! "
—ABBIE FARWELL BROWN : " Love's Calendar."

To get the very perfection of repetends and refrains we must, however, go back to the seventeenth century.

[1] From " Poems of Sidney Lanier." Copyright 1884, 1895, by Mary Day Lanier, and published by Charles Scribner's Sons.

Nothing more spontaneously dainty than the following exists. Such a lilt cannot quite be caught to-day.

> " Why so pale and wan, fond lover ?
>   Prithee, why so pale ?
> Will, when looking well can't move her,
>   Looking ill prevail ?
>   Prithee, why so pale ?
>
> " Why so dull and mute, young sinner ?
>   Prithee, why so mute ?
> Will, when speaking well can't win her,
>   Saying nothing do't ?
>   Prithee, why so mute ? "
>   —Sir John Suckling: " Why so Pale and Wan ? "

But the scope of the refrain is, in the end, limited, and limits the verse. It would handicap strong emotion, so

Scope of the refrain limited

that in really fervid verse we never find it used. The utterance of passion cannot pause for studied mellifluence.

Besides the details of verse-music already illustrated, a poem should have a certain tonal homogeneity—which homogeneity is the result of unity in its controlling purpose—making its movements appeal to us as a whole. In the perfect poem, stanza will modulate into stanza sequently and harmoniously, in confluent waves of sound, so that not one could be omitted and the poem remain quite perfect; for the *lyric unity* of a poem is its final test. This quality of homogeneity, or lyric unity, may rightly be called *harmony*, because here the word is used in its universal sense of concord, or completeness of balance.

Thus, having followed to their conclusion the underlying laws, the formative principles, of verse, we find that verse has *motion, melody,* and *harmony;* but *not pitch.*[1]

[1] I must once more emphasise the fact that there can be in verse no such thing as musical tonality, or pitch, although some teachers of metre claim for it this quality. As I have elsewhere pointed out, verse is a single voice, a melody. It is a melody because it has rhythmic vibration and tonal inter-relation ; but the exact point in which the melody of verse differs from the melody of music is just this one of pitch. Music has definite pitch, but verse has no such quality. The modulations of the voice in reading or re-citing poetry—dependent as they are upon the perceptive and interpretive genius of the reader or reciter—cannot be so considered.

CHAPTER V

METRIC FORMS

CERTAIN metrical denominations have been used by certain poets in certain lands, and have found such popular acceptance that other poets have imitated the forms, not only in the same languages and lands but sometimes in other languages and lands; so that they have been adopted from literature to literature, and become as it were cosmopolitan.

Italy was the fountain-head, not only of the literary thought of the early Renaissance, but of most of the
Italy the fountain-head of metric forms forms into which that thought crystallised. From Italy these art forms filtered through other countries, often undergoing local changes which carried them into still further evolutions, and multiplied variants of the originals. England— opened to all these new influences by the Norman Conquest—proved a grateful soil and readily assimilated all which came to it; using some forms imitatively while transforming others to fit the peculiar demands of her language and her muse, until they ceased to be alien, became germane to her thought and a part of her literature. While some of the forms—blank verse, for instance —were imported directly from Italy, the immediate channel for most of them was France, where, throughout the middle ages and the early Renaissance, minstrelsy of all sorts reigned supreme. Indeed the Romance poets of

southern France had no little hand in shaping the nascent literatures of Europe.

In this chapter it is proposed to consider first those so assimilated as to be distinctively English, and afterwards those which have been used in direct imitation of foreign models, and so have preserved their identity.

No consideration of English forms would be complete without an examination of the one indigenous verse-form, **Anglo-Saxon** the Anglo-Saxon; although it is true that the **epic form** Anglo-Saxon, further than by bestowing upon English poetry the melodic factor of alliteration, has furnished to it no forms, and has left upon it no imprint. This is obviously because of the more artistic genius of the continental forms, which prevailed inevitably by reason of their inherent fitness. In nothing is this more clearly evidenced than in the fate of two great works, almost contemporaneous, of the fourteenth century;— William Langland's "The Vision of Piers the Plowman" (about 1362), and Geoffrey Chaucer's "Canterbury Tales" (about 1374–1382). Between the ethical significance of the two works there can be no comparison. "Piers the Plowman" is a great and solemn allegorical epic; the "Canterbury Tales" is a cycle of breezy metrical romances. But to-day—four centuries later—the "Canterbury Tales" is delightful reading, full of a fresh realism and a sparkling humour whose charm never palls; while, except for the profounder researches of the student, the great allegory lies forgotten upon dusty shelves. Now what is the cause of the survival of the lesser work in face of the oblivion which has overtaken the greater? Simply the difference in the *forms* into which they were cast.

"The poem of Langland was forgotten. Nor was any other destiny possible to it. Consciously or uncon-

sciously, Langland rejected all elements of the common
life offered from above, from culture, learning, knighthood. His 'Visions' are uncouth, primitive, amorphous; redolent of the soil, but heavy with it as well.
He wrote in a revival of the old alliterative metre dear to
his Saxon forefathers; and the movement of his verses
is that of the labourer in the field, not that of the lady
in the dance:—

> " ' Duke of this dim place, anon undo the gates,
> That Christ may comen in, the Kingë's son of heaven.'

" It was a noble metre; it had held sway over English
poetry for six hundred years—a far longer reign than that
of the heroic blank verse, its upstart successor. Splendid passions had found expression in its surging, swaying
lines. Yet when Langland chose it for his vehicle it was
already doomed. Its grave inward music, its slow un-
relieved majesty, were of pure Teuton strain. They
could not satisfy the community into which was gradually filtering from above a new element and a new
spirit." [1]

In the Anglo-Saxon versification there is perceivable
a rough triple movement. The verse may be described
as 3/4, with a sharp cæsura in the middle. The notation
of the bars is very irregular, there sometimes being two
syllables only, and at others more than three.

Also occasionally the line runs out longer. This verse
was recited, or chanted, by the bards to the accompaniment of their harps; and it is easy to see how the volume
of syllables could be prolonged or shortened to a given
cadence, exactly as is the case in church chanting to-day,
thus giving what Lanier calls " an ordered riot of sounds."

[1] VIDA D. SCUDDER: "Social Ideals in English Letters," chapt. i.
part iv.

The scheme of alliteration—the only binding element which this verse shows—is in general two alliterated letters in the first section, and one in the second, though this rule does not seem absolute. Here is a short quotation from " The Battle of Maldon," sometimes called " The Death of Byrhtnoth," a poem dating about 993.[1]

> " Byrhtnoth mathelode, bord hafenode,
> wand wacne aesc, wordum maelde,
> yrre and anraed, ageaf him andsware;
> 'Gehyrst thu, saelida, hwaet this folc segeth ?
> Hi willath eow to gafole garas syllan,
> aettrene ord and ealde swurd,
> tha heregeatu the eow aet hilde ne deah.
> Brimmana boda, abeod eft ongean;
> sege thinum leodum micle lathre spell,
> thaet her stent unforcuth eorl mid his werode,
> the wile geealgian ethel thysne,
> Æthelraedes eard, ealdres mines,
> folc and foldan : feallan sceolan
> haethene aet hilde ! ' "

To this Lanier furnishes the accompanying translation:

" Byrhtnoth cried to him, brandished the buckler, shook the slim ash, with words made utterance, wrathful and resolute, gave him his answer: ' Hearest thou, sea-rover, that which my folk sayeth ? Yes, we will render you tribute in javelins—poisonous point and old-time blade—good weapons, yet forward you not in the fight.

---

[1] Of the versification of " Byrhtnoth," Lanier says: " In most lines the three first bars or feet begin with the same consonant ; in others the three first bars begin with a vowel, though not necessarily the same vowel ; in others the two middle bars begin with the same consonant ; in others the first and third bars begin with the same consonant. These four alliterative types are rarely departed from."—" Science of English Verse," page 145.

Herald of pirates, be herald once more: bear to thy people a bitterer message,—that here stands dauntless an earl with his warriors, will keep us this country, land of my Lord Prince Athelraed, folk and field: the heathen shall perish in battle.' "

The earliest, most wide-spread, and, in one way most important, verse-form developed in England is the English Ballad. It differs from others in that it was not an expression of literary or cultured feeling, but of the thoughts, desires, and impulses of the people. Therefore is it more spontaneous, and less an achievement of artistic craftsmanship than a popular growth. In essence it had for progenitor the bardic epics of the earliest ages. " The minstrels were an order of men in the Middle Ages, who subsisted by the arts of poetry and music, and sang to the harp verses composed by themselves or others. They also appear to have accompanied their songs with mimicry and action, and to have practised such various means of diverting as were much admired in those rude times, and supplied the want of more refined entertainment. These arts rendered them extremely popular in this (England) and all the neighbouring countries; where no high scene of festivity was deemed complete that was not set off with the exercise of their talents; and where, so long as the spirit of chivalry subsisted, they were protected and caressed, because their songs tended to do honour to the ruling passion of the times, and to encourage and foment a martial spirit." [1]

Genesis of the ballad The earliest ballads which we possess are of much antiquity and considerably antedate Chaucer. This form of poetry obtained its greatest

The English Ballad

---

[1] THOMAS PERCY: " Reliques of Ancient English Poetry," vol. i.; " Essay on the Minstrels."

dominance in the northern shires of England and in
southern Scotland, thus partaking of the rugged northern spirit. As it made its way southward and was
adopted into courtly circles, it became a more polished
instrument, but was also shorn of much of the native
vigour and spontaneity of the earlier verse.

Ballads were doubtless passed orally from mouth to
mouth, perhaps from generation to generation, and came
at last to be written—those which *were* written, for pre-
sumably many were not—by persons quite other than
those who composed them.

The metric *form* which the ballad took had of necessity
a foreign origin. The so-called *English Ballad Metre* is
technically a verse of seven bars of 2-beat rhythm (2/7)
with a strong central cæsura which naturally divides it
into two sections. Written in full it stands as follows:

"Ye gen-tle-men of England   who live at home at ease

How little   do ye think up - on the   dangers of   the seas."

This form was developed from the *Latin Septenary*,
which found its way to England with other foreign influ-
The Latin ences at the time of the Conquest. "In late
Septenary Latin poetry a metre had become common
which consisted of a half-verse of four accents, the last
accent falling on the last syllable, joined to a half-verse
of three accents with double (feminine) ending: on
account of the seven accents of the whole verse the

---

[1] The central bar may be full, or may be filled out with a rest.

metre was called *Septenarius*. It was furnished with end-rime. Both in the church hymns, and in the songs of wandering ' clerks,' who strolled from nation to nation secure in their common language, this metre was very popular. Cf. the following opening couplet of a convivial song:—

> " ' Méum ést propósitúm   ín tabérna móri
> Ét vinúm appósitúm   sítiénti óri ! '

" This measure was soon used for English verse." [1]
In becoming adopted as an English metric medium it suffered, however, a certain transformation. For the feminine ending of the Latin, there was substituted the sterner masculine ending, for which the English poets have always had a strong instinct; and, correlatively with the docking the last bar of its unaccented syllable, there comes the prefixing to the verse of the anacrusis. The cadence of the verse is thereby radically altered. There is a certain sing-song quality inherent in this measure which rendered it well adapted to the simple airs to which the ballads were sung.

Sometimes we find the ballad metre written out in couplets of 2/7 verse, as in the foregoing example. More often, however, it is divided by the central pause, and appears in a quatrain of alternating 2/4 and 2/3 verse. Doubtless the former was the *original* form of the English Septenary. Percy mentions that a number of ballads which he gives in the " Reliques " as quatrains, appear in the " Folio " as long couplets. Chapman, in his translation of Homer, has selected these long, swinging lines, which indeed seem to carry more dignity than when split into quatrains. " The rushing gallop of the

[1] FRANCIS B. GUMMERE : " A Handbook of Poetics," chap. vii.

long fourteen-syllable stanza in which it is written has the fire and swiftness of Homer,'' comments Stopford Brooke.

" But, ere stern conflict mixed both strengths, fair Paris stepped
    before
  The Trojan host; athwart his back a panther's hide he wore,
  A crooked bow, and sword, and shook two brazen-headed darts,
  With which, well armed, his tongue provoked the best of
    Grecian hearts
  To stand with him in single fight. Whom when the man
    wronged most
  Of all the Greeks, so gloriously saw stalk before the host;
  As when a lion is rejoiced, with hunger half forlorn,
  That finds some sweet prey, as a hart, whose grace lies in his
    horn,
  Or sylvan goat, which he devours, though never so pursued
  With dogs and men; so Sparta's king exulted when he viewed
  The fair-faced Paris so exposed to his thirsted wreak
  Wherof his good cause made him sure.''
      —GEORGE CHAPMAN : " The Iliad,'' book III.

And here is a fine modern specimen:

" Come, see the Dolphin's anchor forged—'tis at a white heat
    now;
  The bellows ceased, the flames decreased, though on the
    forge's brow
  The little flames still fitfully play through the sable mound,
  And fitfully you still may see the grim smiths ranking round,
  All clad in leathern panoply, their broad hands only bare;
  Some rest upon their sledges here, some work the windlass
    there.''
      —SAMUEL FERGUSSON : " The Forging of the Anchor.''

The earliest ballads are extremely loose in versification, sometimes running the line out beyond metrical **Ancient** limits, and often crowding extra syllables into **ballads** the bar, so that in places the verse seems for a time to depart into triple rhythm. Indeed some ballads—" Mary Ambree," for instance—are distinctly triple throughout.[1]

But we find as the ballad approaches its entrance into literature, it grows smoother and more carefully proportioned. I give a few extracts from Percy's " Reliques of Ancient Poetry." Many ballads were divided into parts, anciently called *fits*.

> " The Persè owt of Northombarlande,[2]
>   And a vowe to God mayd he,
>   That he wolde hunte in the mountayns
>   Off Chyviat within dayes thre
>   In the mauger of doughtè Dogles,
>   And all that ever with him be.

> " The fattiste hartes in all Cheviat
>   He sayd he wold kill, and cary them away :
>   Be my feth, sayd the dougheti Dogles agayn,
>   I wyll let that hontyng yf that I may.

> " Then the Persè owt of Banborowe cam,
>   With him a myghtye meany :
>   With fifteen hondrith archares bold ;
>   The wear chosen out of shyars thre.

[1] There are also many ballads cast not in ballad metre, but in other stanzaic forms : " A Ballad of Luther," " On Thomas, Lord Cromwell," " Little John Nobody," " Guy and Amarant," etc.

[2] Percy assigns " Chevy Chace " to the early part of the fifteenth century ; but there are fragmentary ballads of greater antiquity.

" This begane on a monday at morn
  In Cheviat the hillys so he ;
  The chyld may rue that ys un-born,
  It was the mor pittè.

" The dryvars thorowe the woodes went
  For to reas the dear ;
  Bomen bickarte uppone the bent
  With ther browd aras cleare.

" Then the wyld thorowe the woodes went
  On every syde shear ;
  Grea-hondes thorowe the greves glent
  For to kyll thear dear."
—The Ancient Ballad of " Chevy Chace," The First Fit.

" Nowe on the Eldridge hilles Ile walke
  For thy sake, fair ladìe ;
  And Ile either bring you a ready tokèn
  Or Ile never more you see.

" The lady is gone to her own chaumbère,
  Her maydens following bright :
  Syr Cauline lope from care-bed soone,
  And to the Eldridge hills is gone,
  For to wake there all night.

" Unto midnight that the moone did rise,
  He walked up and downe ;
  Then a lightsome bugle heard he blowe
  Over the bents soe browne :
  Quoth hee, ' If cryance come till my heart,
  I am ffar from any good towne.'

" And soone he spyde on the mores so broad,
   A furyous wight and fell ;
A ladye bright his brydle led,
   Clad in a fayre kyrtèll.

ı " And soe fast he called on syr Caullne,
   ' O man, I rede thee flye,
For, but if cryance come till thy heart,
   I weene but thou mun dye.'

" He sayth, ' No cryance comes till my heart,
   Nor, in faith, I wyll not flee ;
For, cause thou minged not Christ before,
   The less me dreadeth thee.' "
                         —" Sir Cauline," Part First.

" I can beleve, it shall you greve,
   And somewhat you dystrayne ;
But, aftyrwarde, your paynes harde
   Within a day or twayne
Shall sone aslake ; and ye shall take
   Comfort to you agayne.

" Why sholde ye ought ? for, to make thought,
   Your labour were in vayne.
And thus I do ; and pray you to,
   As hartely as I can ;
For I must to the grene wode go,
   Alone, a banyshed man.

" Now syth that ye have shewed to me
   The secret of your mynde,
I shall be playne to you agayne,
   Lyke as ye shall me fynde.

Syth it is so, that ye wyll go,
  I wolle not leve behynde;
Shall never be sayd the Not-browne Mayd
  Was to her love unkynde:
Make you redy, for so am I,
  Although it were anone;
For, in my mynde, of all mankynde
  I love but you alone."
             —" The Not-browne Mayd."

" He armed rode in forrest wide
  And met a damsell faire,
Who told him of adventures great
  Whereto he gave good eare.

" Such wold I find, quoth Lancelot:
  For that cause came I hither,
Thou seemst, quoth she, a knight full good,
  And I will bring thee thither.

" Whereas a mighty knight doth dwell,
  That now is of great fame:
Therefore tell me what wight thou art,
  And what may be thy name.

" My name is Lancelot du Lake,
  Quoth she, it likes me than;
Here dwelles a knight who never was
  Yet matcht with any man:

" Who has in prison threescore knights
  And four, that he did wound;
Knights of King Arthur's court they be,
  And of his table round."
             —" Sir Lancelot du Lake."

The smoother movement of this last excerpt betrays its more modern composition. There is also a " Chevy Chase" dating from Elizabeth's day, which was, until the discovery by Bishop Percy, regarded as the original. A brief comparison of the two shows the gain in versification of the later one, and also its loss in native aroma.

> " God prosper long our noble king,
>   Our lives and safetyes all ;
> A woefull hunting once there did
>   In Chevy-Chace befall ;

> " To drive the deere with hound and horne,
>   Erle Percy took his way ;
> The child may rue that is unborne
>   The hunting of that day.

> " The stout Erle of Northumberland
>   A vow to God did make,
> His pleasure in the Scottish woods
>   Three summer days to take ;

> " The cheefest harts in Chevy-Chace
>   To kill and beare away.
> These tydings to Erle Douglas came,
>   In Scotland where he lay."
>   —The Modern Ballad of " Chevy-Chace."

The most remarkable ballad of modern times—from a literary point of view, of any time—is Coleridge's
Coleridge's " Rime of the Ancient Mariner." In its sub-
ballad jective weirdness and horror it is quite unique, its effect being heightened by the somewhat broken rhythms, whose antique atmosphere Coleridge has wonderfully reproduced.

" It is an ancient Mariner,
  And he stoppeth one of three.
  ' By thy long grey beard and glittering eye,
  Now wherefore stopp'st thou me ?

" ' The Bridegroom's doors are opened wide,
  And I am next of kin ;
  The guests are met, the feast is set :
  May'st hear the merry din.'

" He holds him with his skinny hand,
  ' There was a ship,' quoth he.
  ' Hold off ! unhand me, grey-beard loon ! '
  Eftsoons his hand dropped he.

" He holds him with his glittering eye—
  The Wedding-Guest stood still,
  And listens like a three years' child :
  The Mariner hath his will."
                —" Rime of The Ancient Mariner," Part I.

  . . . . .

" And the good south wind still blew behind,
  But no sweet bird did follow,
  Nor any day for food or play
  Came to the mariner's hollo !

" And I had done a hellish thing,
  And it would work 'em woe :
  For all averred I had killed the bird
  That made the breeze to blow.
  ' Ah wretch ! ' said they, ' the bird to slay,
  That made the wind to blow ! ' "   —*Ibid.*, Part II.

  . . . . .

" With throats unslaked, with black lips baked,
  We could nor laugh nor wail ;

Through utter drought all dumb we stood!
I bit my arm, I sucked the blood,
And cried, ' A sail! a sail!'

" With throats unslaked, with black lips baked,
Agape they heard me call:
Gramercy! they for joy did grin,
And all at once their breath drew in,
As they were drinking all.

" ' See! see! (I cried) she tacks no more
Hither to work us weal,—
Without a breeze, without a tide,
She steadies with upright keel!'

" The western wave was all aflame,
The day was well nigh done!
Almost upon the western wave
Rested the broad bright sun;
When that strange shape drove suddenly
Betwixt us and the sun."   —*Ibid.*, Part III.

.   .   .   .   .

" Alone, alone, all, all alone,
Alone on a wide, wide sea!
And never a saint took pity on
My soul in agony.

" The many men, so beautiful!
And they all dead did lie:
And a thousand thousand slimy things
Lived on; and so did I.

" I looked upon the rotting sea,
And drew my eyes away;
I looked upon the rotting deck,
And there the dead men lay.

" I looked to heaven, and tried to pray;
  But or ever a prayer had gusht,
  A wicked whisper came, and made
  My heart as dry as dust."   —*Ibid.*, Part IV.

**Macaulay's
ballads** Later Macaulay, in his " Lays of Ancient
Rome," has given us some ringing ballad music.

" Lars Porsena of Clusium
      By the Nine Gods he swore
  That the great house of Tarquin
      Should suffer wrong no more.
  By the Nine Gods he swore it,
      And named a trysting day,
  And bade his messengers ride forth,
  To east and west and south and north,
      To summon his array.

" East and west and south and north
      The messengers ride fast,
  And tower and town and cottage
      Have heard the trumpet's blast.
  Shame on the false Etruscan
      Who lingers in his home
  When Porsena of Clusium
      Is on the march for Rome."
              —T. B. MACAULAY : " Horatius."

" Ho ! maidens of Vienna;
      Ho ! matrons of Lucerne ;
  Weep, weep, and rend your hair for those
      Who never shall return.
  Ho ! Philip, send, for charity,
      Thy Mexican pistoles,

> That Antwerp monks may sing a mass
>   For thy poor spearmen's souls.
> Ho ! gallant nobles of the League,
>   Look that your arms be bright ;
> Ho ! burghers of St. Genevieve,
>   Keep watch and ward to-night.
> For our God hath crushed the tyrant,
>   Our God hath raised the slave,
> And mocked the counsels of the wise,
>   And the valour of the brave.
> Then glory to his holy name,
>   From whom all glories are ;
> And glory to our Sovereign Lord,
>   King Henry of Navarre."
>   —T. B. MACAULAY : " Ivry."

Alongside of the ballad, and coeval with it, there grew up another measure called the *Short Couplet*. This is **The short couplet** a rhymed couplet of 2/4 verse, usually strict. It is indirectly of Latin origin, but came into England directly from France, where it was much in vogue. It became a great favourite. An early example may be seen in " The Owl and the Nightingale " (about 1250). Chaucer employs it in " The House of Fame " and " The Boke of the Duchesse."

> " Now herkneth, as I have you seyd,
> What that I mette or I abreyd.
> Of Decembre the tenthe day,
> Whan hit was night, to slepe I lay
> Right ther as I was wont to done,
> And fil on slepe wonder sone
> As he that wery was for-go
> On pilgrimage myles two—"
>   —CHAUCER : " The House of Fame."

We perceive this to be the favourite metre of Scott, Byron, Wordsworth, and others, which was mentioned on page 70 as being monotonous and without much motion.

The *Alexandrine*, or strict 2/6 verse, is also an old metre, and came into England with those already de-**The Alexandrine** scribed. In France it grew to be the classical standard; but in England it has not put down vital roots, and, although much verse has been written in it, it embalms nothing with the stamp of immortality. The cause is not far to seek. It is clumsy, heavy, in-elastic, and the cæsura, falling always exactly in the middle of the line, seems to *jerk* it into two wooden metric periods. " The droning old Alexandrine," Lowell calls it. Here is a sample:

> " Upon a thousand swans the naked Sea-Nymphs ride
> Within the oozy pools, replenish'd every tide :
> Which running on, the Isle of Portland pointeth out
> Upon whose moisted skirt with sea-weed fring'd about,
> The bastard coral breeds, that, drawn out of the brack,
> A little stalk becomes, from greenish turn'd to black :
> Which th' ancients, for the love that they to *Isis* bare
> (Their Goddess most ador'd) have sacred for her hair.
> Of which the *Naïdes*, and the blue *Nereids* make
> Them tawdries for their necks : when sporting in the lake,
> They to their sacred bow'rs the Sea-gods entertain."
> —MICHAEL DRAYTON : " Polyolbion," Second Song.

But, although the Alexandrine is ill adapted for sustained movement, an occasional one contrasts well with some other metres. Robert Mannyng (about the beginning of the fourteenth century) wrote a Chronicle of England in Alexandrines. They were common in the miracle plays, and even up to the time of Elizabeth were greatly in favour; so we are not surprised to find the early drama well tinctured with them. Marlowe abounds in Alexandrines. There is also a fair sprinkling of them in Shakespeare; and, though it has been pointed out that these generally occur divided between two speakers, this is not always the case; witness Hamlet's:

"What's Hecuba to him or he to Hecuba,"

The Alexandrine was often combined with the ballad metre, as in the lines of Surrey's:

"Layd in my quiet bed, in study as I were,
    I saw within my troubled head a heape of thoughtes appeare."

A halting metrical movement enough; as if one should **Poulter's** yoke a camel with an ox. This Gascoigne **measure** calls "Poulter's measure."[1]

The superiority of heroic verse[2]—strict 2/5 verse—over either 2/4 or 2/6 is easily manifest. It has more move- **The heroic** ment than the latter, more strength than the **rhymed** former, and combines plasticity with dignity. **couplet** Although domesticated in England rather later than the other continental forms, it seems to have been used empirically even before Chaucer gave it the mint-stamp of his genius. The heroic rhymed couplet has by its very adaptedness been a favourite medium for metrical romance, and eventually prevailed above all others.

---

[1] "Because the poulterer giveth XII for one dozen and XIIII for another."

[2] Observe the metric sequence, so early perfected : in the short couplet, 2/4 verse ; in the heroic couplet, 2/5 verse ; in the Alexandrine, 2/6 verse ; in the ballad metre, 2/7 verse. But any contemporary use of triple measure would seem to be accidental, and remains unclassified.

Chaucer's use of it is spontaneous and quaintly charming.

> "Whan that Aprille with his shoures sote
> The droghte of Marche hath perced to the rote,
> And bathed every veyne in swich licòur,
> Of which virtu engendred is the flour;
> Whan Zephirus eek with his swete breeth
> Inspired hath in every holt and heeth
> The tendre croppes, and the yonge sonne
> Hath in the Ram his halfe cours y-ronne,
> And smale fowles maken melodye,
> That slepen al the night with open yë,
> (So priketh hem nature in hir corages):
> Than longen folk to goon on pilgrimages—"
> —CHAUCER: Prologue to "Canterbury Tales." [1]

The heroic rhymed couplet was in use for early drama and was not readily displaced by the more adapted dramatic medium of blank verse. Shakespeare's earlier plays abound with rhymed couplets. It is only by the time of his middle period—the period of the great tragedies—that we find these entirely disappearing.

> "*Helena.* Call you me fair? that fair again unsay.
> Demetrius loves your fair: O happy fair!
> Your eyes are lode-stars, and your tongue's sweet air
> More tuneable than lark to shepherd's ear,
> When wheat is green, when hawthorn buds appear.
> Sickness is catching: O, were favour so,
> Yours would I catch, fair Hermia, ere I go;
> My ear should catch your voice, my eye your eye,
> My tongue should catch your tongue's sweet melody."
> —SHAKESPEARE: "Midsummer Night's Dream," i., 1.

[1] Skeat has been followed in the quotations from Chaucer.

" *Romeo.* Good heart, at what ?
" *Benvolio.*   At thy good heart's oppression.
" *Romeo.* Why, such is love's transgression.

> Griefs of mine own lie heavy in my breast,
> Which thou wilt propagate, to have it prest
> With more of thine ; this love that thou hast shown
> Doth add more grief to too much of mine own.
> Love is a smoke rais'd with the fume of sighs ;
> Being purg'd, a fire sparkling in lovers' eyes ;
> Being vex'd, a sea nourish'd with lovers' tears :
> What is it else ? a madness most discreet,
> A choking gall, and a preserving sweet—
> Farewell, my coz.

" *Benvolio.*   Soft ! I will go along;

> An if you leave me so, you do me wrong."

> —SHAKESPEARE : " Romeo and Juliet," i., 2.

In the period of the Restoration, the heroic rhymed couplet again comes to the front; but it is an emasculated rhymed couplet, shorn of *enjambement*. Revived with authority by Waller and his pupil, Denham, perfected by Dryden, and polished to the facets of a gem by Pope, it was made to sing every strain, grave or gay. But no amount of scholarship or cleverness could save it from seeming an artificial and mechanical movement; the epigrammatic periods falling upon the ear with the wearisome regularity of a machine.[1]

> " Those antique minstrels sure were Charles-like kings,
> Cities their lutes, and subjects' hearts their strings,
> On which with so divine a hand they strook
> Consent of motion from their breath they took."

> —EDMUND WALLER : " Upon His Majesty's Repairing of Paul's."

[1] The distinguishing characteristic of the romantic poetry had been overflow, that of the didactic, which followed it, was the end-stopped distich.

" O could I flow like thee, and make thy stream
My great example, as it is my theme !
Though deep, yet clear; though gentle, yet not dull;
Strong without rage, without o'erflowing full.''
—Sir John Denham : " Cooper's Hill.''

" ' Thy praise (and thine was then the public voice)
First recommended Guiscard to my choice;
Directed thus by thee, I look'd, and found
A man I thought deserving to be crown'd;
First by my father pointed to my sight,
Nor less conspicuous by his native light;
His mind, his mien, the features of his face,
Excelling all the rest of human race : ' ''
—John Dryden : " Sigismonda and Guiscardo.''

" Force first made conquest, and that conquest law;
Till superstition taught the tyrant awe,
Then shar'd the tyranny, then lent it aid,
And gods of conquerors, slaves of subjects made;
She, midst the lightning's blaze and thunder's sound,
When rock'd the mountains and when groan'd the ground,—
She taught the weak to bend, the proud to pray
To power unseen, and mightier far than they : ''
—Alexander Pope : " Essay on Man,'' iii., iv.

In our own century, once more freed and with the
overflow restored to it, the heroic couplet has been made
to do fine things. One of the most beautiful examples
may be studied in Keats's " Lamia.'' But no poet, ancient or modern, has handled the heroic couplet with
greater mastery than Browning. He swings his periods
along with a broad, free movement, which, if not always
rounded to perfect grace, is yet entirely without taint
either of formalism or sugariness. He employs it exten-

sively in his romantic poems.   I have room for only one
quotation:

> " ' Since I could die now of the truth concealed,
> Yet dare not, must not die,—so seems revealed
> The Virgin's mind to me,—for death means peace,
> Wherein no lawful part have I, whose lease
> Of life and punishment the truth avowed
> May haply lengthen,—let me push the shroud
> Away, that steals to muffle ere is just
> My penance-fire in snow!   I dare—I must
> Live by avowal of the truth—this truth—
> I loved you.   Thanks for the fresh serpent's tooth
> That, by a prompt new pang more exquisite
> Than all preceding torture, proves me right!
> I loved you yet I lost you!   May I go
> Burn to the ashes, now my shame you know ? ' "
>   —ROBERT BROWNING : " A Forgiveness."

Very different from the foregoing is the stately and
melodious Spenserian stanza in that far from being in

The Spenserian stanza   any sense an evolution or a growth, it is the
deliberate invention of a single gifted mind.
Edmund Spenser, experimenting with the various new Italian forms which had recently found their
way to England and bewitched the fancy of men of letters, produced alone this noble metric form.   Lowell
thus gives us Spenser's processes:

" The delicious abundance and overrunning luxury of
Spenser appear in the very structure of his verse.   He
found the *ottava rima* too monotonously iterative; so,
by changing the order of his rhymes, he shifted the
couplet from the end of the stave, where it always seems
to put on the brakes with a jar, to the middle, where it
may serve at will as a brace or a bridge.   He found it
not roomy enough, so first ran it over into another line,

and then ran that added line over into an alexandrine,
in which the melody of one stanza seems forever longing
and feeling forward after the one to follow. There is no
ebb and flow in his metre more than on the shores of the
Adriatic, but wave follows wave with equable gainings
and recessions, the one sliding back in fluent music to be
mingled with and carried forward by the next." [1]

Professor Corson repudiates the idea that the Spenserian stanza is built upon the *ottava rima*. " If Spenser

Corson's idea of the origin of Spenserian stanza was indebted to anyone for the eight lines of
his stanza, he was indebted to his master
Chaucer, who, in the ' Monk's Tale,' uses an
eight-line stanza with a rhyme-scheme identical with that of the eight heroic lines of the Spenserian
stanza, that scheme being *a b, a b, b c, b c.* Chaucer also
uses this stanza in his ' A B C ' (a Hymn to the Virgin)
in ' L'Envoy de Chaucer à Bukton,' and in ' Ballade
de Vilage sauns Peynture.' The Envoy to his ' Compleynte of a Loveres Lyfe ' (or the Complaint of the
Black Knight) is also in this stanza. The following is a
stanza from the ' Monk's Tale ' according to the Ells-
mere text :

> " ' Allas, fortune ! She that whilom was
> Dredful to kinges and to emperoures,
> Now gaureth al the peple on hir, allas !
> And she that helmed was in starke stoures,
> And wan by force tounes stronge and toures,
> Shal on hir heed now were a vitremyte ;
> And she that bar the ceptre ful of floures
> Shal bere a distaf, hir cost for to quyte.'

" By this rhyme-scheme the couplet instead of being at
the end is brought in the middle, where it serves to bind

---

[1] JAMES RUSSELL LOWELL : Essay on Spenser, "Among my Books,"
vol. ii.

together the two quatrains. That is in fact what the eight verses are, namely, two quatrains, with the last

Formula of Spenserian stanza line of the first and the first line of the second rhyming together. To these the poet added as a supplementary harmony, and in order to impart a fine sweeping close to his stanza, the alexandrine, making it rhyme with the second and fourth verses of the second quatrain.'' [1]

It would not be possible to define more clearly than does the foregoing eloquent passage, just what the Spenserian stanza *is*, in metric dignity being worthy to stand beside the sonnet, while in rich melodious flow it certainly surpasses it.

> " A gentle Knight was pricking on the plaine,
>   Ycladd in mightie armes and silver shielde,
>   Wherein old dints of deepe woundes did remaine,
>   The cruell markes of many a bloody fielde ;
>   Yet armes till that time did he never wield :
>   His angry steede did chide his foming bitt,
>   As much disdayning to the curbe to yield :
>   Full jolly knight he seemd, and faire did sitt,
> As one for knightly giusts and fierce encounters fitt.

> " And on his brest a bloodie crosse he bore,
>   The deare remembrance of his dying Lord,
>   For whose sweete sake that glorious badge he wore,
>   And dead, as living ever, him ador'd :
>   Upon his shielde the like was also scor'd,
>   For soveraine hope which in his helpe he had.
>   Right, faithfull, true he was in deede and word ;
>   But of his cheere did seeme too solemne sad ;
> Yet nothing did he dread but ever was ydrad.''
>   —" Faerie Queene,'' book i., canto i.

[1] Hiram Corson : " Primer of English Verse,'' chap. vii.

" Eftsoones they heard a most melodious sound,
 Of all that mote delight a daintie eare,
 Such as attonce might not on living ground,
 Save in this Paradise, be heard elsewhere :
 Right hard it was for wight which did it heare,
 To read what manner musicke that mote bee ;
 For all that pleasing is to living eare
 Was there consorted in one harmonee ;
Birdes, voices, instruments, windes, waters, all agree.

" The joyous birdes, shrouded in chearefull shade
 Their notes unto the voice attempred sweet ;
 Th' Angelicall soft trembling voyces made
 To th' instruments divine respondence meet ;
 With the base murmure of the waters fall ;
 The waters fall with difference discreet,
 Now soft, now loud, unto the wind did call ;
The gentle warbling wind low answered to all."
    —" Faerie Queene," book ii., canto xii.

Spenser was the teacher of many subsequent poets, even of those who did not directly imitate him; for his elaborate effects are an education in themselves.[1] We trace his influence peculiarly in some of the modern poets. In the revival of artistic feeling, which began in the latter end of the eighteenth century, and culminated in the noble music of the early part of the nineteenth, the Spenserian stanza came greatly into favour.

Professor Corson points out its " signal adaptedness to elaborate pictorial effect; " and therefore it offers a good medium to the objective poet, especially the objective poet of exotic imagination. It requires a preëminent

---

[1] " No man contributed so much to the transformation of style as Spenser. By the charm of his diction, the harmonies of his verse, his ideal method of treatment, and the splendour of his fancy, he made the new manner popular and fruitful."—LOWELL : Essay on Spenser, " Among my Books," vol. ii.

feeling for colour as well as an immense mastery of rhyme-effects; and these qualities the Georgian poets to **Followers** an unusual degree possessed. " I was enticed," **of Spenser** says Shelley, "by the brilliancy and magnificence of sound which a mind that has been nourished upon musical thoughts can produce by a just and harmonious arrangement of the pauses of this measure." Thomson, Shenstone, Beattie, Burns, Campbell, Scott, Wordsworth, Shelley, Keats, and Byron have all used this measure with more or less splendour. It seems rather strange that Tennyson and Browning, with their abounding vocabularies, and great mastery of metric and tonal effects, have not affected the Spenserian stanza. The five opening stanzas of the " Lotos Eaters " move in it, but the theme quickly melts into a looser and more fluid movement. The student who desires to sound the heights and depths of this verse-form will find it treated at great length and with superlative luminousness in Professor Corson's " Primer of English Verse," chapters vii. and viii.

I append a few modern examples. Keats's verse will be seen to be the closest in sensuous melody to that of the master; Byron's, full of a fire and vigour of which the master never dreamed; Shelley's, touched with that ethereal, almost disembodied quality which it was his privilege alone among poets to infuse into verse.

> " Then by the bedside, where the faded moon
> Made a dim, silver twilight, soft he set
> A table, and, half-anguish'd, threw thereon
> A cloth of woven crimson, gold, and jet :
> O for some drowsy Morphean amulet !
> The boisterous, midnight, festive clarion,
> The kettledrum, and far-heard clarionet,
> Affray his ears, though but in dying tone :
> The hall door shuts again, and all the noise is gone.

" And still she slept an azure-lidded sleep,
In blanchèd linen, smooth and lavender'd,
While he forth from the closet brought a heap
Of candied apple, quince, and plum, and gourd ;
With jellies smoother than the creamy curd,
And lucent syrops, tinct with cinnamon ;
Manna and dates, in argosy transferr'd
From Fez ; and spicèd dainties, every one
From silken Samarcand to cedar'd Lebanon."
— KEATS : " The Eve of St. Agnes."

" There was a sound of revelry by night,
And Belgium's capital had gather'd then
Her Beauty and her Chivalry, and bright
The lamps shone o'er fair women and brave men ;
A thousand hearts beat happily ; and when
Music arose with its voluptuous swell,
Soft eyes look'd love to eyes which spoke again
And all went merry as a marriage bell ;
But hush ! hark ! a deep sound strikes like a rising knell !

" Did ye not hear it ?—No ; 'twas but the wind
Or the car rattling o'er the stony street ;
On with the dance ! Let joy be unconfined ;
No sleep till morn, when Youth and Pleasure meet
To chase the glowing Hours with flying feet—
But hark !—that heavy sound breaks in once more,
As if the clouds its echo would repeat ;
And nearer, clearer, deadlier than before !
Arm ! Arm ! it is—it is—the cannon's opening roar ! "
— BYRON : " Childe Harold," iii.

" Peace, peace ! he is not dead, he doth not sleep !
He hath awakened from the dream of life.
'Tis we who, lost in stormy visions, keep
With phantoms an unprofitable strife,

And in mad trance strike with our spirit's knife
Invulnerable nothings. *We* decay
Like corpses in a charnel ; fear and grief
Convulse us and consume us day by day,
And cold hopes swarm like worms within our living clay.

" He has out-soar'd the shadow of our night.
Envy and calumny and hate and pain,
And that unrest which men miscall delight
Can touch him not and torture not again.
From the contagion of the world's slow stain
He is secure ; and now can never mourn
A heart grown cold, a head grown grey, in vain—
Nor, when the spirit's self has ceas'd to burn,
With sparkless ashes load an unlamented urn.

" He lives, he wakes—'tis Death is dead, not he ;
Mourn not for Adonaïs.—Thou young Dawn,
Turn all thy dew to splendour, for from thee
The spirit thou lamentest is not gone !
Ye caverns and ye forests, cease to moan !
Cease, ye faint flowers and fountains ! and, thou Air,
Which like a mourning veil thy scarf hadst thrown
O'er the abandoned Earth, now leave it bare
Even to the joyous stars which smile on its despair !

" He is made one with Nature.   There is heard
His voice in all her music, from the moan
Of thunder to the song of night's sweet bird.
He is a presence to be felt and known
In darkness and in light, from herb and stone ;
Spreading itself where'er that Power may move
Which has withdrawn his being to its own,
Which wields the world with never-wearied love,
Sustains it from beneath, and kindles it above."
                                    —SHELLEY : " Adonaïs."

" The blasts of autumn drive the wingèd seeds
  Over the earth,—next come the snows, and rain,
  And frosts, and storms, which dreary Winter leads
  Out of his Scythian cave, a savage train;
  Behold! Spring sweeps over the world again,
  Shedding soft dews from her ethereal wings;
  Flowers on the mountains, fruits over the plain,
  And music on the waves and woods she flings,
And love on all that lives, and calm on lifeless things.

" O Spring! of hope and love and youth and gladness
  Wind-wingèd emblem! brightest, best, and fairest!
  Whence comest thou, when with dark Winter's sadness
  The tears that fade in sunny smiles thou sharest?
  Sister of joy! thou art the child who wearest
  Thy mother's dying smile, tender and sweet;
  Thy mother Autumn, for whose grave thou bearest
  Fresh flowers, and beams like flowers, with gentle feet
Disturbing not the leaves which are her winding sheet." [1]
                              —SHELLEY : " Revolt of Islam," ix.

It is Professor Corson's opinion that the resources of
the Spenserian stanza are far from exhausted. Perhaps
future poets will come to it, and, with that concentrated
spiritual power which ever-advancing thought brings to
the soul of genius, touch this rich and responsive instrument into a music still undreamed.

The Eliza-   I place the Elizabethan sonnet—often called
bethan or   the Shakespearean sonnet—here, rather than
Shake-
spearean   after its great Italian congener, because it is
sonnet   *sui generis*—specifically English, and has a
beauty all its own. It consists indeed of a lyric of four-

---

[1] The feminine endings in this stanza simply double the melody; and,
with the fine instinct of the great artist, Shelley does not persist in them to
the end, which would make weakness of the stanzaic climax, but comes
back in the finish-rhyme to the masculine ending.

teen lines of heroic verse, but there the relation ends; for it conforms neither to the structural canons of the legitimate sonnet nor to its organic sequence.

Surrey is generally conceded to have brought the sonnet to England, and both he and Wyat made early essays in this form,[1] but its technicalities appear to have made small impression upon the teeming Elizabethan genius, fecund enough for all its own needs. The Elizabethan poets adopted the outline only, and filled out the details to suit themselves.

The Elizabethan sonnet is really an aggregation of three quatrains capped by a couplet. There is generally no tonal connection between the quatrains, although occasionally we find one in which the finish-rhyme of the first quatrain is made the off-rhyme of the second; and in Spenser's "Amoretti" this scheme extends even into the third quatrain. Drummond uses two *alternating* rhymes through the first two quatrains. There appears to have been no fixed model, but each singer followed his own feeling for tone. The couplet is again distinct tonally, and, quite contrary to the spirit of the Italian sonnet, enfolds the subjective climax.

This loosely-hung framework was admirably adapted to the independent genius of the age, which for the most part preferred evolving its own art-forms to imitating those already formulated. Most of the contemporary poets seem to have tried their hands at sonnet writing, prominent names being those of Shakespeare, Spenser, Sidney, Daniel, Drummond, Drayton, Donne, Chapman, etc. Among these, Shakespeare is easily first.

---

[1] There are other Elizabethan sonnets which follow the Italian model as far as the octave is concerned, but become loose in the sestet. Of such is Sidney's famous and beautiful " With how wan steps, O Moon," which ends with the characteristic Elizabethan and non-Italian couplet.

" Shall I compare thee to a summer's day ?
Thou art more lovely and more temperate :
Rough winds do shake the darling buds of May,
And summer's lease hath all too short a date :
Sometime too hot the eye of heaven shines,
And often is his gold complexion dimm'd ;
And every fair from fair sometime declines,
By chance or nature's changing course untrimm'd ;
But thy eternal summer shall not fade,
Nor lose possession of that fair thou owest,
Nor shall death brag thou wander'st in his shade,
When in eternal lines to time thou grow'st ;
   So long as men can breathe, or eyes can see,
   So long lives this, and this gives life to thee."
                 —SHAKESPEARE : XVIII.

" When to the sessions of sweet silent thought
I summon up remembrance of things past,
I sigh the lack of many a thing I sought,
And with old woes new wail my dear time's waste :
Then can I drown an eye, unused to flow,
For precious friends hid in death's dateless night,
And weep afresh love's long since cancell'd woe,
And moan the expense of many a vanish'd sight :
Then can I grieve at grievances foregone,
And heavily from woe to woe tell o'er
The sad account of fore-bemoaned moan,
Which I new pay as if not paid before.
   But if the while I think on thee, dear friend,
   All losses are restored, and sorrows end."
                 —SHAKESPEARE : XXX.

" Let me not to the marriage of true minds
Admit impediments.   Love is not love
Which alters when it alteration finds,
Or bends with the remover to remove :

O no ! it is an ever-fixed mark
That looks on tempests and is never shaken ;
It is the star to every wandering bark,
Whose worth's unknown, although his height be taken.
Love's not Time's fool, though rosy lips and cheeks
Within his bending sickle's compass come ;
Love alters not with his brief hours and weeks,
But bears it out even to the edge of doom.
   If this be error, and upon me proved,
   I never writ, nor no man ever loved."

                       —SHAKESPEARE : CXVI.

" Like as a ship that through the ocean wide
By conduct of some star doth make her way,
Whenas a storm hath dimm'd her trusty guide,
Out of her course doth wander far astray,—
So I, whose star, that wont with her bright ray
Me to direct, with clouds is over-cast,
Do wander now in darkness and dismay,
Through hidden perils round about me plac'd :
Yet hope I well that when this storm is past,
My Helice, the lodestar of my life,
Will shine again and look on me at last,
With lovely light to clear my cloudy grief.
   Till then I wander careful, comfortless,
   In secret sorrow and sad pensiveness."

                        —SPENSER : XXXIV.

" Dear, why should you command me to my rest,
When now the night doth summon all to sleep ?
Methinks this time becometh lovers best :
Night was ordain'd together friends to keep.
How happy are all other living things,
Which though the day disjoin by several flight,

The quiet Evening yet together brings,
And each returns unto his love at night!
O thou that art so courteous unto all,
Why shouldst thou, Night, abuse me only thus,
That every creature to his kind dost call,
And yet 'tis thou dost only sever us ?
   Well could I wish it would be ever day,
   If, when night comes, you bid me go away."
            —MICHAEL DRAYTON.

" Dear quirister, who from those shadows sends,
Ere that the blushing dawn dare show her light,
Such sad lamenting strains, that night attends
(Become all ear), stars stay to hear thy plight;
If one whose grief even reach of thought transcends,
Who ne'er (not in a dream) did taste delight,
May thee importune who like case pretends ;
And seems to joy in woe, in woe's despite ;
Tell me (so may thou fortune milder try,
And long, long sing) for what thou thus complains,
Sith, winter gone, the sun in dappled sky
Now smiles on meadows, mountains, woods and plains ?
   The bird, as if my questions did her move,
   With trembling wings sobb'd forth, I love, I love !"
            —WILLIAM DRUMMOND.

Alien metric forms We now pass to the consideration of alien metric forms.

The Italian, or legitimate sonnet, is the greatest of ex-**The Italian or legitimate sonnet** istent fixed metric forms. It has endured in undimmed lustre for five centuries, has penetrated to many lands, and been adopted into many literatures. It appears to be of Provençal origin,[1]

---

[1] " The sonnet passed through many changes, in the length of the verses, the order of the rhymes, the addition of tails or *rondellos ;* but there is no doubt that the regular sonnet of fourteen lines, with the rhymes as in Type

and to have passed through a moulding process in various hands until, in Dante's, it became the perfectly attuned instrument.

Petrarch, in his famous cycles to Laura, gave it its final polish, and made it universally popular. Even to his time this and kindred forms seem to have been always allied with music, and to have been not recited but *sung*.[1] Mr. Tomlinson tells us that " Petrarch sang his verses to the sound of his lute, which he bequeathed in his will to a friend, and we are told that his voice was sweet and flexible, and of considerable compass; it is also said that such was the magic of his song that the gravest persons were accustomed to go away repeating or humming the words." Other great sonnet writers were Tasso, Ariosto, and, later, Michael Angelo and Vittoria Colonna.

The sonnet is a lyric of fourteen lines of heroic verse in special tonal arrangement. There must be one leading or governing idea or sentiment. Metrically it is divided into two sections, the octave and the sestet. In the octave the motive or theme is developed, finding its climax there. The sestet becomes a sort of commentary

III, was in use as early as 1321, such a sonnet being written by Guglielmo degli Amalricchi in honour of Robert, King of Naples. In Italy, the sonnet, in the hands of Fra Guittone d'Arezzo, Dante, Cino, and, lastly, Petrarch, was perfected ; and it seems probable that these great masters received from the Provençal poets the form of the sonnet as well a that of the *canzone*, the *sestina*, the *ballata*, etc."—CHARLES TOMLINSON · " The Sonnet ; its Origin, Structure, and Place in Poetry," part i., p. 16

[1] " As the words *sonetto* and *canzone* imply (from *picol suono*, a small sound or composition, and *dal canto*), they were sung with a musical accompaniment, in common with all lyric poetry, and had reference to the composer's own feelings. As the Horatian lyrics merged into the rhyming verses of the monks, and scansion gave way to accent, these probably gave rise to the poems of the troubadours (trovatori ; *i.e.*, inventors) of the early part of the eleventh century."—CHARLES TOMLINSON : " The Sonnet," part i., p. 9.

or reflection—the moral as it were—upon the octave, declining in stress of feeling so that the poem ends tranquilly.[1] One might characterise the octave as a *crescendo* passage, and the sestet as a *diminuendo*.

Mr. Theodore Watts has thus beautifully symbolised the spirit of the sonnet.

> " Yon silvery billows breaking on the beach
>   Fall back in foam beneath the star-shine clear,
>   The while my rhymes are murmuring in your ear
> A restless lore like that the billows teach ;
> For on these sonnet-waves my soul would reach
>   From its own depths, and rest within you, dear,
>   As through the silvery billows yearning here
> Great Nature strives to find a human speech.

> " A sonnet is a wave of melody :
>   From heaving waters of the impassioned soul
>   A billow of tidal music one and whole
> Flows in the ' octave ' ; then, returning free,
>   Its ebbing surges in the ' sestet ' roll
> Back to the deeps of Life's tumultuous sea."
>   —THEODORE WATTS : " The Sonnet's Voice."

The severest idea of the sonnet makes a subdivision of the octave and also of the sestet, halving the former into two quatrains (*Basi* or bases), and the latter into two tercets (*Volte* or turnings), all of which divisions are periodically distinct from each other. But it is noticeable that the animus of the sonnet in English is against subdivision and toward entire unity of movement, thus differentiating somewhat from its model. Octave flows

---

[1] " In short, the quatrains should contain the proposition and proof, the tercets, its confirmation and conclusion."—CHARLES TOMLINSON : " The Sonnet," part i., p. 28.

into sestet in one continuous thought-wave. And I may state here that *all* Italian forms in assuming English dress substitute the typical English masculine ending for the typical Italian feminine ending.

The rhyme-scheme of the sonnet is a strict one, the octave admitting of two rhymes only; the sestet, of either **Formula of** two or three. The arrangement of rhymes in **the legiti-** the octave is always the same, only those in **mate sonnet** the sestet permitting variation. Furthermore, the colours of the rhymes in octave and sestet should be as far as possible contrasted. Mr. Tomlinson, in his study of the Petrarchan sonnet, classes these in three typic groups.[1] Thus:

	TYPE I.	TYPE II.	TYPE III.
Octave	1221, 1221,	1221, 1221,	1221, 1221,
Sestet	345, 345,	343, 434,	345, 435.

Of these the first type is regarded as the purest. Professor Corson, in Chapter X. of the "Primer of English Verse," gives a detailed and careful analysis of a great number of sonnets upon these lines.

It is not until Milton that we find the Italian sonnet reproduced in its purity in England. Milton's visit to **Milton's** Italy (1638), his intimate reception there, and **sonnets** his predilection for the literature of the land would naturally saturate him with a feeling for its predominant form, while the severe type of the lyric, with its measured cadences, would appeal to his classically-trained intellect. The Miltonic sonnets were thrown out from time to time between the stress of other work and as occasion prompted. We find Milton's sonnets ele-

[1] Twenty-seven others are outside of these formulas and classed as irregular.

vated, stately, and resonant;—full of " a mighty sweep
of music," as Mr. Hall Caine hath it.

The next name identified with the sonnet is that of
Wordsworth. There is a certain order of mind and a
Words-
worth's
sonnets
certain quality of subject to which the sonnet
form presents itself as a specially fitting instrument. This order of mind and this quality of
subject were Wordsworth's to a superlative degree; and
his exercise of them places him at the head of English
sonnet writers. Wordsworth's sonnets are looser in form
than Milton's, but wider in sympathy, and strike a higher
spiritual note. He moved serenely and easily in that
upper stratum of air where many suffer from shortness
of breath—metrically as well as metaphorically—and
where others still never find their way at all.

We have also noble sonnets from the hands of Keats,
Shelley, and Byron; since which time a mighty inunda-
tion has loosed itself upon the world.

Among Victorian sonneteers, Dante Gabriel Rossetti
is by many considered preëminent. Mrs. Browning's
Modern
sonnets
" Sonnets from the Portuguese," though somewhat loose in form, take high rank for their
power, passion, and purity.

> " Lady, that in the prime of earliest youth
>   Wisely hast shunn'd the broad way and the green,
>   And with those few art eminently seen,
> That labour up the hill of heavenly truth,
> The better part with Mary and with Ruth
>   Chosen thou hast; and they that overwean,
>   And at thy growing virtues fret their spleen,
> No anger find in thee, but pity and ruth.
> Thy care is fix'd, and zealously attends
>   To fill thy odorous lamp with deeds of light,
>   And hope that reaps not shame. Therefore be sure

Thou, when the bridegroom with his feastful friends
Passes to bliss at the mid hour of night,
Hast gain'd thy entrance, virgin wise and pure.''
—MILTON : " To a Virtuous Young Lady.''

" Avenge, O Lord, thy slaughter'd saints, whose bones
Lie scatter'd on the Alpine Mountains cold ;
Even them who kept thy truth so pure of old,
When all our fathers worshipp'd stocks and stones,
Forget not : in thy book record their groans
Who were thy sheep, and in their ancient fold
Slain by the bloody Piedmontese that roll'd
Mother with infant down the rocks.   Their moans
The vales redoubled to the hills, and they
To heaven.   Their martyr'd blood and ashes sow
O'er all the Italian fields, where still doth sway
The triple tyrant ; that from these may grow
A hundred fold, who, having learn'd thy way,
Early may fly the Babylonian woe.''
—MILTON : " On the Late Massacre in Piedmont.''

" The world is too much with us ; late and soon,
Getting and spending, we lay waste our powers :
Little we see in Nature that is ours ;
We have given our hearts away, a sordid boon !
This sea that bares her bosom to the moon ;
The winds that will be howling at all hours
And are up-gather'd now like sleeping flowers ;
For this, for everything we are out of tune ;
It moves us not.   Great God ! I'd rather be
A pagan suckled in a creed outworn ;
So might I, standing on this pleasant lea,
Have glimpses that would make me less forlorn,
Have sight of Proteus coming from the sea,
Or hear old Triton blow his wreathèd horn.''
—WORDSWORTH.

" Milton ! thou shouldst be living at this hour ;
 England hath need of thee : she is a fen
 Of stagnant waters : altar, sword, and pen,
Fireside, the heroic wealth of hall and bower,
Have forfeited their ancient English dower
 Of inward happiness. We are selfish men :
 Oh ! raise us up, return to us again ;
And give us manners, virtue, freedom, power.
Thy soul was like a star, and dwelt apart :
 Thou hadst a voice whose sound was like the sea ;
 Pure as the naked heavens, majestic, free ;
So didst thou travel on life's common way,
 In cheerful godliness ; and yet thy heart
The lowliest duties on itself did lay."
—WORDSWORTH.

" And wilt thou have me fashion into speech
 The love I bear thee, finding words enough,
 And hold the torch out, while the winds are rough,
Between our faces to cast light on each? —
I drop it at thy feet. I cannot teach
 My hand to hold my spirit so far off
 From myself—me—that I should bring thee proof
In words, of love hid in me out of reach.
Nay, let the silence of my womanhood
 Commend my woman-love to thy belief,—
Seeing that I stand unwon, however wooed,
 And rend the garment of my life, in brief,
By a most dauntless, voiceless fortitude,
 Lest one touch of this heart convey its grief."
—ELIZABETH BARRETT BROWNING : XIII.

" When our two souls stand up erect and strong,
 Face to face, silent, drawing nigh and nigher,
 Until the lengthening wings break into fire
At either curved point,—what bitter wrong

Can the earth do to us, that we should not long
 Be here contented ? Think. In mounting higher,
 The angels would press on us, and aspire
To drop some golden orb of perfect song
Into our deep, dear silence. Let us stay
 Rather on earth, Beloved,—where the unfit
Contrarious moods of men recoil away
 And isolate pure spirits, and permit
A place to stand and love in for a day,
 With darkness and the death-hour rounding it."
   —Elizabeth Barrett Browning : XXII.

" O Lord of all compassionate control,
 O Love ! let this my lady's picture glow
 Under my hand to praise her name, and show
Even of her inner self the perfect whole :
That he who seeks her beauty's furthest goal,
 Beyond the light that the sweet glances throw
 And refluent wave of the sweet smile, may know
The very sky and sea-line of her soul.

" Lo ! it is done. Above the long lithe throat
 The mouth's mould testifies of voice and kiss,
 The shadowed eyes remember and foresee.
Her face is made her shrine. Let all men note
 That in all years (O Love, thy gift is this !)
 They that would look on her must come to me."
   —Dante Gabriel Rossetti : " The Portrait."

" Dusk-haired and gold-robed o'er the golden wine
 She stoops, wherein, distilled of death and shame,
 Sink the black drops ; while, lit with fragrant flame,
Round her spread board the golden sunflowers shine.
Doth Helios here with Hecaté combine
 (O Circe, thou their votaress !) to proclaim
 For these thy guests all rapture in Love's name,
Till pitiless Night give Day the countersign ?

" Lords of their hour, they come. And by her knee
 Those cowering beasts, their equals heretofore,
 Wait; who with them in new equality
 To-night shall echo back the unchanging roar
 Which sounds forever from the tide-strown shore
 Where the dishevelled seaweed hates the sea."
  —DANTE GABRIEL ROSSETTI : " The Wine of Circe."

The sonnet has very little motion, and—Wordsworth
to the contrary notwithstanding—it is not " a trumpet."
Rather is it a silver flute through which the adept may
breathe an esoteric music,—and the adepts are fewer
than is commonly supposed. For, while it is compara-
tively easy to write to the formal metric requirements, it
is another thing to strike real music therefrom. Person-
ally I am somewhat inclined to side with Ben Jonson,
who has likened the sonnet to the bed of Procrustes.
This is not to defame the truly great sonnets which en-
rich our literature, but merely to suggest that the average singer will be likely to sing more notably if he clothe
the average idea in a few short stanzas of looser and more
mobile construction.

Sonnet writing is valuable metric drill, and it is well
for the student to master the form; but the sonnet *habit*
is a bad one to acquire, as it tends to impede growth to
larger flights.

The *ottava rima* has already been noticed as occupying
the attention of the Elizabethans. It is the measure of
The ottava Tasso and of Ariosto, and consists, as its name
rima   indicates, of an octave, or stanza of eight lines
—these lines being of heroic verse. The rhyme-scheme
is two alternating rhymes in the first six lines, the final
two being a rhymed couplet: thus;—*a, b, a, b, a, b, c, c.*

It has nothing like the dignity and melodious flow of
the Spenserian stanza, and the iterated rhymes of the

first six lines are inclined to cloy the English ear, attuned to more virile tone-contrasts; but its facility as a form naturally invites experiment, and it is a measure often employed by our own poets. In 1600 Fairfax published a stanza-for-stanza translation of Tasso's " Gerusalemme Liberata," which still holds high rank in our literature. Fairfax's muse was much influenced by the " Faerie Queene," published a few years earlier. Milton drops into *ottava rima* in the epilogue to "Lycidas," although, not being stanzaically separated, this is not very patent to the eye. Byron employs it in " Don Juan," " Beppo," " Morgante Maggiore," and " The Vision of Judgment." Keats uses it for " Isabella and the Pot of Basil;" and Shelley, in " The Witch of Atlas." Keats and Shelley have wrung the most music from it; but to Byron it seems to have stood for the medium of satire and mockery.

> " The purple morning left her crimson bed,
>   And donned her robes of pure vermilion hue,
> Her amber locks she crowned with roses red,
>   In Eden's flowery gardens gathered new.
> When through the camp a murmur shrill was spread,
>   Arm, arm, they cried; arm, arm, the trumpets blew,
> Their merry noise prevents the joyful blast,
> So hum small bees, before their swarms they cast.

> " Their captain rules their courage, guides their heat,
>   Their forwardness he stayed with gentle rein;
> And yet more easy, haply, were the feat
>   To stop the current near Charybdis main,
> Or calm the blustering winds on mountains great,
>   Than fierce desires of warlike hearts restrain;
> He rules them yet, and ranks them in their haste,
> For well he knows disordered speed makes waste.

" Feathered their thoughts, their feet in wings were dight,
    Swiftly they marched, yet were not tired thereby,
For willing minds make heaviest burdens light.
    But when the gliding sun was mounted high,
Jerusalem, behold, appeared in sight,
    Jerusalem they view, they see, they spy,
Jerusalem with merry noise they greet,
With joyful shouts and acclamations sweet.''
—EDWARD FAIRFAX : " Jerusalem Delivered,'' book iii.[1]

" And tall and strong and swift of foot were they,
    Beyond the dwarfing city's pale abortions,
Because their thoughts had never been the prey
    Of care or gain : the green woods were their portions.
No sinking spirits told them they grew grey ;
    No fashion made them apes of her distortions ;
Simple they were, not savage ; and their rifles
Though very true, were not yet used for trifles.

" Motion was in their days, rest in their slumbers,
    And cheerfulness the handmaid of their toil ;
Nor yet too many nor too few their numbers ;
    Corruption could not make their hearts her soil ;
The lust which stings, the splendour which encumbers
    With the free foresters divide no spoil ;
Serene, not sullen, were the solitudes
Of this unsighing people of the woods.''
            —BYRON : " Don Juan,'' viii., 66, 67.

" All day the wizard lady sat aloof ;
    Spelling out scrolls of dread antiquity
Under the cavern's fountain-lighted roof ;
    Or broidering the pictured poesy

---

[1] These stanzas are taken from Morley's 1890 edition, " The Carisbrooke Library.''

12

Of some high tale upon her growing woof,
   Which the sweet splendour of her smiles could dye
In hues outshining heaven—and ever she
   Added some grace to the wrought poesy :—

" While on her hearth lay blazing many a piece
   Of sandal wood, rare gums, and cinnamon.
Men scarcely know how beautiful fire is ;
   Each flame of it is as a precious stone
Dissolved in ever-moving light, and this
   Belongs to each and all who gaze thereon.
The witch beheld it not, for in her hand
She held a woof that dimmed the burning brand.

" This lady never slept, but lay in trance
   All night within the fountain—as in sleep.
Its emerald crags glowed in her beauty's glance :
   Through the green splendour of the waters deep
She saw the constellations reel and dance
   Like fireflies—and withal did ever keep
The tenour of her contemplations calm,
With open eyes, closed feet, and folded palm."
                    —SHELLEY : " The Witch of Atlas."

A third prominent Italian form is the *terza rima*, the
verse-form of Dante's " Divina Commedia." It is really

The terza   a much greater form than the *ottava rima*, but
rima   has been less imitated in English, owing to its

technical difficulties. The successive interlaced triplets
of rhyme are so taxing that it requires power of a high
order to maintain a *sostenuto* movement which shall never
either descend into the trivial nor hack out into the
mechanical. The *terza rima* (literally third rhyme) is an
unending succession of interlaced tercets, the rhyme-
scheme being *a b a, b c b, c d c, d e d*, etc., *ad infini-
tum*. Thus the first line and the third of each tercet

rhyme, while between them is constantly introduced a new tone which is to serve in turn as the binding rhyme of the next tercet.[1] We are told that Dante chose this verse-form because its interlaced triplets symbolised the trinity—three in one.

The verse of *terza rima* is usually written solidly, like our blank verse, but in English we sometimes see the tercets separated into little stanzas. There is an old poem of Surrey's in this measure. In modern times Byron has used it for his " Prophecy of Dante," Shelley for his " Ode to the West Wind," and Browning in " The Statue and the Bust;" the last two poems showing special modifications.

> " The spirit of the fervent days of old,
>   When words were things that came to pass, and thought
>   Flash'd o'er the future, bidding men behold
> Their children's children's doom already brought
>   Forth from the abyss of time which is to be,
>   The chaos of events, where lie half-wrought
> Shapes that must undergo mortality ;
>   What the great Seers of Israel wore within,
>   That spirit was on them, and is on me ;
> And if, Cassandra-like, amidst the din
>   Of conflict none will hear, or hearing heed
>   This voice from out the Wilderness, the sin
> Be theirs, and my own feelings be my meed,"
>   —BYRON : " The Prophecy of Dante," canto ii.

Shelley has divided his poem into stanzas by interpolating at the end of every twelve lines a rhymed couplet. It makes a very noble stanza.

[1] " There were also *serventesi*, a kind of satirical poetry, in various metres and orders of rhyme, so incatenated that a rhyme of the preceding tercet or quatrain is brought into the succeeding one. In this way arose the ordinary *terza rima*."—CHARLES TOMLINSON : " The Sonnet," p. 16.

" Make me thy lyre, even as the forest is :
What if my leaves are falling like its own ?
The tumult of thy mighty harmonies
Will take from both a deep autumnal tone,
Sweet though in sadness.   Be thou, Spirit fierce,
My spirit !   Be thou me, impetuous one !
Drive my dead thoughts over the universe,
Like withered leaves, to quicken a new birth ;
And by the incantation of this verse
Scatter, as from an unextinguished hearth
Ashes and sparks, my words among mankind !
Be through my lips to unawakened earth
The trumpet of a prophecy !   O Wind,
If Winter comes, can Spring be far behind ? ''
                    —SHELLEY : " Ode to the West Wind.''

Browning departs from the rhythmic and metric canons
—the typical verse being heroic—and uses a triple measure with excellent musical effect.

" There's a palace in Florence the world knows well,
    And a statue watches it from the square,
    And this story of both do our townsmen tell.

" Ages ago, a lady there,
    At the farthest window facing the east,
    Asked, ' Who rides by with the royal air ? '

" The bridesmaids' prattle around her ceased ;
    She leaned forth, one on either hand :
    They saw how the blush of the bride increased—

" They felt by its beats her heart expand—
    As one at each ear and both in a breath
    Whispered, ' The Great Duke Ferdinand.'

" That selfsame instant, underneath,
The Duke rode past in his idle way,
Empty and fine, like a swordless sheath.

" Gay he rode, with a friend as gay,
Till he threw his head back—' Who is she ? '
' A bride the Riccardi brings home to-day.' "
—BROWNING : " The Statue and the Bust."

Ever since the new learning in the early Renaissance
days reached England, many efforts have been made by
many scholars and poets to domesticate the Homeric
dactylic hexameter. These efforts cannot be said to
have been crowned by signal success.

Classically defined, the dactylic hexameter is a verse
of six feet; the first four of which may be either a dactyl
The Homeric or its metrical equivalent, the spondee; the
dactylic fifth *must* be a dactyl, and the sixth a spon-
hexameter dee.[1] The cæsural pause comes after the
thesis, or in the arsis, of the third foot. According to
our accentual mensuration, the dactylic hexameter may
be defined as a line of six bars of 3-beat rhythm, with
the direct attack and the feminine ending. Like all
long lines, it tends to divide itself in the middle, giving
a natural pause or cæsura there. Coleridge exemplified
it thus:

" Strongly it bears us along in swelling and limitless billows,
Nothing before and nothing behind but the sky and the ocean."

The reason assigned by many metrists for the un-
adaptability of the hexameter to English verse is the

[1] For the definitions of dactyl and spondee, I must refer the reader to
the classical prosodies, as it is quite without the scope of this work to enter
into these details.

scarcity of true spondees in the English language; but the cause undoubtedly lies deeper. In becoming an English measure it ceases to be quantitative and becomes accentual, and thus its organic character is destroyed. Volume of sound takes the place of measures of quantity, and this is not easy to preserve in purity of classic values for any prolonged period; so that, though we have plenty of short flights of noble character in this measure, nothing of large moment exists in it. Its inherent feebleness, as an English medium, for sustained action is well illustrated in Longfellow's "Evangeline," whose pathetic theme covers a multitude of metrical deficiencies. The British ear is, however, more closely trained to classic values than the American. Following is a spirited passage from Kingsley.

> " As when an osprey aloft, dark-eyebrowed, royally crested,
> Flags on by creek and by cove, and in scorn of the anger of Nereus
> Ranges, the king of the shore; if he see on a glittering shallow,
> Chasing the bass and the mullet, the fin of a wallowing dolphin,
> Halting, he wheels round slowly, in doubt at the weight of his quarry,
> Whether to clutch it alive, or to fall on the wretch like a plummet,
> Stunning with terrible talon the life of the brain in the hindhead:
> Then rushes up with a scream, and stooping the wrath of his eyebrows,
> Falls from the sky like a star, while the wind rattles hoarse in his pinions.
> Over him closes the foam for a moment; then from the sandbed

Rolls up the great fish, dead, and his side gleams white in the
sunshine.
Thus fell the boy on the beast, unveiling the face of the Gor-
gon."

CHARLES KINGSLEY : " Andromeda."

Another classical form frequently imitated in English
is the *Ovidian elegiac distich.* This consists of a dactylic
hexameter followed by a dactylic pentameter.
The Ovidian elegiac distich Allen and Greenough define the pentameter
as the same as the hexameter, omitting the
last half of the third and sixth feet. " The pentameter
verse is thus to be scanned as *two half-verses,* of which
the latter always consists of two dactyls followed by a
single syllable."
Coleridge gives us this English exemplar of the Ovidian elegiac distich.

| ♭ ♭ ♭| ♭ ♭ ♭| ♭ ♭ ♭| ſ ♭ | ♭ ♭ ♭| ♭ ♭ ≯ |
" In the hex-am-e-ter rises the fountain's   silvery   column :

| ♭ ♭ ♭| ♭ ♭ ♭| ſ ≯ | ♭ ♭ ♭| ♭ ♭ ♭| ſ ≯
In the pen-tam-e-ter aye   falling in   melody   back."

I have given the notation of this to demonstrate that,
measured by accents, the second line has also *six* bars,
and not five. Half a bar in the middle of a moving
phrase is a rhythmic impossibility; all the *time* is there
even if filled by a rest or silence. Here is a melodious
bit in this measure.

" Grant, O regal in bounty, a subtle and delicate largess ;
Grant an ethereal alms, out of the wealth of thy soul :
Suffer a tarrying minstrel, who finds, not fashions his numbers.
Who, from the commune of air, cages the volatile song,—

Here to capture and prison some fugitive breath of thy descant,
Thine and his own as thy roar lisped on the lips of a shell,
Now while the vernal impulsion makes lyrical all that hath
    language,
While through the veins of the Earth, riots the ichor of Spring,
While, with throes, with raptures, with loosing of bonds, with
    unsealings,—
Arrowy pangs of delight, piercing the core of the world,—
Tremors and coy unfoldings, reluctances, sweet agitations,—
Youth, irrepressibly fair, wakes like a wondering rose."
                    —WILLIAM WATSON : " Hymn to the Sea."

In the last quarter century a good deal of attention has
been paid to old French forms, Austin Dobson, Edmund
Old French Gosse, and others having made essays in these
verse-forms fanciful and graceful verse-forms. Of these,
Mr. Dobson's are undoubtedly the most finished and have
the most " go." It is now not uncommon in our current literature to run across a *Ballade*, a *Rondeau*, or a
Triolet ; but these forms cannot yet be regarded as incor-
porate in our literature, and therefore I do not give them
place here. The reader will find them all—*Rondeau*,
Rondel, Triolet, Villanelle, Ballade, Huitain, Dixain, and
the splendid *Chant Royale*—in Austin Dobson's " Vi-
gnettes in Rhyme." They are one and all conditioned
by intricate rhyme-schemes, and upon repetitions and
refrains,—each stanza carrying exactly the same melodic
tones as every other. They are fascinating to write, and
are very exacting metric drill—the man who is quite
master of the *Chant Royale* need never baulk at any metric
form—but it is evident that such close tone-schemes
must be constrictive, and, while being a good field for
the play of what is known in the poetic art as " conceits," offer none at all for the development of real
thought or passion.

The student should experiment in, and gain mastery of, *all* forms, but permit himself to become enslaved by none. Thus will the spirit, playing freely in every key, always find for the special inspiration the special expression.

Setting aside blank verse—which is a genus of itself, and will be treated separately in the next chapter—un-**With regard** rhymed verse in English has not, as a rule, **to unrhymed** proved very successful. This is because, if we **verse** discard the great fusing and unifying element of rhyme, we have left only rhythm to guide us to the verse-form—primary rhythm, or motion within the bar, and the larger rhythm of metrical division. Without the first we could not have even the pretence of verse; but the second seems of equal importance, for upon the nice adjustment and balance of the cæsural effects and the natural metric pauses or end-stops is conditioned the musical swing, not only of the whole line, but of the whole stanza. Therefore upon this factor it depends whether the ear shall receive an impression of verse at all or merely of dislocated prose periods. I give herewith three examples of unrhymed verse which have this pronounced musical swing, and which therefore seem entirely satisfying to the ear.

> " Thus they see you, praise you, think they know you!
> There, in turn I stand with them and praise you—
> Out of my own self, I dare to phrase it,
> But the best is when I glide from out them,
> Cross a step or two of dubious twilight,
> Come out on the other side, the novel
> Silent silver lights and darks undreamed of,
> Where I hush and bless myself with silence.

> " Oh, their Rafael of the dear Madonnas,
> Oh, their Dante of the dread Inferno,

Wrote one song—and in my brain I sing it,
Drew one angel—borne, see, on my bosom!''
—BROWNING : " One Word More.''

" And the evening sun descending
Set the clouds on fire with redness,
Burned the broad sky, like a prairie,
Left upon the level water
One long track and trail of splendour,
Down whose stream, as down a river,
Westward, westward Hiawatha
Sailed into the fiery sunset,
Sailed into the purple vapours,
Sailed into the dusk of evening.''
—LONGFELLOW : " Hiawatha's Departure.''

" Lo, with the ancient
Roots of man's nature
Twines the eternal
Passion of song.

" Ever Love fans it,
Ever Life feeds it ;
Time cannot age it,
Death cannot slay.

" Deep in the world-heart
Stand its foundations,
Tangled with all things,
Twin-made with all.

" Nay, what is Nature's
Self, but an endless
Strife toward music,
Euphony, rhyme ?

¹ The measure of *Hiawatha* is said to be imitated from the Finnish *Kalevala.*

" Trees in their blooming,
Tides in their flowing,
Stars in their circling,
Tremble with song.

" God on His throne is
Eldest of poets :
Unto His measures
Moveth the Whole."
—WILLIAM WATSON : " England, My Mother."

These extracts were selected at random, without any
regard to their correlation, and merely because they present harmonious and proportioned movement; yet, if we
study them, we shall find that they possess three elements in common:

1. They are metrically symmetrical; that is, every line
is the length of every other line. This impresses upon
the ear at the outset the harmonious movement of the
larger rhythms.

2. They all have the direct attack, which we have
already noted (page 47) as a potent factor of verse-
motion.

3. They all have the feminine ending, which also we
have observed to be a concomitant of motion as well as
of melody.[1] Thus we perceive that the writers of these
poems, though they have dispensed with melodic
cadence-correspondence, have, consciously or unconsciously, availed themselves of every other element which
could unify their verse. And in unrhymed verse, without this metrical symmetry and exactness, this melodious
systole and *diastole*, it seems to me we cannot have *verse*

---

[1] The third extract may be considered equi-metric notwithstanding the
masculine ending of every fourth line. This merely points off the groups or
stanzas. This poem has the added movement of triple rhythm.

at all.   For, in a *rhymed* poem which is metrically irregular, the rhyme gives tonal correspondence and cohesion; but an *unrhymed* poem, which is metrically irregular, runs much risk of being metrical chaos.

In these latter days strange things find their way into print under the classification of poetry; some writers, who value sensation above art, rushing into the *bizarre* and amorphous.   But it is always well to bear in mind that no idea, however beautiful, or however true and vital, unless it conform to those organic laws which govern and condition the musical motion of verse, can of itself and by itself constitute a poem.

Forms are not fetters, but opportunities.

CHAPTER VI

HEROICS

THE dividing line between the larger forms of poetic art and the smaller is the personal one. By this they **Objective and subjective poetry** are made to fall naturally into groups of the objective or subjective order, according as they are either the record of observer or observed. In lyric verse the singer is himself the protagonist, and it is his personal emotions and experiences to which he is giving voice. The peculiarity of lyric poets, says Professor Masson, is " that their poems are vehicles for certain fixed ideas in the minds of the authors, outbursts of their personal character, impersonations, under shifting guises, of their wishes, feelings, beliefs." On the other hand, in the epic and drama, the central figure is sought for outside of self; and, although the poet so flings himself into the personality of his creations that he may be said to feel and act in them, and for the nonce to *be* one or another of them, in the larger sense he remains forever outside of them, an impersonal observer of characters and events. Personality melts into imagination. To quote again from Masson, the objective poets " fashion their creations by a kind of inventive craft, working amid materials supplied by sense, memory and reading, without any distinct infusion of personal feeling."

Thus it comes about that the suitable media for expression also differentiate themselves; those which most fittingly express the personal emotion are not suited to the impersonal; and vice-versa. In brief, lyric verse is *song*, pure and simple, and demands singable and motive forms; while the epic and the drama are *recitatives* and demand a verse-form fitted to the long-sustained chords of action.

The lyric, though probably not so old as the epic— because the impulse of savage man to celebrate his heroes would fore-run his self-conscious impulse to **The lyric** express himself—is very ancient. We have noted (page 3) how " lyrical poetry, like all art in Greece, took its origin in connection with nature worship;" and from " the Æolian lyrists, with Sappho at their head, and the so-called Dorian lyrists, who culminate in Pindar," to our own day, it has remained the favourite form for man's intimate expression.

Lyric poetry has practically no metrical limitations, and may employ any and all poetic forms. Objective **Forms** poetry is obviously limited to the very few **suited to** forms which are large enough to embody its **objective** **poetry** prolonged action without wearying the ear. Such forms are the Greek dactylic hexameter, the modern heroic blank verse, or, very occasionally, the same stately iambic employed in a full, rhymed stanza, as in the " Faerie Queene."

The foregoing chapters have been mainly concerned with lyric forms; in this chapter we shall consider the larger medium of objective verse.

Objective art groups itself naturally into two general divisions; viz.: (1) the epic,[1] with its cognate miniatures, **Divisions of** in which the story of the personages concerned **objective** is *told* or *narrated;* and (2) the drama, with its **poetry** cognate miniatures, in which the story *tells itself* through the speech and action of the personages

---

[1] Greek : Epikos, from epos, *word.*

concerned. Aristotle's definition of drama is *imitated action*.

The smaller forms of the epic are:

1. The Metrical Romance, such as most of Scott's and many of Byron's poems, Keats's " Eve of St. Agnes" and " Lamia," Browning's " Ivan Ivanovitch," **Epic forms** " Donald," etc. The Metrical Romance, by far the largest class in imaginative poetry, was introduced into English literature by Chaucer with his " Canterbury Tales."

2. The Idyll. The Idyll is epical in character, in that it is large and simple, but, as its name indicates, it should be tranquil, and be less a matter of action than of situation and sentiment. Under this head we may consider Arnold's " Balder Dead;" Wordsworth's " Laodamia;" Tennyson's " Ulysses" and " Ænone;" Landor's " Dryope," " Cupid and Pan," " Chrysaor," etc. Such poems as Burns's " Cotter's Saturday Night" are also classed as Idylls, though they are strictly speaking merely Pastorals. The Pastoral Poem might be called a small Idyll. Tennyson's " Idylls of the King" are not really Idylls, as they deal with action and approach too near the true epic.

3. The Ballad. The Ballad has already been treated in the preceding chapter. It partakes of the nature of the lyric, in that, though objective in substance, it is lyrical in external character.

The epic takes its dawn beyond the horizon of civilisation. Barbaric peoples, desirous of celebrating the ex- **Origin of** ploits of their heroes, or the attributes of their **the epic** deities, or both mythically interwoven, would naturally break into rude song, more or less vocal, and rendered rhythmic by the length of a suspiration, or the rough steps of an accompanying dance. Such celebra-

THE MUSICAL BASIS OF VERSE

tions we may observe to-day in the song-dances of our own North American Indian tribes. These songs would be at first largely ejaculatory, but, as the scope of human speech widened, they would become rhetorically fuller and more rounded. By and by as man became more civilised and settled, we can see that these recitals would cease to be chanted by the whole people, and would be relegated to specialists, whose trained memories could retain the prodigious chronicles, and whose function it would be to polish and reduce them to an artistic—natively artistic—homogeneity. Hence the minstrel, or poet-singer. The next step in development would be the reduction of these recitatives to writing, by which they would take on fixity of form and become *literature*.

From the first self-consciousness of literature on, we have plenty of epics; they, however, are no longer endogenous, **The literary** but exogenous; not an internal, but an external, **epic** growth. The material is no longer organic, evolved with the development of the people, but is selected and arranged and expressed by a single mind. The literary epic may therefore be called a composition. An early example of a composition is Virgil's " Æneid," which, though attempting to follow the great Greek models, cannot attain to their heroic spontaneity.

The earliest as well as the noblest epics which have come down to us are the " Iliad " and the " Odyssey," **Earliest** attributed to Homer. We have other exam- **epics** ples in the great Norse " Sagas," [1] and in the early Anglo-Saxon (heathen) poem of " Beowulf."

With the Christian era a new element is introduced **Christian** into epic poetry, viz.: the spiritual. It is no **epics** longer brute force which is to be celebrated and extolled, but that something in man, larger and finer,

---

[1] Saga—something said.

which impels him to shed the material and to press forward to ever higher and higher ideals. In his " Divina Commedia " Dante opened the new literary era with the grandest music to which the world has ever listened. The " Divina Commedia " is also called a Didactic Allegory. One may ask, since its motive is profoundly subjective, why this poem takes the rank of the epic. It takes rank as an epic because of its construction, because of the largeness of its scope, and because, notwithstanding the underlying subjectivity, its expression is objective, unrolling before us a panorama of vivid concrete pictures.

James Russell Lowell says of Dante, " He would not have been the great poet he was if he had not felt intensely and humanly, but he could never have won the cosmopolitan place he holds had he not known how to generalise his special experience."

English literature is rich in epics. To name only a few: Layamon's " Brut " (eleventh century); Lang- **English** land's " Vision of Piers the Plowman " (four- **epics** teenth century); Spenser's " Faerie Queene " (also Allegories); Milton's " Paradise Lost;" Keats's splendid fragment, " Hyperion;" and, in our own day, Tennyson's " Idylls of the King," now called " The Arthuriad." While, taken separately, the " Idylls " are not individually large enough to stand as epics, together, and as a whole, they make a most noble epic setting of these immortal Celtic legends.

There is a large class of poems which, though epical in scope and treatment, are wanting in the action and move- **Pastoral** ment of the true epic. Of such are Words- **epics** worth's " Excursion," Goldsmith's " Traveller " and " Deserted Village," Thomson's " Seasons," etc. These are known as Pastoral Epics.

13

The union of largeness of conception with simplicity in execution is the distinguishing characteristic of the **Character of** epic.   There is usually a central figure round **the epic** which the general movement groups itself. Such are Achilles in the " Iliad," Ulysses in the " Odyssey," Fridthjof in the "Fridthjof Saga," Sigurd in the "Volsung " legends, Beowulf in "Beowulf," etc.   In the Christian epics, Dante himself is the heroic figure of the " Divina Commedia; " Satan, of " Paradise Lost; " Arthur, of the " Idylls of the King."

The epic is discursive, and abounds with episodes, or interpolated narratives of events not closely related to the main theme.   Dialogue is a great feature of the epic, and gives life to the canvas, but its dialogue is discursive and expansive, and not the concentrated utterance of the drama.   It is not so much the action or character of special personages as the impression of the whole which is of importance in the epic.

The epic is sculptured upon heroic lines—large, simple, severe—like a colossal statue which is designed to produce its effect by massiveness of outline rather than by delicacy of detail.   In its largeness of form and tonic austerity of movement, it may be likened to the symphony in music, each representing in its own department of art the loftiest sustained effort of which the composer is capable; for the epic poet is the " poet of life, sublimity, action."

The one feature which modern drama has in common with ancient is that both had their origin in religious **Origin of the** ceremonial.   Such mimetic art as India and **drama**   Egypt possessed was centred about the mysteries of their worship.   In Greece, as we have already noted (page 3), " the Bacchic songs of alternating mirth and sadness gave birth through the dithyramb to tragedy, and through the Comus-hymn to comedy." " In the religious life of Egyptians, Indians, Chinese, and Greeks, the deepest conceptions of death in life and life in death veiled themselves under dramatic forms which were at once jealously guarded from contact with the multitude, and remained to it objects of unutterable reverence. Wherever in religious rites a dramatic element asserted itself—as in the worship of Osiris, of Buddha, of Dionysus,—it sprang from an endeavour to symbolise in mysterious forms conflict and solution, passion and expiatory action." [1]

Christian dramatic art also had its beginning in the church, and primarily strove to present to the vulgar an **Early Christian drama** idea of the divine mysteries for which the symbolised worship stood. But in form nothing could be farther from the classical standards. Greek art—severe, one might even say sculpturesque, and single in idea—did not serve as model for the mediæval *Mysteries* or *Miracle-plays*, which, like the lyric poetry of the same epoch, developed waywardly, in consonance with the racial feeling of the new civilisations.

The first distinct dramatic representations of the Christian world are to be found in the *Mysteries* and *Miracle-plays*, common in the middle ages, which consisted of portions of scripture, or sacred legends, loosely hung together and often strangely assorted. At first exclusively an ecclesiastical prerogative, these came afterwards into the hands of purely secular performers. A rare instance of the survival of this mediæval form is found in the famous " Passion Play " of Oberammergau, in the Tyrol, performed at intervals down to our own time.

[1] A. W. WARD : "History of English Dramatic Literature," Introduction.

But there were certain connecting links with ancient art.   Classical traditions and classical volumes lingered **Previous to** in odd monastic corners, and were browsed **the Norman** upon by occasional inquiring minds.   There **Conquest no** **impulse** exist crude essays in dramatic form and with **toward** Latin text, always of a theological character, **formal** **drama** and probably never seen outside the walls of the cloisters.   Conspicuous among such were the works of Hroswitha, the Benedictine nun of Gandersheim, who modelled herself in form upon Terence, endeavouring to adapt this to the requirements of Christian theology.   In England the development of dramatic entertainments, though not beginning until the Norman conquest, was cognate and coeval with that of the continent.   Previous to the conquest there seems to have been no impulse towards dramatic form;[1] this came in, with other continental culture, with the Normans.   " French ecclesiastics, who filled the English monasteries, brought with them the literary tendency of the times.   Thus it would be in accordance with probability that Latin religious dramas, treating of the legends of the saints, should have been performed in the English monasteries in the latter part of the eleventh century, as they had been performed at Quedlinburg, and perhaps at Gandersheim. And as these performances would be in the first instance treated as part of the education of the children committed to the care of the religious foundations, the legends of the patron-saints of boys and girls, St. Nicholas and St. Catharine, would be expected to have been treated with especial predilection."[2]

---

[1] Because, as Professor Ward has well pointed out, mere dialogue, without implied action, has none of the elements of drama.   If it had, Isaac Walton's " Compleat Angler" could be regarded as a drama.

[2] WARD : " History of English Dramatic Literature," chap. i.

The elementary stages of English dramatic art are not difficult to trace. It seems to have been early the cus-
Early church mimetic ceremonials tom to add to the ceremonial of church functions on special occasions tableaux representing biblical subjects. Some mimetic elements would next creep in, then the vernacular would be substituted for the Latin texts; and we are well on the way towards elementary drama. The joining together of a number of *Mysteries* into a collective *Mystery* is another long step in the line of dramatic construction.

" ' The Ludus de S. Katherina,' the earliest religious play of which we have nominal mention, and which the Norman Geoffrey (afterwards Abbot of St. Albans) caused to be represented about the year 1110, is usually supposed to have been written in French. The supposition, however, is not proved." [1]

There appear to have been Miracle-plays [2] in London in 1170–1182, but it is not known in what language they
First miracle-plays were written; probably Latin. Professional players are heard of in 1258. From this time on the Miracle-plays multiplied and came eventually to be performed in great numbers in centres like Chester, Coventry, York, Newcastle-on-Tyne, Leeds, Lancaster, Preston, Kendal, Wymondham, Dublin, and London.

Three series of English Collective Mysteries have come down to us: the Towneley, the Chester, and the Coventry collections. The Coventry plays have more literary form than the others, for which reason it is supposed that they were written by the clergy, while the Chester

---

[1] WARD : " History of English Dramatic Literature," chap. i.

[2] Strictly speaking, the *Mystery* deals with purely scriptural subjects, and the *Miracle-plays* with legends of the saints ; but the two were a good deal mixed, and in England the term *Mystery* (a corruption of *ministerium*) seems never to have been used at all.

plays, being more popular in style, probably came from secular sources.

Each separate play was called a *pageant* and began upon a Sunday at six o'clock in the morning. Rogers (about the end of the sixteenth century) says of the Chester plays, " Every company had his pageant, which pageants were a high scaffold with two rooms, a higher and a lower, upon four wheels. In the lower they apparelled themselves, and in the higher room they played, being all open on the top that all beholders might see and hear them. The places where they played them was in every street. They began first at the Abbey gates, and when the first pageant was played, it was wheeled to the high cross before the Mayor, and so to every street."

But the public temper demanding a more humanised element in its mimetic art—something nearer to every-

Evolution of the morality day life—there was developed the *Morality*, wherein merely ethical subjects supersede the sacred. Human virtues, vices, attributes of all sorts, are herein personified, and act out their artificial, often grotesque, parts; yet from the nature of it the *Morality* was more dramatically coherent than anything which preceded it. In the *Morality* also we trace the rudiments of character drawing.

With the increase of learning and the consequently heightened literary taste, the Morality, as well as the

Into the interlude Miracle-play, ceased to satisfy; and the next dramatic evolution is into the *Interlude* The Interlude was light in character and, as its name indicates, served to fill the intervals at feasts and other entertainments. It was the progenitor of comedy proper. The most notable early Interludes are by John Heywood. Good examples of the Interlude may be seen in "Midsummer-Night's Dream," "Love's Labour's Lost," and the "Tempest," though the latter might better come under the head of the *Mask*. The more elaborate Interludes were called Masks, and were popular throughout the reign of Elizabeth, having been introduced from Italy, where they were known as "masked dramas." They were usually pastoral in character and interspersed with dancing. Ben Jonson wrote many elaborate Masks, the most famous of them being "Cynthia's Revels." The greatest English Mask is, however, Milton's "Comus."

The Miracle-play, the Morality—the Morality survived till the end of the sixteenth century—and the Interlude continued in a manner side by side until all were superseded by legitimate drama. It was during the reign of Henry VIII. that tragedy and comedy,[1] which had heretofore been strangely jumbled, became, through the influence of classical study and of Italian dramatic models, differentiated into their respective fields and forms, comedy seeming to have taken shape before tragedy. The earliest original English comedy is "Ralph Roister Doister" (1551 or earlier); and "Gammer Gurton's Needle" (printed in 1575) is generally regarded as chronologically the next.

Differentiation of tragedy and comedy

[1] Greek *Komodia*, from *Komos*, revel + *ode*. Tragedy is derived from the Greek *Tragodia*, this word having its origin in *Tragos*, a goat, from the fact that originally tragic singers were dressed in goat-skins to represent Satyrs.

"According to Aristotle, that which distinguishes tragedy as a dramatic species is the importance and magnitude of its subject, the adequate elevation of its literary form, and the power of the emotions—pity or terror—by means of which it produces its effects. Comedy, on the other hand, imitates actions of inferior interest ('neither painful nor destructive'), and carried on by characters whose vices are of a ridiculous kind."—WARD: "History of English Dramatic Literature," chap. ii.

Comedy has tended to prose, therefore it is generally in the great tragedies that we must look for the highest achievements of dramatic verse.

The first English tragedy proper of which we have record is " Gorboduc "—also called " Ferrex and Porrex "

The first English tragedy —from the hands of Thomas Sackville, Lord Buckhurst (1567).[1] This play, although the first legitimate English drama, " moves without ease or variation," and is full of " moral reflections of excessive length." It is the first *drama* in blank verse, Surrey's "Æneid" having preceded it by fifteen years.

But it was the fiery genius of Marlowe which, with its " Tamburlaine the Great," ushered in the splendid drama of the golden age of Elizabeth; and, though he did not reach the stature of Shakespeare, nor the technical finish even of a number of others, he must be reckoned as the first of the Titans of English dramatic literature.

A mighty decadence follows the great Elizabethan music. Inspiration faded and artifice took its place;

Decadence until at last all art became obscured in the Puritan twilight. And we find the revived drama of the Restoration meretricious both in matter and manner.

In the nineteenth century, literature and the stage would seem to have become entirely divorced; but there are hopeful signs to-day of a change in this respect.[2]

The two axes upon which the spirit of drama moves are action and character; character prompting action, and action organically elucidating character. The great-

[1] The first three acts are said to have been written by Thomas Norton, the last two by Sackville.

[2] The reader will bear in mind that this book concerns itself exclusively with English drama. In France the literary drama has always obtained ; as, largely, in other countries of Europe.

ness of Shakespeare is in nothing more demonstrated than in his power of drawing a character and making

Principles of the drama it act itself. Furthermore true drama is potentially *human*, stirring the chords of laughter or tears, love, pity, or terror, to which men's passions vibrate the world over; and only in proportion as it is human can it be intrinsic or great. It is of no consequence to us that Rosalind is assumedly a French-woman, Portia a Venetian, Hamlet a Dane, Othello a Moor, etc., because these, in their large delineations, are not particular types but cosmopolitan types, playing out universal life-dramas upon a universal stage. Characterisation is a development of modern drama, and is one of the salient features which distinguish it from ancient art.

In the ancient drama—simple, direct, austere—the persons seem to be rather the sport of an inexorable

Comparison of ancient with modern drama destiny, and the action moves upon inevitable lines. In the modern drama the *dramatis personæ* mould their own destinies, and give us many surprises. "The motive of ancient drama," says Lowell, "is generally outside of it, while in the modern it is within."

Underplots, which only crept into classic literature in its decadence, form the very woof of modern drama. The latter borrowed from the Romans the system of dividing a play into five sections, or acts, but has beautifully disregarded the traditions of the Greek unities of time, place, and action, moving upon lines of its own.

Modern drama is far more complex than the ancient, and introduces not only more personages but more motives. Naturally this admits of much subjectivity; but the objective side of the art must ever dominate, else will the art as art suffer deterioration. We call

"Hamlet" a subjective drama, and so are all of Ibsen's plays subjective dramas; but, with all their power, no one could think of comparing the latter with the great Shakespearean play, for the simple reason that, in "Hamlet," the perfect objective dominance, the high artistic poise—which was indeed in the very air the Elizabethans breathed—lifts it far above the atmospheric stratum in which modern realism moves.

Drama has its miniatures in the one-act play; in poetic literature, in the *scena* and *gran scena*, for which **Dramatic** Aldrich's lovely "Pauline Paulovna" and **miniatures** Browning's "In a Balcony" may stand as types. Certain other poems, semi-dramatic in form but lyrical in movement—such as Arnold's "Empedocles on Ætna" and Browning's "In a Gondola"—we may class as *dramatic lyrics*. Shelley's "Prometheus Unbound" is called a *lyrical drama;* and there are other works which defy classification, such as Browning's "Pippa Passes" and "Paracelsus," the latter being defined by Miss Scudder as "drama moving toward monologue."

There was a form of Dramatic Idyll, imitated from the Italian,[1] and called Pastoral Drama, which had vogue in Elizabeth's time, but which has long gone by. Fletcher's "Faithful Shepherdess" and Ben Jonson's "Sad Shepherd" are examples. Spenser's "Shepherd's Calendar" is slighter and belongs rather to the department of the Eclogue.

Imitations of pure Greek drama are found in Swinburne's "Atalanta in Caledon" and "Erechtheus," and

---

[1] The Pastoral Drama, which was, in other words, the bucolic idyll in dramatic form, and freely lent itself to the introduction both of mythological and allegorical elements, flourished in Italy at the close of the fifteenth century. Its origin was purely literary.

in Milton's "Samson Agonistes," the latter a master-piece well comparable to its models.

With this necessarily brief survey of the field of objective art we shall have to pause and transfer our attention to the medium employed for its expression.

It is obvious that any long-sustained theme, such as we find in objective art, would demand for its expression
The five-foot iambic some medium whose motion could be indefinitely prolonged, and whose periods could be indefinitely varied, so as to charm and not weary the ear. Such a medium was early found in European verse in the so-called five-foot iambic. Stanzaic verse of any kind is unsuited to long-sustained themes because the exigencies of the rhyme and the greater metric uniformity and exactness make prolonged stanzaic movements cloying or wearisome to the ear. There have been a few successful exceptions, such as Chapman's Homer, whose strong, rugged numbers catch Homeric echoes; and Spenser's "Faerie Queene," which endures, not because it is best adapted to epic art, but by virtue of its wonderful music. We have only to place beside the latter "Paradise Lost" to recognise the immensely greater power and virility of blank verse. It is indeed not a little due to the selection of blank verse as a medium—a process of natural selection, since it was not easily adopted, and only made its way as its superior fitness manifested itself—that English poetic art has established its preëminence.

The iambic measure seems to have been evolved by the Greeks quite as early as the dactylic, but it was not considered by them of sufficient dignity for a heroic medium, and was relegated to the expression of satire. The Latins used it imitatively; but, with all elements of

classic culture, it became obscured in the mists of mediæ-
valism.   When it emerges again to view in the literature
of the early Italian Renaissance, it is seen to be a very
different medium from the classic form.   Quantity no
longer dictates.   It is dominated solely by the nascent
musical ear of the new culture, and measures its numbers
by the recurrent and interconsistent accent.   In the polished verse of Dante and Petrarch it becomes a wonderfully elastic medium—is indeed often so loosely hung as
almost to seem dithyrambic; yet are the musical unities
ever preserved.   For so fluent is the limpid Tuscan
tongue, with such a superabundance of warm vowel tones
and the ever-inherent tendency of the southern larynx
to soften consonants, that it permits marvellous elisional
effects, the measures seeming to melt one over the other,
as it were, in waves of harmoniously modulated sound.

Of the modern five-foot iambic, Professor Mayor, quot-
ing Zarncke, says: " We have no ground for tracing the
Modern   metre back either to the Greek five-foot iambic
five-foot   or five-foot trochaic with anacrusis, nor to the
iambic   Latin hendecasyllabic, which is quite opposed
to it in rhythm.   We can say no more of it than that
it was in all probability the ordinary metre of the
Romance epic [1] and spread from France into other countries.   .   .   .   This will give an idea:

> " ' Enfánts en díes forén omé felló
> Qu'el éra cóms mólt onráz e ríx
> Nos jóve ómne quandiús que nós estám
> Donz fó Boécis córps ag bó e pró.' [2]

---

[1] Whence did the Romance poets evolve it?   It is more likely that they
had an idea of the classic form enfeebled by the attrition of the Middle-Age
ignorance, but uttered it in their own way with the dawn of a new music in
their souls.   See page 21.

[2] The reason for omitting the scansion marks in the originals of these
quotations will be obvious.

"In the 'Alexius' and 'Song of Roland,' dating from the eleventh century, we meet with examples of feminine ending, as—

"'Faités la guérre cum vós l'avéz empríse,'

. . . "From about the middle of the twelfth century the five-foot verse gave place to the four-foot and the six-foot (Alexandrine), but was still retained for lyric poetry, undergoing however two changes: (1) the cæsura, which occurs regularly after the fourth syllable, was treated simply as a metrical, not a logical pause; (2) the preceding accent was often thrown back or inverted, making the second foot a trochee, as:

"'Bona dómna per cui planc e sospir'

. . . "Later on all the accents except the last became liable to inversion, as:

"'Bélha dómna válham vóstra valórs,'

. . . "From 1500 the feminine cæsura disappears altogether, owing to the growing weakness of the final *e*. The more regular form of the five-foot iambic became known as *vers commun*, and was employed by Ronsard for epic and by Jodelle for tragedy. By the end of the sixteenth century, however, there was a reaction in favor of the Alexandrine, the stiff monotony of the rhyming five-foot, with its fixed pauses after the fourth and tenth syllables, being felt to be unsuitable for the more animated styles of poetry.

"The Italian hendecasyllabic metre had been developed out of the Provençal lyric poetry long before it was made famous by Dante. It differs from the French (*a*) in the constant feminine ending; (*b*) the freedom of the cæsura, which may be either masculine or feminine, and either after the second or third foot; (*c*) the use of *enjambement*, i.e. the absence of a final pause, so as to allow one verse to run on into another; (*d*) the transposition of the accent in any foot except the last, but especially the fourth foot, as:

> " ' Le Donne i Cavalier l'árme gli amore,'

" This freedom of rhythm is accompanied by greater freedom in the rhyme, so as to connect together not merely two consecutive lines but whole stanzas." [1]

Thus we perceive that the medium was perfected long before England had use for it.

The five-foot iambic is generally considered to have been introduced into England by Chaucer, although, as English five-foot iambic, or heroic verse we have seen, echoes of it had been wafted across the Channel even earlier; but Chaucer's was the first artist hand upon it. He used it in rhymed couplets, very free, and delicately balanced. From his time until we approach the golden age of Elizabeth, there is nothing notable; yet it was undoubtedly a period of metric as well as literary gestation. The concentrated hour never arrives by accident. Even if the earthquake seem sudden and unprepared, we may be sure that the seismic forces have long been gathering.

The first use we find made of blank verse, or the unrhymed five-foot iambic, is in the translation of the second and fourth books of the " Æneid" by Henry Howard, Earl of Surrey (about 1540). Surrey brought blank verse from Italy, where it had recently been introduced by Trissino; but, although his introduction of it into English literature marks an epoch in the history of English metre, the versification of the " Æneid" is so

---

[1] JOSEPH B. MAYOR: " English Metre:—Postscript."

harsh and crude that it cannot take high rank as a work
of art.

The first work of real genius in blank verse is Marlowe's " Tamburlaine the Great " (printed 1590), in which
First great he handles his medium with a masterliness
work in which stamped it as the preëminent one for
blank verse drama. Marlowe has not wholly sloughed the
empiric roughness, yet such virile music does he give us
that we may easily pardon a few barbaric echoes.

And from Marlowe's moribund hands the lyre fell into
those of the master musician—the Protean Shakespeare,
as he has been felicitously called.   Beneath his consummate touch the five-foot iambic suddenly expands into
a mighty instrument; and so does he play upon it and
manipulate it, so toss it back and forth like a shuttle-
cock, so combine and break and re-combine, so invent
and diversify, so riddle it with mysterious sweet har-
monics, that he has wrung from it a music at which,
in three centuries, the world has never ceased wondering.

Shakespeare and Milton are the acknowledged masters
of English blank verse, Milton in the field of the epic,
Shakespeare Shakespeare in that of the drama.   Milton ex-
and Milton cels in the large sonority of his verse—" the
the masters
of blank long-breathed periods of Milton," Lowell calls
verse them,—and Shakespeare by his melodious,
forceful, and apt diversity.   Milton's verse is full of the
echo of mighty organ tones; Shakespeare has a whole
orchestra beneath his fingers.

And we observe that the objective poets who have followed these two, though they have left us noble and
resonant blank verse, have never quite touched the same
artistic heights.

After Beaumont and Fletcher the writing of blank

verse declines, being to a great extent replaced by the rhymed couplet. Dryden in his later dramas reverts to blank verse; but his work is tinctured by the false taste of the age, and is not of the first order.

In our own century Wordsworth, Keats, Shelley,—the two 'latter with an auroral promise which deepens the **Modern** tragedy of their early deaths,—and later, **blank verse** Browning, Swinburne, and Tennyson have given us noble heroic verse. Not every one will agree with Professor Corson that Browning was " one of the greatest masters of language-shaping." The radical defect of Browning is that he has regarded too little the *unity* of his verse, and so indulges a propensity to break up his periods as to give much of his verse a jolting effect.[1] Yet when he pleases he can give us such magnificent bursts of organic verse-music as to make us regret that he could not have held in more importance the purely æsthetic side of his art.

Tennyson must be considered the modern master of the technique of blank verse as well as of the lyric forms; for, if he somewhat lack the virile force of his great contemporary, he is so rich in diction, so fertile in every metric resource, so fluid and melodious in movement, so faultless in his management of cæsural effects, such a master, in short, in the unity of verse, as to place him,

[1] " Browning inclines to a strong masculine realism, apparently careless of sound, and only too happy to startle and shock and puzzle his readers. . . . The extreme harshness of many of his lines is almost a match for anything in Surrey, only what in Surrey is helplessness seems the perversity of strength in Browning. . . . I hardly know whether it is fancy or not, but to me there is no poetry which has such an instantaneously solemnising power as Browning's. We seem to be in company with some rough rollicking Silenus, and all of a sudden the spirit descends upon him, the tone of his voice changes, and he pours out strains of the sublimest prophecy."—JOSEPH B. MAYOR : " English Metre," chap. xii.

for purposes of metrical study, next to Shakespeare and Milton.

The typical five-foot iambic is

The absolutely simple form of it is found in such a line as this:

" And swims, or sinks, or wades, or creeps, or flies ; "

because not only is every bar normal in notation, but each bar, as well as the line, is syllabically complete. Yet more than a line or two in monosyllables is obviously harsh, and artistically impossible; therefore art makes use of a judicious mixture of monosyllables, dissyllables, and polysyllables. (See chap. vii. for remarks upon the ponderable values of words.)

Construction of blank verse

A very pure example of normal five-foot iambic may be studied in the quatrain from Gray's " Elegy," on page 34. We find here every syllable, down to the anacrusis, exactly in place and of the right weight; every line end-stopped;[1] and the stanza itself rounded to its finish. This absolute metrical exactness—a survival of the arbitrary dictum of Dryden's day, which decreed that everything, from a love-lay to a satire, should be cast in the end-stopped heroic rhymed couplet—is not unsuited to a certain formal quality inherent in elegy; but long-prolonged it would become tiresome. Successive end-stopped lines obviously make versification stiff and mechanical. Blank verse was so written by those who

[1] Verse is called *end-stopped* when there comes a natural or rhetorical pause at the end of the line, marking off every five bars uniformly. When this terminal pause is absent, and one has to carry the meaning on into the next line, the verse is called *run-on*. Overflow is another name for the latter ; and we also use the French word *enjambement.*

used it first, and in Shakespeare's earlier work we find
a great predominance of end-stopped lines; but by his
middle period—the period of the great tragedies—we
see his use of the run-on line in full force.

The masters of blank verse have found means to escape
from the monotony of the typic scheme, and to give flexi-
Ways of bility and expressiveness to their verse in two
varying ways, viz.: by varying the bar-notation, and
normal
scheme by varying the cæsural effects.   The bar-notation may be varied (1) by dropping the anacrusis, (2) by
doubling a note, (3) by an occasional suspended syllable,
(or the prolonging of a single syllable through a bar),
(4) by the use of the feminine ending.   These features
accelerate or retard the movement of the verse so as to
allow a free play for feeling.

The cæsural effects are varied by the use of *enjambement*—overflow—which carries the sense into the line
beyond, putting a pause or cæsura there.

The cæsura plays a most important part in blank verse,
since upon its nice adjustment depends the cadence of
Part played the verse,—those larger rhythms of single
by cæsura phrases, and the great rhythmic swing of whole
periods.   Unless the poet fully understands cæsural
effects he will not be able to write organic and harmonious blank verse.[1]

---

[1] It is interesting here to compare Gascoigne's rule of metre, as given
forth in his " Instruction Concerning the Making of Verse in English,"
published in 1575.   " There are certain pauses or rests in a verse, which
may be called cæsures, whereof I should be loth to stand long, since it is
at the discretion of the writer, and they have been first devised, as should
seem by the musicians ; but yet thus much I will adventure to write that in
mine opinion, in a verse of eight syllables the pause will stand best in the
midst, in a verse of ten it will be best placed at the end of the first four
syllables."   And again : " nowadays in English rimes we use none other
order but a foot of two syllables, whereof the first is depressed or made
short and the second elevate or made long."

Classical canons fixed the cæsural pause in the third
foot (bar), though it might be in the fourth; but modern
poets follow no rule, and place it variously, according to
the exigencies of the verse. An examination of " Paradise Lost " shows us that Milton generally uses the
cæsura normally, in the third or fourth bars—thereby
preserving the balance of the prolonged *enjambement* of
many of his periods;—but we also find plenty of instances
of cæsura in any other bar. A favourite pause with Shakespeare is before the last accented syllable of a verse.
Tennyson much affects a pause after the first accented
syllable.

The so-called feminine cæsura is the pause after an
unaccented syllable. Thus:

" Then fearing rust or soilure, fashioned for it "

Surrey and Sackville made almost no use of the internal pause, and Marlowe not nearly so much as the
masters who followed him; but in all blank verse we find
plenty of lines without an internal pause, while many
others carry more than one.

Modern art tends to make the cæsura a rhetorical,
rather than a merely metrical pause, or more correctly to
make them coincide.

In all cases where variation is made from the normal
verse-scheme, we shall find that the metrical balance is
Metrical   restored by some other device,—a doubling of
balance   notes, or a peculiarly heavy syllable, in the
bar preceding or following the irregular one.[1] Thus the
verse is made interconsistent, and the volume of sound

---

[1] This license in the arrangement of syllables in a bar is not admissible
in stanzaic forms, because the very nature of the stanza demands a uniform
flow, and to break it would destroy the proportioned rhythmic effect necessary to *song*.

preserved.   This is peculiarly true of Shakespeare, whose variants are especially daring.

Many metrists speak of these variants as " the shifting of the accent," which is misleading.   The rhythmic accent is *never* shifted, for it is what marks the measurements of the bar; nor in good blank verse is the rhetorical accent shifted, for we do not now admit wrenched accents; but the number of syllables to a bar *is* shifted, throwing occasionally a heavier burden than the normal in one, or a lighter burden than the normal in another.

Discarding now classical nomenclatures, we will state that English blank verse is composed of a succession of **Basic** verses, or lines, in *free 2/5 verse*, in each of **formula of** which lines the pause may be either final, in-**blank verse** ternal, or both final and internal, or in some cases altogether absent.   But the typical scheme must reappear with sufficient persistence to dominate the verse and give it the organic stamp, thus preserving its unity. " All metrical effects are to a great extent *relative*," says Professor Corson, " and relativity of effect depends, of course, upon having a standard in the mind or the feelings.   In other words, there can be no variation of any kind without something to vary from.   Now the more closely the poet adheres to his standard,—to the even tenor (modulus) of his verse,—so long as there is no *logical* nor *æsthetic* motive for departing from it, the more effective do his departures become when they *are* sufficiently motived.   All non-significant departures weaken the significant ones.   In other words, all non-significant departures weaken or obscure the standard to the mind and the feelings.   . . .   But a great poet is presumed to have metrical skill; and where ripples occur in the stream of his verse, they will generally be found to justify themselves as organic; i.e. they are a part of the expression."

" The secret of complex and melodious blank verse,"
says John Addington Symonds, " lies in preserving the
balance and proportion of syllables while varying their
accent and their relative weight and volume, so that each
line in a period shall carry its proper burden of sound,
but the burden shall be differently distributed in the successive verses."

In brief, heroic blank verse is a five-stringed instrument, to which the poet brings the sole gauge of an
attuned and experienced ear, and upon which he may
make music according to the inspiration of his particular
genius.

Following are a number of examples of blank verse
notations ranging from Marlowe to Tennyson. In those
from Shakespeare, Milton, and Tennyson, I have endeavoured to give groups illustrative (1) of simple doubled
notes, (2) of direct attack, and (3) of suspended syllables,
i.e. a single syllable to a bar,—effects not really separable,
since the presence of either the second or third generally
involves the first,—adding to those from Shakespeare
three longer periods taken from his early, his mature,
and his latest works, as evidencing distinct modifications
in technique. The two extracts from Browning are
selected to show extremes of style. Note in the last line
of the quotation from Keats a remarkable circumstance.
Here we have the anacrusis omitted, but there are no
balancing doubled notes. The ear of the poet did not,
however, betray him; for the feminine ending would of
itself balance the line; but besides this, the fact of its
being an invocation throws a peculiar emphasis upon the
first three words, which are all of light syllables, thus
increasing the general volume of sound.

In all the examples please notice how the use of the
direct attack gives a certain dynamic force to the verse;

also **how a** suspended syllable stimulates emotion and
intensifies the animus of the moment.   The imagination
hangs as it were breathless, awaiting the next word.

MARLOWE

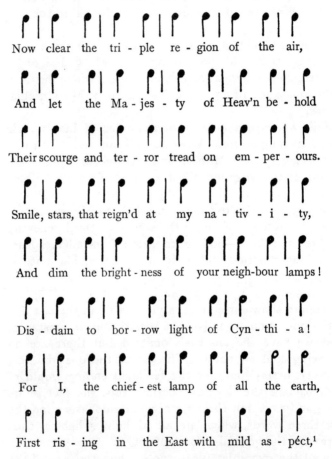

Now clear the tri - ple re - gion of   the air,

And let   the Ma - jes - ty   of Heav'n be - hold

Their scourge and ter - ror tread on   em - per - ours.

Smile, stars, that reign'd at   my na - tiv - i - ty,

And dim   the bright - ness of   your neigh-bour lamps !

Dis - dain to bor - row light of Cyn - thi - a !

For   I,   the chief - est lamp of   all   the earth,

First ris - ing in   the East with mild as - péct,[1]

[1] A *wrenched* accent, common in Elizabethan times, but not now
admitted.

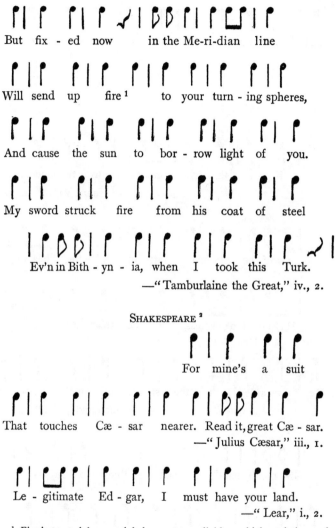

But fix - ed now   in the Me-ri-dian   line

Will send up   fire [1]   to your turn - ing spheres,

And cause the sun   to bor - row light of   you.

My sword struck   fire   from his   coat of   steel

Ev'n in Bith - yn - ia, when   I   took this   Turk.

—"Tamburlaine the Great," iv., 2.

SHAKESPEARE [2]

For   mine's   a   suit

That   touches   Cæ - sar   nearer. Read it, great Cæ - sar.

—"Julius Cæsar," iii., 1.

Le - gitimate   Ed - gar,   I   must have your land.

—"Lear," i., 2.

[1] *Fire* is treated here and below as two syllables, which, strictly speaking, it is not.

[2] The Rolfe edition has been used in these extracts.

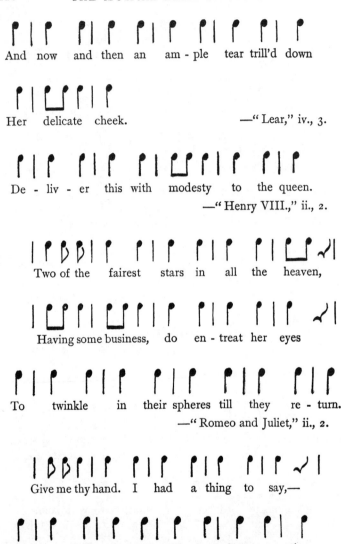

And now and then an am - ple tear trill'd down

Her delicate cheek.   —" Lear," iv., 3.

De - liv - er this with modesty to the queen.
—" Henry VIII.," ii., 2.

Two of the fairest stars in all the heaven,

Having some business, do en - treat her eyes

To twinkle in their spheres till they re - turn.
—" Romeo and Juliet," ii., 2.

Give me thy hand. I had a thing to say,—

But I will fit it with some bet - ter time.
—" King John," iii., 3.

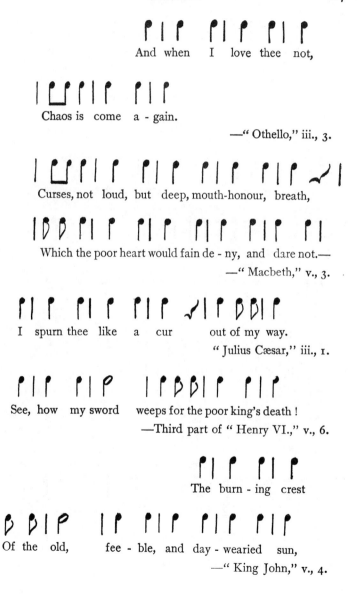

And when I love thee not,

Chaos is come a - gain.

—" Othello," iii., 3.

Curses, not loud, but deep, mouth-honour, breath,

Which the poor heart would fain de - ny, and dare not.—

—" Macbeth," v., 3.

I spurn thee like a cur out of my way.

" Julius Cæsar," iii., 1.

See, how my sword weeps for the poor king's death !

—Third part of " Henry VI.," v., 6.

The burn - ing crest

Of the old, fee - ble, and day - wearied sun,

—" King John," v., 4.

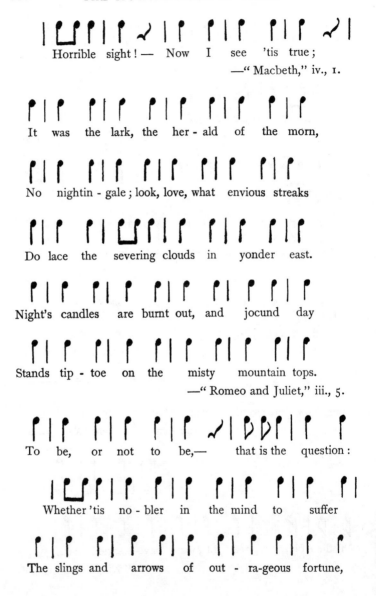

Horrible sight! — Now I   see   'tis true;

—" Macbeth," iv., 1.

It   was   the lark, the   her - ald   of   the   morn,

No   nightin - gale ; look, love, what   envious streaks

Do lace   the   severing clouds in   yonder   east.

Night's candles   are burnt out, and   jocund   day

Stands tip - toe   on   the   misty   mountain tops.

—" Romeo and Juliet," iii., 5.

To   be,   or not   to be,—   that is the   question :

Whether 'tis no - bler   in   the mind   to   suffer

The slings and   arrows   of   out - ra-geous fortune,

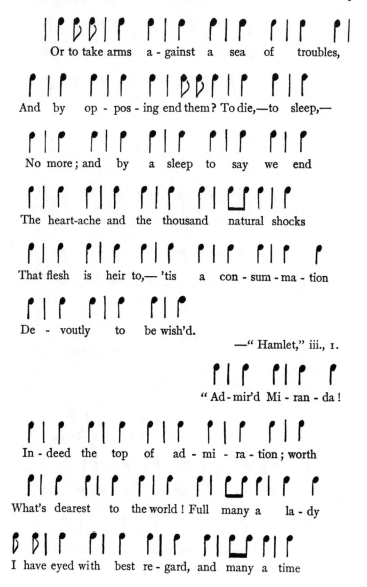

Or to take arms a - gainst a sea of troubles,

And by op - pos - ing end them? To die,—to sleep,—

No more ; and by a sleep to say we end

The heart-ache and the thousand natural shocks

That flesh is heir to,— 'tis a con - sum - ma - tion

De - voutly to be wish'd.

—" Hamlet," iii., 1.

" Ad - mir'd Mi - ran - da !

In - deed the top of ad - mi - ra - tion ; worth

What's dearest to the world ! Full many a la - dy

I have eyed with best re - gard, and many a time

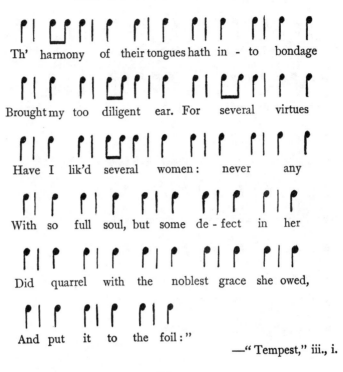

Th' harmony of their tongues hath in - to bondage

Brought my too diligent ear. For several virtues

Have I lik'd several women : never any

With so full soul, but some de - fect in her

Did quarrel with the noblest grace she owed,

And put it to the foil : "

—"Tempest," iii., i.

MILTON

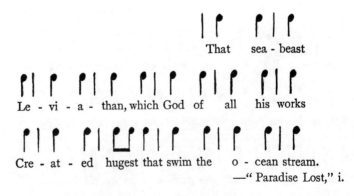

That sea - beast

Le - vi - a - than, which God of all his works

Cre - at - ed hugest that swim the o - cean stream.

—"Paradise Lost," i.

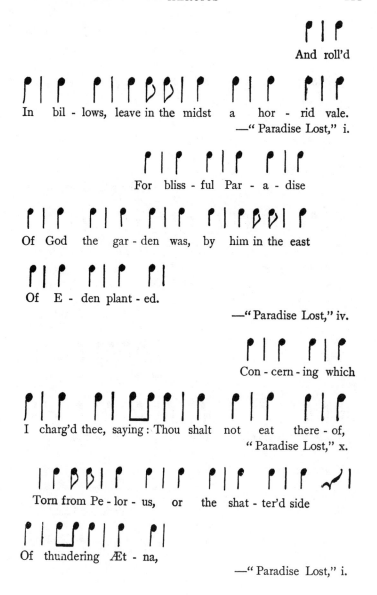

And roll'd

In bil - lows, leave in the midst a hor - rid vale.

—" Paradise Lost," i.

For bliss - ful Par - a - dise

Of God the gar - den was, by him in the east

Of E - den plant - ed.

—" Paradise Lost," iv.

Con - cern - ing which

I charg'd thee, saying : Thou shalt not eat there - of,

" Paradise Lost," x.

Torn from Pe - lor - us, or the shat - ter'd side

Of thundering Æt - na,

—" Paradise Lost," i.

Part, huge of bulk,

Wallowing un-wieldy, e - nor - mous in   their gait,

Tempest the   o - cean:

—" Paradise Lost," vii.

Laden with fruit of   fair - est col - ours mix'd,

Ruddy and gold.

—" Paradise Lost," ix.

And the fresh field

Calls us ; we lose   the prime, to mark how spring

Our   tended plants,

" Paradise Lost," v.

Millions of flam - ing swords, drawn from the thighs

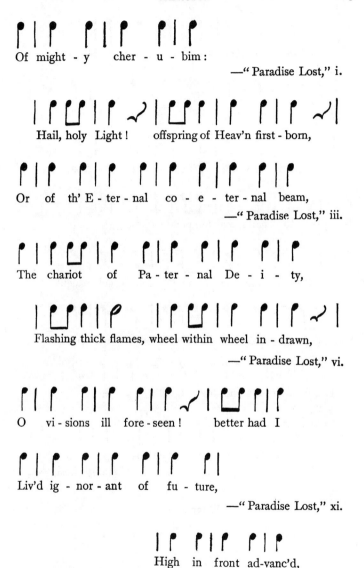

Of might - y cher - u - bim :

—" Paradise Lost," i.

Hail, holy Light ! offspring of Heav'n first - born,

Or of th' E - ter - nal co - e - ter - nal beam,

—" Paradise Lost," iii.

The chariot of Pa - ter - nal De - i - ty,

Flashing thick flames, wheel within wheel in - drawn,

—" Paradise Lost," vi.

O vi - sions ill fore - seen ! better had I

Liv'd ig - nor - ant of fu - ture,

—" Paradise Lost," xi.

High in front ad-vanc'd,

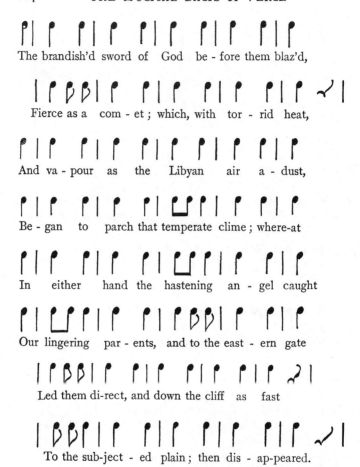

The brandish'd sword of God be - fore them blaz'd,

Fierce as a com - et; which, with tor - rid heat,

And va - pour as the Libyan air a - dust,

Be - gan to parch that temperate clime; where-at

In either hand the hastening an - gel caught

Our lingering par - ents, and to the east - ern gate

Led them di-rect, and down the cliff as fast

To the sub-ject - ed plain; then dis - ap-peared.

—"Paradise Lost," xii.

WORDSWORTH

For I have learn'd

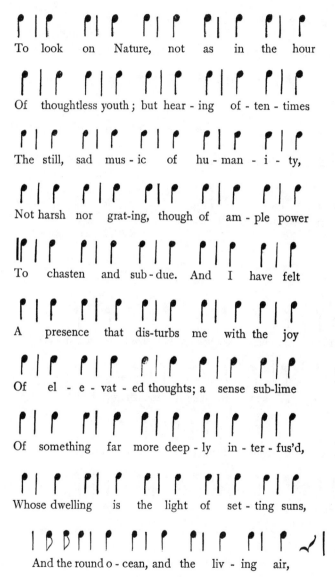

To look on Nature, not as in the hour

Of thoughtless youth; but hear - ing of - ten - times

The still, sad mus - ic of hu - man - i - ty,

Not harsh nor grat-ing, though of am - ple power

To chasten and sub - due. And I have felt

A presence that dis-turbs me with the joy

Of el - e - vat - ed thoughts; a sense sub-lime

Of something far more deep - ly in - ter - fus'd,

Whose dwelling is the light of set - ting suns,

And the round o - cean, and the liv - ing air,

15

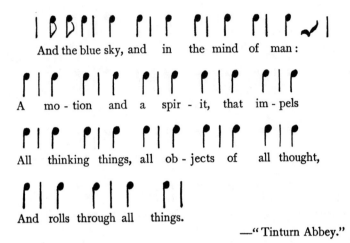

And the blue sky, and   in   the mind of   man :

A   mo - tion   and   a   spir - it,   that   im - pels

All   thinking things, all   ob - jects of   all thought,

And   rolls through all   things.

—"Tinturn Abbey."

SHELLEY

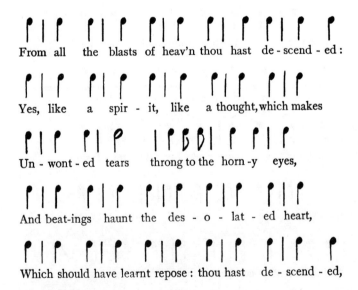

From all   the blasts of heav'n thou hast   de - scend - ed :

Yes, like   a   spir - it,   like   a thought, which makes

Un - wont - ed   tears   throng to the horn -y   eyes,

And beat-ings haunt   the   des - o - lat - ed heart,

Which should have learnt repose : thou hast   de - scend - ed,

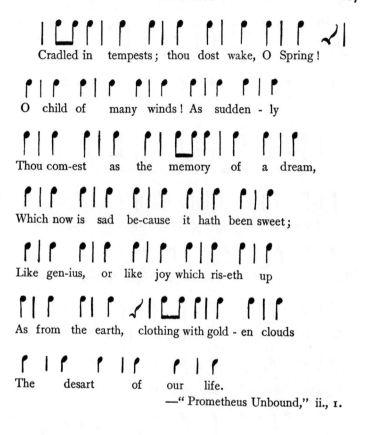

Cradled in tempests; thou dost wake, O Spring!

O child of many winds! As sudden - ly

Thou com-est as the memory of a dream,

Which now is sad be-cause it hath been sweet;

Like gen-ius, or like joy which ris-eth up

As from the earth, clothing with gold - en clouds

The desart of our life.

—"Prometheus Unbound," ii., 1.

KEATS

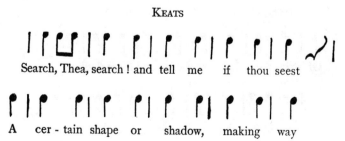

Search, Thea, search! and tell me if thou seest

A cer - tain shape or shadow, making way

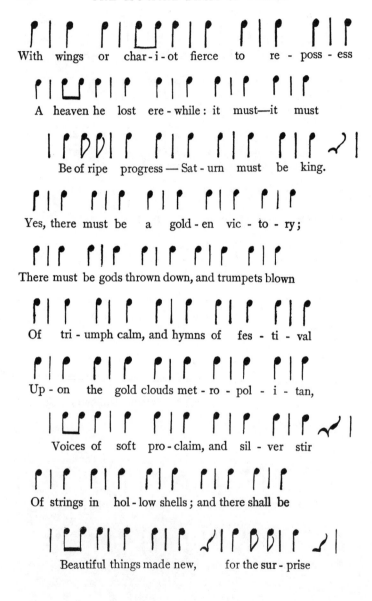

Of the sky - children ;   I   will   give   command :

The - a !   The - a !   The - a !   where   is   Saturn?

—" Hyperion," i.

BROWNING

I

I   haste

To   contem - plate   un - daz - zled some one   truth,

Its   bearings   and   ef - fects   a - lone—at   once

What   was   a   speck ex - pands   into   a   star,

Asking a   life   to   pass   ex - plor - ing   thus,

Till   I   near craze.   I   go   to   prove my   soul !

I see my way as birds their track - less way—

I shall ar - rive! what time, what cir - cuit first,

I ask not: but un - less God send his hail

Or blinding fire - balls, sleet, or stifling snow,

In some time—his good time—I shall ar - rive:

He guides me and the bird. In his good time!

—" Paracelsus."

II

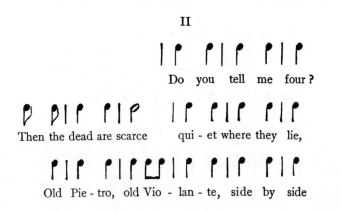

Do you tell me four?

Then the dead are scarce qui - et where they lie,

Old Pie - tro, old Vio - lan - te, side by side

At the church Lo - ren - zo,—oh, they know it well!

So do I. But my wife is still a - live,

Has breath e - nough to tell her sto - ry yet,

Her way, which is not mine, no doubt at all.

And Ca - pon - sac - chi, you have summoned him,—

Was he so far to send for ? Not at hand ?

I thought some few o' the stabs were in his heart,

Or had not been so lav - ish: less had served.

Well, he too tells his sto - ry,—flor - id prose

As smooth as mine is rough. You see, my lords,

There will be a   lying in - tox - i - cat - ing smoke

Born of the blood,—con - fus - ion pro - ba - bly,—

For lies breed lies — but all that rests with you!

The trial is no con - cern of mine; with me

The main of the care is   o - ver: I   at least

Recognize who took that huge burden   off,

Let me be-gin to live a - gain.

—" The Ring and the Book.—Count Guido Franceschini."

TENNYSON

And while   I look'd

And   listen - ed, the full-flowing river of speech

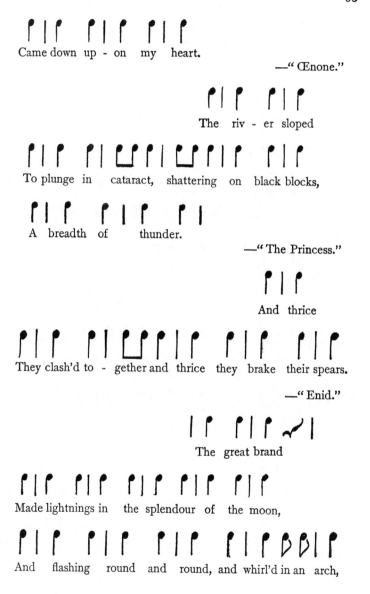

Came down up - on my heart.

—" Œnone."

The riv - er sloped

To plunge in cataract, shattering on black blocks,

A breadth of thunder.

—" The Princess."

And thrice

They clash'd to - gether and thrice they brake their spears.

—" Enid."

The great brand

Made lightnings in the splendour of the moon,

And flashing round and round, and whirl'd in an arch,

Shot like a   streamer of   the northern morn,

—"The Passing of Arthur."

Oaring one arm, and bearing   in   my left

The weight   of   all   the hopes of   half   the world

Strove   to   buffet to land in vain.

—"The Princess."

"How he went down," said Gareth, "as a false knight

Or   e - vil king be - fore my lance, if lance

Were mine   to   use—"

—"Gareth and Lynette."

The   voice   of   E - nid,   Yniol's   daughter, rang

Clear thro' the o - pen casement of the hall,

singing;

—" Enid."

Stabb'd thro' the heart's af - fec - tions to the heart!

Seeth'd like the kid in its own mother's milk!

Kill'd with a word worse than a life of blows!

—" Vivien."

As if the flower

That blows a globe of af - ter ar - row - lets,

Ten thousand - fold had grown, flash'd the fierce shield,

All sun;

—" Gareth and Lynette."

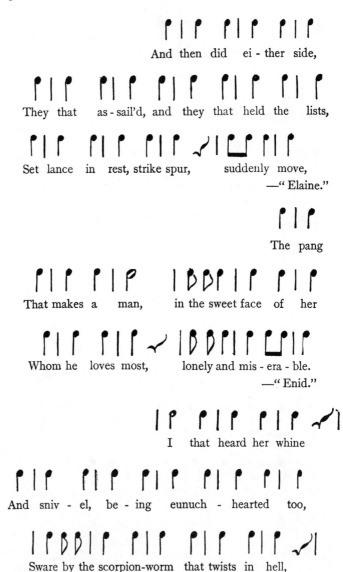

And then did ei - ther side,

They that   as - sail'd, and they that held the   lists,

Set lance in   rest, strike spur,   suddenly move,

—" Elaine."

The pang

That makes a   man,   in the sweet face of   her

Whom he   loves most,   lonely and mis - era - ble.

—" Enid."

I   that heard her whine

And sniv - el, be - ing   eunuch - hearted   too,

Sware by the scorpion-worm that twists in   hell,

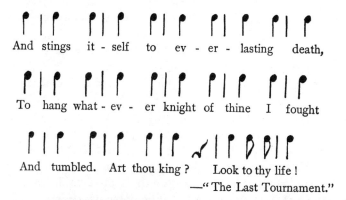

And stings it - self to ev - er - lasting death,

To hang what - ev - er knight of thine I fought

And tumbled. Art thou king ? Look to thy life !

—"The Last Tournament."

From the foregoing tables—which the student may in-definitely multiply for himself—it will be apparent that all true or organic blank verse is easily divided and analysed by the system of musical notation.

There have not been wanting, from Dryden's day to ours, plenty of critics to cry out against, and declare "illegitimate," a great deal of the verse of Shakespeare and Milton; though it remains a paradox why verse which is illegitimate should have become world-classic. But, an-alysed by bar and note, we find rhythmic diffi-culties melt into thin air. Those age-long bugaboos of the conventional metrist, *extra syllables*, are perceived to be not extra syllables at all, but variants of *free verse ;* and we see that " looked at musically," and their longi-tude reckoned by the accents and not by the arbitrary foot-divisions, they settle themselves into place as har-moniously as the *passing notes* of a musical composition. It is no longer necessary to slur syllables in order to scramble them into a fixed metrical space (indeed the genius of the English language does not really permit of such things as slurring or eliding), nor to chop

All blank verse mensurable by the foregoing method

them in two in order to drag them to the conventional limits.

Shakespeare, writing for the boards and not for the literary critic, adjusts the music of his verse to appeal to the ear rather than to the eye; and we must remember too, one great fact, viz.: that Shakespeare and Milton (indeed to an extent all the great poets) rhythmise, not only single verses, but whole passages, and that, for impartial criticism, whole passages and not fragments of them must therefore be taken into consideration.

In Shakespeare a steady growth is observable in the mastery of his instrument. The later work not only **Shake-** shows more metric daring, but also greater **speare's use** fluency, more use of *enjambement*, and an in- **of feminine** **endings** creased tendency to the use of the feminine ending. The limits of the latter he never oversteps, as does Fletcher,[1] and it adds richness to the cadence of his verse without ever impairing its virility. Thus a table of Mr. Fleay's gives an average of feminine endings in " Love's Labour's Lost" of one to sixty-four and one-third lines; in " Cymbeline," of one to three and one-half lines.

Coincident with his adoption of *enjambement*, and for the same reason—freedom—Shakespeare drops rhyme. Rhyme not only hampers drama tonally, but to a great extent it involves the end-stop. The Dryden and Pope rhymed couplets are carefully and uniformly end-stopped, giving to the verse a trip-hammer effect. But there are plenty of narrative poems in rhymed couplets with con-

---

[1] " By the use of the feminine ending the poet endeavours to reproduce the easy tone of ordinary life ; and this no doubt explains its frequency in Fletcher, the poet of society. There is felt to be something formal, stilted, high-flown, poetic, in the regular iambic metre."—JOSEPH B. MAYOR : "English Metre," chap. xi.

siderable use of *enjambement,* which are most graceful
and charming. (See preceding chapter.)

The period of Shakespeare's breaking loose from tradition is further characterised by his free adoption of light
Shake- and weak endings, i.e. the ending of a line upon
speare's use an insignificant syllable. Thus such words as
of weak
and light *am, are, be, do, has, I, they,* etc., are called light
endings endings, while still less significant words, such
as *and, for, in, if, or,* etc., are called weak endings. The
latter are more " fugitive in character," and both so tend
to precipitate the reader forward that there is no possible
chance to pause after it, but the ear must hurry on into
the next line to find a cæsura to rest upon. Such lines
as the following are typical:

> " ' It sounds no more ; and sure it waits upon
> Some god o' the Island,"   —" Tempest," i., 2.

> " A most majestic vision, and
> Harmonious charmingly."   —" Tempest," iv., 1.

The weak ending is very liable to abuse, and we observe that later poets employ it much more sparingly
than Shakespeare.[1]

---

[1] " It should be noted that commonly a pause occurs before the weak
final monosyllable, after which the verse, as it were, leaps forward. This
structure, as has been said, gives to the verse something of the bounding
life which Ulysses describes Diomed as showing in the manner of his gait:

> ' He rises on the toe ; that spirit of his
> In aspiration lifts him from the earth.'

It conduces to liveliness and variety, and so is hardly appropriate to tragedy of the deeper sort ; but it is admirably adapted to the romantic drama
of Shakspere's latest stage, and here alone it appears in a conspicuous
degree."—EDWARD DOWDEN : " Shakspere " (Literature Primer), chap.
iv., 30.

Blank verse offers the best medium for long-sustained themes because of its nearness to prose, and because it **Blank verse** does not cloy the ear as long poems in rhymed **the best** couplets or in stanzas are apt to do.   Further-**medium for** **objective** more, the stricter pause exactions of the stanza **poetry** interrupt the action and the flow of dialogue, which blank verse favours.

Lanier indeed claims that the use of blank verse is " an attempt to escape from metre." Not so.   For if a writer desire to escape from metre, he has nothing to do but to write plainly in prose; whereas the very selection of blank verse betrays that his fundamental thought is rhythmic.   Blank verse is not an escape from metre, but the use of the largest, most elastic, and most universal metric form we have.

We observe in Shakespeare that, when the tone of the drama is lowered—as by the introduction of a comic, or a colloquial element—the movement drops into periods of prose, resuming verse with the deepening of the artistic emotion.   The demarcation is as sharp as if cut with a knife; there is never a syllable's confusion.

" For " (says Mr. A. J. Ellis), " as Dionysius and Cicero well put it, verse is *in rhythm*, and prose is merely *rhythmical;* that is, verse follows a conscious and mainly enunciable law in the juxtaposition of syllables of different kinds, and prose follows a subjective, and mainly non-enunciable feeling."

I know of no better way for the student of verse to obtain a mastery of blank verse technique than by memorising a great number of notable passages, and saturating himself, as it were, with the cadences, so that they become a part of him.   For objective art is an esoteric art, an art of the chosen few, only to be learned by long apprenticeship and the finest of perception.

Carlyle defines poetry as " the heroic of speech." This is certainly a true definition of blank verse; for, if heroic subjects demand a heroic medium, so does the heroic medium demand a heroic subject. It is not suited to lyric expression and should never be used for it. A short chop of blank verse does not constitute a poem. To comprehend the scope of its modulations we require to get it in the mass; exactly as the effect of a great orchestral composition could not be obtained by hearing fragments from two or three instruments, but only from the rounded volume of the full orchestra.

Objective art demands of the poet, not only metrical skill of the highest order, but also a great shaping or **Objective art** constructive faculty, as well as a consummate **demands of** sense of proportion. He must bring to his **the poet the** **architectonic** work, not only the finest conception of art, **faculty** but an universal perception of men and things, and of their eternal relations. For it is only when a man becomes merged in the universal, and creates outside of himself—steps from the leading-strings of the personal into the illimitability of the impersonal—that the canvas of life truly unrolls beneath his hands; and only then, when he has power to create action wedded to proportion, is in fact an intrinsic *artist*. This is the quality which Matthew Arnold, borrowing the term from the Germans, designates as the *architectonic faculty ;* and by the canons of the architectonic Time ruthlessly sits in judgment upon all art. Only as it is structurally great shall it endure.

16

CHAPTER VII

BEAUTY AND POWER

THERE seems at the present day to be a largely preva-
lent idea to the effect that originality and development
in art—all forms of art—consist in the despis-
ing, often the outraging, of *form*. But what
is form ? Is it not expression *per se;* the reduction of
the abstract to the concrete ? Can anything tangible
exist without form ?

The progress of human thought has been a unifying
process. Investigation on all sides proves to us not so
much that there are laws as that there is law.
The scientist to-day postulates life in all its
manifestations as molecular motion; the meta-
physician postulates thought as molecular motion. Molecular motion is, in another word, vibration, and vibration we have seen to be the basis of the two highest
expressions of human thought—poetry and music. Science teaches us further that the forces of nature can
interchange. Colours turn to sound; sound again to
form. If we attach a delicate pencil to the wires of
a pianoforte, place the point in contact with a prepared
paper, and then strike major chords upon the keyboard,
we shall find the vibrations of the harmonies transferred
to the paper in loveliest geometric and decorative de-
signs. This ratiocination brings us round in a circle,
and demonstrates that between science and art there is

no real base of conflict; because they are in fact only different projections of one central cause.

When we turn to nature for hints we find the inevitable procession of law and order, whether we consider the orbits of the planets, the sequence of day and night, the changes of the sidereal year, or contemplate the marvellously packed crystals of a geode, or the delicately balanced petals and sepals of a flower. There is no haphazard about it all. Crystals fall always into the same geometric patterns. Plants produce bud and bloom, and perfect their seed, each after its kind, always in the same way. There is unity throughout creation; everywhere we find the order and balance without which nothing, not even the universe, could exist at all.

"In the beginning God created the heaven and the earth. And the earth was without form and void; and darkness was upon the face of the deep: and the spirit of God moved upon the face of the waters."

Over the inconceivableness of chaos moved the inspiration of divine thought, evolving therefrom the con-

Form, the law of expression ceivable—organisation, measure, proportion, symmetry, coördination ; in another word *form*.

Form, then, is merely the law of expression.

What we find true of nature is equally so of art; for nature and art are basically alike in that they are *form* infused with *life*. What we call nature is the direct creation of Deity; what we call art is the indirect creation of Deity—nature sifted through the consciousness of man. Nature is creation upon the lines of, and in harmony with, great fundamental laws. Art too must be upon the lines of, and in harmony with, great fundamental laws, or it will not be true art; for the laws themselves are an integral part of the creation.

Form being the law of expression, we cannot then, if we are to express ourselves at all, escape the use of form;

Form an integral part of the creation we can only choose between a good form and a bad form, a lower form and a higher form, a beautiful form and an ugly form, an adapted form and an uncouth or incongruous form. Great art is achieved, not by disobedience to and outraging of law, but by inflection and variation within the lines of the law. With the masters of poetic art this use of form becomes in a manner self-selective; for of course the true artist does not primarily take cognisance of his mechanism as he works. He is already master of his tools— a skilled craftsman; but it is exactly by reason of, and in proportion to, this mastery—so fixed in the subconsciousness that it has become an instinctive factor of expression—that he may in a sense ignore detail. It is the lesser craftsman who is ever conscious of his tools, and must be forever at his measuring and grinding.

" Form," says Eckermann (" Beiträge zur Poesie " [1]), " is the result of the efforts, through thousands of years, of the most excellent masters, which everyone cannot too soon appropriate to himself. It were a most insane delusion of misconceived originality if each one were to go about on his own account fumbling for that which is already on hand in great perfection. Form is handed down, learned, imitated; otherwise progress in art would be out of the question,—everyone would have to begin anew." As a corollary to the above we may quote the words of Robert Schumann, a critic of great acumen not only of his own art, but of its sister art. " The history of all arts and artists has proven that *mastery of form* leads talent to continually increasing freedom."

" The writer of verse is afraid of having too much

[1] See " Theory and Practice of Musical Form," by J. H. Cornell.

form, of having too much technic; he dreads it will inter-
fere with his spontaneity.   No more decisive confession
of weakness can be made.   It is only cleverness and
small talent which is afraid of its spontaneity; the genius,
the great artist, is forever ravenous after new forms, after
technic; he will follow you to the ends of the earth if
you will enlarge his artistic science." [1]

Elizabeth Barrett Browning has epitomised the foregoing ideas in a notable passage of " Aurora Leigh ":

> " Without the spiritual, observe,
> The natural's impossible ;—no form,
> No motion ! Without sensuous, spiritual
> Is inappreciable :—no beauty or power !
> And in this twofold sphere the twofold man
> (And still the artist is intensely a man)
> Holds firmly by the natural, to reach
> The spiritual beyond it,—fixes still
> The type with mortal vision, to pierce through,
> With eyes immortal, to the antetype
> Some call the ideal,—"

Every age has had its generic art-form; that by which
its individual thought and aspiration can best be expressed and made concrete.   These reflect not
only contemporary manners, but reveal the
spiritual development of their epoch.   They
are organic forms of genius; and the high achievements
of one age or race cannot be consummated by another
age or race.   Thus the distinctive art-form of Greece
was sculpture.   The fervid religious thought of the Middle Ages found its expression in the Scripture of Stone
—architecture; an architecture the most soaring and
ideal, which we endeavour to-day to imitate but whose

Every age has had its generic art-form

---

[1] SIDNEY LANIER : " The English Novel," chap. ii.

informing spirit we cannot catch. The Art-form of the
Renaissance was painting; and the restless, inquiring,
aspiring modern world pours its soul out in music.

But close along with the other arts, shoulder to shoulder, moves also and always literature, the perennial and
universal art-form. Thus, beside Phidias and
Praxiteles, we find Æschylus, Sophocles, Eu-
ripides. In the Renaissance, with her great
painters, Italy had her Dante, her Petrarch, her Ariosto,
her Tasso; and in the great world of modern music, we
have a Goethe, a Victor Hugo, a Pushkin, a Robert
Browning.

In an interesting work by Wilhelm August Ambros
(translated by J. H. Cornell), called " The Boundaries of
Music and Poetry," there is a synthetic comparison of the different arts, graduated by the
relative resistance to the idea of the medium employed.
Thus, of the fine arts, architecture stands at the bottom
of the scale, because in it there is the greatest resistance
of crude material, and also because it is the art least individually expressive of the conceiving artist. A Greek
temple is a Greek temple, a Gothic cathedral a Gothic
cathedral. The monument survives its creator,—survives as a type and not as an individuation. Sculpture
resembles architecture in the element of crude material
to be overcome, but greatly transcends it in the power
of the artist for individual expression. Yet here also he
is necessarily limited by material conditions; and while
of ancient masterpieces a few have reached us labelled,
a thousand others have nothing individually distinguish-
able, and may be only uncertainly classed with special
art-epochs. When we come to painting, we find the
artist greatly freed of his crude material, and able to express the personal ideal to a very great degree. Thus

(marginal notes) Literature the univer-sal art-form — Comparison of art-forms

the works of Cimabue, Fra Angelico, Raphael, Michael Angelo, Titian, Correggio, etc., are so distinct from each other, and so instinct with the personal bias of the creative artist, that it would not be possible for the trained observer ever to mistake one for the other. In poetry the resistance of crude material is virtually *nil*. It, of all the arts, permits the closest and most direct following of the abstract concept by its concrete expression. Therefore is poetry the freest and most disembodied, as well as the most personal, of all the arts.

And how shall we define the larger of the Arts of Sound, the at once most intangible yet most scientific of the arts,—music? Upon its concrete or scientific side the art of music is superlatively complex. Constructively it resembles architecture,[1] being composed of related strata of sound (if I may use so material a term), each conditioned to, and built into, others, in accordance with complex physical laws. Therefore, of all the arts, it is next to architecture and the most architectonic. Yet, essentially, upon its psychic side, music is the very freest medium of which we have cognisance. It is spiritualised sound and motion. It transcends speech. It flies upon the wings of the morning; it throbs in the abysses of night. It links heart to heart, and sphere to sphere, and the heights and depths of man's being awaken and respond. Yet, finally, music lacks definiteness. Something more we have to express to each other for which articulate speech alone serves; nay, music must turn to articulate speech to define its very own inwardness; for music, by what Mr. Huneker defines as an " immediate appeal to the nerve-

Music as an art=form lacks definiteness

---

[1] The famous apothegm " Architecture is frozen music "—Schlegel's, I believe, though frequently attributed to Mme. de Staël—will readily recur to the memory.

centres," awakens feelings rather than ideas.   This is
because sound plays upon human emotion without regu-
lating it.   It is the thought of the listener which regu-
lates; and, for the definite thought of one mind to be
conveyed to another (i.e. performer and listener), words
must intervene.   Words must formulate the ideas which
music desires to promulgate; for music, with all its
wings, is not capable of producing before the mind a
definite and fixed image.   In all programme-music—
which deals ostensibly with definite imagery—the idea
Words
finally
needed
which the music is to express is explained by
words; either by definitions of the separate
parts—as in Beethoven's " Pastoral Symphony," Spohr's symphony, " The Consecration of
Sound," [1] and kindred works; or, in the freer forms now
in vogue, the poem from which the composer drew his
inspirational thought is prefixed to the score, and usually
printed in the concert programme.   Such are Raff's
" Lenore," César Franck's " Les Éolides," Richard
Strauss's " Thus Spake Zarathustra," etc.
    In short,

> " Music is Love in search of a Word,"

only for *love* read *spirit*.

The associa-
tive power
of words
There is an immense associative power in
words; and herein lies the virtue of the trope.
Words do not stand isolated in the mental
chambers, but are so much a part of special trains of

---

[1] " ' Die Weihe der Töne ' has generally been accounted Spohr's most
successful symphony.   The sub-title of the score is ' A Characteristic
Tone-Painting in the Form of a Symphony, after a poem by Carl Pfeiffer.'
On a fly-leaf of the score is printed a ' Pre-reminder by the Composer,' to
the effect that he wishes the poem to be printed on concert-programs and
distributed among the audience."—WILLIAM F. APTHORP : " Symphony
Notes," 1900.

thought that the use of a word, or a group of words, will call up, not only the direct image which it stands for, but a dozen associated images which the mind ever holds, as it were, in solution.

When we consider what language *is*, that it is not an invention but an organic growth, and that every word is a sound-vibration closely related to its thought-vibration, we shall realise that, instead of being accidental or arbitrary figures, words are living forces; the more dynamic, the more closely they are correlated to their thought; for words are energised by thought. This is why words of conventional meaning, used by the artificial manufacturers of so-called literature, never move us; there is no living force behind them.

Figures and tropes play a great part in all literary expression, but they are the very sinew of poetry. One **The trope** could not in fact conceive of poetry without the trope; it would be but metric dry bones; for the trope is thought idealised. We can hardly use every-day speech without an infusion of imagery, for adjectives are in themselves a simple form of trope. We should indeed not get a definite image of the object named by the substantive without the qualifying suggestiveness of the adjective. The more unusual, or unusually apt and descriptive the adjective, the more vivid the image which it calls up. Mr. Kipling's adjectives, for instance, are often simply dynamic, and put before one a whole picture, as it were, by a lightning flash. It is, however, very easy, working upon these lines, to slip over the borders of true art into the slough of mere impressionism.

The trope [1] is the figurative use of a word, or of words, in some meaning other than the normal one. It is lit-

[1] Greek : *tropos,* from *trepo,* turn.

erally a turning out of the direct course of language in
order to express the thought in some more vivid manner.
The poet makes by this means a more swift and definite
impression upon the mind than can be achieved by direct
description.   Thus Wordsworth says:

> " The good die first,
> And they whose hearts are dry as summer's dust
> *Burn to the socket.*"

And we have a more vivid picture than if he had said:
" The good die first, and those who have no emotions or
sympathies live to a good old age."
So when the guilty and excited Macbeth cries out:

> " Methought I heard a voice cry, ' Sleep no more !
> Macbeth does murther sleep !' ' "

we get an infinitely deeper sense of the horror of the
situation than if he had said:
" Macbeth has slain his guest in sleep, therefore he
himself shall never again find rest."
And when Gloster exclaims:

> " See how my sword *weeps* for the poor king's death !"

what a picture is painted for us by a single word!
The trope belongs to the domain of rhetoric, and does
not in any way affect metrical laws; therefore this is no
Metaphor place to enter in detail into its qualities and
functions.   But I will state briefly that tropes
are of two general classes: the direct compared image,
or *metaphor*, and the indirect compared image, or *simile*.
In the metaphor one thing is directly called another.
Thus:

" When I will wear a garment all of blood
And stain my favour in a bloody mask,
Which, wash'd away, shall scour my shame with it."
—SHAKESPEARE : First part of " Henry IV.," iii., 2.

" Sometime too hot the eye of heaven shines,
And often is his gold complexion dimm'd ;
And every fair from fair sometimes declines,
By chance or nature's changing course untrimm'd ;
But thy eternal summer shall not fade."
—SHAKESPEARE : Sonnet XVIII.

" Elegies
And quoted odes, and jewels five-words-long
That on the stretched forefinger of all Time
Sparkle forever."
—TENNYSON : " The Princess."

" Out went the taper as she hurried in ;
Its little smoke in pallid moonshine died."
—KEATS : " The Eve of St. Agnes."

Simile In the simile one thing is compared with another, both being presented or sometimes one being only implied. Thus:

" The barge
Whereon the lily maid of Astolat
Lay smiling, like a star in blackest night."
—TENNYSON : " Elaine."

" I saw young Harry, with his beaver on,
His cuisses on his thighs, gallantly armed,
Rise from the ground like feather'd Mercury,
And vaulted with such ease into his seat,
As if an angel dropp'd down from the clouds,
To turn and wind a fiery Pegasus
And witch the world with noble horsemanship."
—SHAKESPEARE : First part of " Henry IV.," iv., 1.

> " As when far off at sea a fleet descried
> Hangs in the clouds, by equinoctial winds
> Close sailing from Bengala, or the isles
> Of Ternate and Tidore, whence merchants bring
> Their spicy drugs: they on the trading flood
> Through the wide Ethiopian to the Cape
> Ply, stemming nightly toward the pole: so seem'd
> Far off the flying fiend."
> —MILTON: " Paradise Lost," book ii.

> " O Spartan dog,
> More fell than anguish, hunger, or the sea ! "
> —SHAKESPEARE : " Othello," v., 2.

Metaphors and similes will often be found intermingled in the same passage; as in the quotation from Henry IV. just above, " I saw young Harry," etc.

The metaphor being the more concentrated image is the more swift and dynamic. The simile is a more diffuse image, and carries its point of comparison by weight, rather than by swiftness, of evidence. The simile is of oriental, the metaphor of occidental, origin.

The personification of nature   A beautiful and forceful form of metaphor is found in the personification of nature or of natural and impersonal phenomena. Thus:

> " Now morn, her rosy steps in the eastern clime
> Advancing, sowed the earth with orient pearl."
> —MILTON : " Paradise Lost," book v.

> " Oh, good gigantic smile o' the brown old earth,
> This autumn morning ! How he sets his bones
> To bask i' the sun, and thrusts out knees and feet
> For the ripple to run over in its mirth ; "
> —BROWNING : " James Lee's Wife."

This form expanded becomes *Allegory.*

Both metaphor and simile permit of many variants and have suffered technically much subdivision, each division being named after its kind. They may be studied in the standard treatises on rhetoric. The abuse or overloading of diction with tropes is perilously easy. One needs but to compare the lovely and living imagery of Shakespeare with the overdrawn, artificial, and cloying conceits which prevailed afterwards.

But there is connotative potency in the direct use of language as well as in the figurative. What we might call the *ponderable quality* of words greatly influences their suggestive value. Thus monosyllables are terse, incisive, dynamic, and are used by the masters of verse where vigor and virility, or sometimes where mere brute power, are to be conveyed. The following line from Milton, by the succession of heavy, almost crude, monosyllables, presents a more forceful image of naked dreariness than could possibly be obtained by any interspersion of longer words. This is a noticeable point in Milton, who was prone to sonorous diction, and evidences surely how, with the masters of verse, the choice of words is no accident but an absolute instinct for fitness.

The ponderable value of words

" Rocks, caves, lakes, fens, bogs, dens, and shades of death,"

The foregoing remarks are equally applicable to the suggestive force of this line from " Hamlet." The succession of short, weighted words are the direct embodiment of the heavy thought.

" Thoughts black, hands apt, drugs fit, and time agreeing,"

And what could better delineate the sharp, mad agony of Lear than these sharp, hard monosyllables ?

" Howl, howl, howl, howl !   O, you are men of stone !
Had I your tongues and eyes I'd use them so
That heaven's vault should crack.''

Monosyllables have a staccato effect, and, long per-
sisted in, leave upon the ear a strong impression of
harshness and roughness.

The general characteristic of the dissyllable with feminine cadence[1] (i.e. with accent on the first syllable) is
suavity. It links together rougher strokes, and blends
the line into melodious flow.   Its use is conspicuous in
those poets whose predominant characteristic is melody.

I give two illustrative lines from Keats, and two from
Tennyson.

" The carvèd angels, ever eager-eyed,''

" Thea, Thea, Thea, where is Saturn ? ''

" Lightlier move
The minutes fledged with music : ''

" And freedom slowly broadens down.''

Polysyllables impart to verse sonority, stateliness, dignity, elevation.   Witness the abundant use of them by
poets in whom a sense of these qualities predominates.
I give two examples from Milton and two from Wordsworth.

" Thick as autumnal leaves that strew the brooks
In Vallambrosa, where the Etrurian shades
High over-arch'd imbower.''

[1] Because the general effect of dissyllables with masculine cadence is
practically identical with that of monosyllables.

" The Stygian Council thus dissolved, and forth
    In order came the grand infernal peers ;
    Midst came their mighty paramount, and seem'd
    Alone the antagonist of heaven, nor less
    Than Hell's dread emperour,"

" Hail, Twilight, sovereign of one peaceful hour !
    Not dull art thou as undiscerning Night ;
    But studious only to remove from sight
    Day's mutable distinctions."

                                " Near
    The solid mountain shone, bright as the cloud,
    Grain-tinctured, drenched in empyrean light."

Not a little in the nice distribution of words of different ponderable values—each absolutely placed and
adapted, each conveying the definite impression intended
—is the great art of the great artist evidenced.

It is this marshalling of the forces of words—differently
marshalled by different hands—which constitutes what
Apropos we designate as *style*. Individuality of style is
of style a subtle quality not easy to define, but very
conclusively apprehended. Thus Shakespeare's style,
Milton's style, Keats's style, Browning's style, etc., are
as organically native, as unconfusable, and as uncom-
municable as possible.

While poetry deals much more with hyperbole than
prose, and employs many syntactical inversions not per-
Professor missible in prose, the fundamental elements of
Wendell's good writing are the same in both literary
three
fundamental forms. Professor Barrett Wendell, in his mas-
groups terly little book on English Composition,
places these elements very succinctly before us in three
groups; viz.: the intellectual, or quality of *clearness ;* the

emotional, or quality of *force ;* and the æsthetic, or quality of *elegance—beauty.*

The secret of clearness lies in *denotation,* or the direct statement. The writer must have a definite conception **The secret** of that which he wishes to say, and express it **of clearness** in such language that others shall as definitely perceive it. Vagueness and obscurity of expression are to be avoided. True art is deep as a well and clear as crystal. Occasional ridicule has been excited by the homeliness of Wordsworth's diction, and some of his poems are indeed suggestive of the schoolboy's composition; but this is due to the poet's fixed theory that one should compose whether the fountain of inspiration be playing or not, and the pieces in question certainly took shape upon the dry days. In his times of elevation and inspiration, the directness and simplicity of Wordsworth's diction become a powerful instrument of expression. We are sometimes tempted to wish that some of Browning's work could receive an infusion of the same clarifying element.

The emotional element of style is *force,* and in all forms of literature this is the quality which *holds the* **The secret** *attention.* It is of course the power to put the **of force** sense or image of the thing or things treated vividly before the mind of the reader; and it is in *connotation,* or that which is implied or suggested rather than definitely stated, that the secret of force lies. This is because the suggested idea fires trains of thought in the imagination and permits it to construct a cosmos out of a granule. It becomes evident that this division is the field of the trope.

Yet should the ultimate power be kept in reserve, and only exerted at focal moments, lest the impression produced be of the exhaustion of resource.

" In the very torrent, tempest, and, as I may say, the whirlwind of passion, you must acquire and beget a temperance that may give it smoothness," Hamlet exhorts the players.

Clearness should of course always underlie force.

In *adaptation* lies the secret of beauty. This is only another way of defining that which we have more than **The secret** once stated in these pages; viz. : that the lit-**of beauty** erary *form* must be such as to express most concretely the thought of the creating artist. Says Professor Wendell:

" The more exquisitely style is adapted to the thought it symbolises, the better we can make our works and compositions denote and connote in other human minds the meaning they denote and connote in ours, the greater charm style will have, merely as a work of art." [1]

The study of great works of art shows them to be finished and proportioned, but full of underlying strength. Power is not attained either by brutality or by extravagance of diction, but by an art which is masterly, *because* technically finished and proportioned. To the student of poetry I would say: study intelligently; write copiously; prune drastically; and above all be not in haste to rush into print, for this evidences rather a desire for cheap notoriety than a strong art feeling. True art is always characterised by restraint.

> " I hung my verses in the wind,
> Time and tide their faults may find ;
> All were winnowed through and through,
> Five lines lasted sound and true." [2]

A poem should always be measured to the dimensions of its informing idea. If it be longer than its idea it will

[1] " English Composition," chap. viii. [2] EMERSON : " The Test."

17

descend into mere verbiage; but neither should it be so
contracted as to leave room for no ideas.   Although the
voice of the day seems to be for it, an epigram is not
a poem.

But when all is said and done about the *manner* of the
verse, it is of course the genius of the poet, the creative
The creative soul, which infuses the form with life and ren-
soul   ders it not an agglomeration of words and sentences, but a potentiality.   Back of the archetype must
be the informing idea, the essential element which gives
it being—the burning, palpitating, eternal current which
links all causes with all expression.   Genius touches the
every-day, the familiar, the common, and lifts it into the
realm of the ideal, so that it takes on for us a new significance and a new beauty.   What genius *is* no man
rightly knows.   Probably the possessor of it would sub-
scribe to Emerson's postulate that it is a " greater infusion of deity;" for he knows that that which he creates
is not of himself but flows through him from some deeper
reservoir.   " We do not take possession of our ideas, but
are possessed by them," says Heine.   The most compre-
hensive definition of genius which I know is one given
by Miss Sheppard in " Counterparts."   " Genius is that
essence which alone assimilates with the unseen; which
passes into the arcana of knowledge as a part of itself,
and that without preparation, education or experience."

A great deal passes for genius which is nothing higher
than well-trained talent—tricks of mere cleverness.   But
literature, like water, will rise to its own level, and no
higher.   Genius is a compulsive force, no more to be
restrained than is the mountain torrent.   We are obliged
to say with Owen Meredith:

> " Genius is master of man;
> Genius does what it must, talent does what it can."

Within the hand of genius lies that talisman of fire which makes thought candent at the core and casts it into inevitable shapes of passion and power.

Beauty and power are the keys to art.

It is not possible, as some have tried to do, to define power as the subjective element, or soul, and beauty as **Beauty and** the objective element, or body, of art, because **power are** *both* qualities are attributes of the informing **the keys to** **art** spirit as well as of its expression. Power, shorn of beauty, is but elemental force; beauty, shorn of power, is mere sensuousness. True art therefore is a synthetic union of the concrete with the abstract.

In a way beauty is of itself a power; one of the strongest which can sway us. It is by virtue of his beauty—his glowing workmanship, his rich and transporting melody, his superlative imagery—and not by the ethical value of his long-drawn allegory that Spenser endures to-day. It is by the same virtue that Keats lives, and will live as long as appreciation for literary perfection survives. And the secret of Shelley's ethereal charm lies in his passionate love of the beautiful, and his equally burning desire to transmute all life and all experience into beauty.

Beauty is the *alpha* and *omega* of art—by beauty meaning that art which is intrinsically and extrinsically proportioned—and without beauty there could be no art. Ugliness is untrue to art. All distortion is ugliness—untruth—and therefore not art. Amorphousness is not art, cacophony is not art, naked realism unillumined by the fires of the imagination is not art, nor yet is extravagance, nor anything which depends upon sensational effects. Art is that sublime union of the concrete with the abstract which makes always for the elevation of the soul of man; otherwise must it be meretricious work and not true art. The sense of beauty may be for a season obscured, even as vapours cloud the face of the sun, but it is inalienable and imperishable. The desire for it—for that beauty which tranquillises, which enlarges, which uplifts—is at the core of existence. Consciously or unconsciously the soul of man is always reaching forward to more and more sublimated experience; and that age which feeds upon beauty will inevitably rise above its fellows both in the conception of ideals and in the externalisation of their inspiration.

The educational value of poetry cannot be overestimated. All forms of art are " mediators between the soul and the Infinite; " but music and poetry, from their character, playing as they do upon the emotional nature, are the most powerful.

The educational value of poetry

Poetry is really less esoteric than music. It is nearer the universal sympathy and more essentially comprehensible by the general mind. Lines of beautiful poetry will live in the memory like haunting strains of music, wiping out the common and the sordid, and at all times uplifting, purifying, tranquillising, and inspiring. Poetry has its objective side which appeals to the intellect, and its subjective, which appeals directly to the spirit. This latter is a psychic process, and is brought about, exactly as in music, by *virtue of the vibration.* A thought cast in rhythmic form will appeal to the spirit as the same thought in dry prose will not. It becomes a spear of palpitating flame, piercing the crust of the understanding at a blow, and penetrating straight to the heart of things.

The study of poetry has fallen too much into desuetude; has been left to be a recreation for a cultured few, when in fact it ought to be made mental food for the million. One cannot but mark with regret the conspicuous ignorance our undergraduates—and our graduates!—show with regard

The love of poetry should be cultivated

to the noblest masterpieces of our literature; but there is opportunity for reform. Some of the time now spent in the acquisition of material knowledge would be well devoted to developing a taste and appreciation for great literature. We should familiarise our little ones with choice selections of simple verse, and train our young men and women to live lovingly in the society of the great poets. One of the faculties which awake earliest in the child is a feeling for rhythmic motion—dancing, marching, calisthenics, etc. When taught them, they greatly enjoy simple and melodious verses; and such, becoming fixed in the memory at this plastic age, never wholly lose their power. I know of a school whose principal is a lover of Shakespeare, where little ones of six and seven take the greatest delight in memorising and reciting little songs from the dramas of Shakespeare— " O come unto these yellow sands," " Where the bee sucks," etc. Can one doubt that this is the preparation for the more mature and understanding love ? And I know of several boys' clubs in the slums of different cities,—clubs in which a love of noble literature has been carefully inculcated,—where stultified lads of fourteen to twenty (hoodlums is our common name for them) have spent whole winters in studying and performing such plays as Shakespeare's " Julius Cæsar " and " Merchant of Venice," Banim's " Damon and Pythias," etc. Statistics in these wards show a great falling off in juvenile crime. A few facts like these speak for themselves.

Teachers of the future will realise that more important than the study of physical sciences is the study of life; and life is epitomised in the great literatures of the world. History shows us that those ages which have been dominated by great art-ideals have also been the ages of the greatest and noblest material achievement. Emerson affirms that " sooner or later that which is now life shall be poetry, and every fair and manly trait shall add a richer strain to the song." To this we might append Shelley's immortal words: " Poetry is indeed something divine. It is at once the centre and circumference of knowledge; it is that which comprehends all science and that to which all science must be referred. It is at the same time the root and blossom of all other systems of thought; it is that from which all spring, and that which adorns all, and that which, if blighted, denies the fruit and the seed, and withholds from the barren world the nourishment and succession of the scions of the tree of life."

This generation is wandering through the barren reaches of æsthetic decadence, the natural reaction from nearly a century of wonderful production. In the general lowering of the ideal atmosphere we seem to have lost the sense of proportion. Little men loom before the public eye like giants. A meretricious impressionism has taken the place of inspiration. We endeavour to *sting* ourselves into fresh sensation. " Poverty of inventive power," says Nauman, " ever seeks to gloze over its shortcomings by novel and startling effects." One might say that the art of to-day, from the symphonic poem to the poster, has become largely *unresolved dissonances*. But this will not always be so. The world of art, like the physical cosmos, must have its fallow seasons, while the creative spirit slumbers, and the new forces slowly gather for fresh fruition. This is the natural and necessary alternation; the systole and diastole of the universe.

The ideal can never perish. It is the noumenon or core of existence, the axis upon which life ever moves to higher and higher expression. Ideals have varied from age to age, but the general trend has ever been upward. Mephitic vapours of materialism or formalism have at

Renascence

times obscured it, but this is only the darkness before the dawn, the obscuration which leads into the glory of renascence. The night is to usher in the day. Spring leaps up like a diviner phœnix from the frozen ashes of the winter. Then shall arise the new poets, with clarified perceptions and more puissant song. They shall stand upon the Mount of Vision and look backward through the æons and forward into the dazzle of eternal verity. They shall hear all harmonies, from the stupendous choiring of the planets to the mystic palpitation of the æther; they shall unravel real from unreal, true from false; they shall read more clearly yet the meanings of love, beauty, life; and so, with eyes turned toward the sunrise, shall

> " Catch
> Upon the burning lava of a song,
> The full-veined, heaving, double-breasted Age."

INDEX*

ABBOTT, Dr., 22
ACHILLES, 3
ÆNEID, 192
ÆSCHYLUS, 246
ALDRICH, T. B., 202
ALEXANDRINE, 67, 151, 152, 157, 205
ALLEN and GREENOUGH, 28, 183
ALLITERATION, 8, 101, 109, 115–117, 120, 122, 137
AMBROS, Wilhelm August, 246
ANACRUSIS, 29
ANGLO-SAXON, 6, 7, 8; verse, 78, 135, 136
ANGLO-SAXONS, 9, 117
APTHORP, W. F., 24, 248
ARIOSTO, 168, 175, 246
ARISTOTLE, 191
ARNOLD, Matthew, 66, 71, 99, 191, 202, 241; extracts from poems of, 33, 67, 69, 92
ARNOLD, Sir Edwin, 126
ARTS of sound, 16

BACON, 9, 99
BALLAD, the, 10, 138, 141, 191; metre, 139, 140
BALLADS, ancient, 142–146; modern, 146–150
BANIM, 261
BAYNE, Peter, 75
BEATTIE, 160
BEAUMONT and FLETCHER, 13, 120, 207

BEAUTY and power, 242
BEETHOVEN, 248
BEOWULF, 192, 194
BLANK verse, 9, 12, 66; definition of, 209, 213, 237, 239, 240, 241; Marlowe's, 207; Milton's, 208; modern, 208; notations, 214–237; Shakespeare's, 208; Surrey's, 206
BOCCACCIO, 8
BROWN, Abbie Farwell, 131
BROWNING, Elizabeth Barrett, 108, 171, 173, 174, 245
BROWNING, Robert, 18, 47, 55, 66, 86, 96, 97, 108, 114, 160, 179, 191, 202, 208, 246, 256. Blank verse, 229, 230, 252. Extracts from lyrical poetry, 35, 36, 50, 54, 61, 89, 90, 93, 102, 123, 125, 180, 185. Rhymed couplets, 156
BRUT, 193
BURNS, 160, 191
BURROUGHS, John, 120
BYRD, 9, 10
BYRON, 70, 71, 83, 151, 160, 171, 176, 191; extracts from poems of, 65, 84, 85, 161, 177, 179

CADENCE correspondence, 104
CADENCE, imperfect, 106; perfect authentic, 102
CÆSURA, 55, 56, 57, 210, 211
CAINE, Hall, 171

* All extracts from poems will be found under the names of their authors.
Subject classifications not made in Index will be found in the marginal notes.